D1446726

THE MOURNER'S SONG

JAMES TATUM

THE MOURNER'S SONG

WAR AND REMEMBRANCE

FROM THE *ILIAD* TO

VIETNAM

THE UNIVERSITY OF CHICAGO PRESS
CHICAGO AND LONDON

James Tatum is the Aaron Lawrence Professor of Classics at Dartmouth College. He is the author of *Apuleius and the Golden Ass, Plautus: The Darker Comedies,* and *Xenophon's Imperial Fiction: On the Education of Cyrus,* and the editor of *The Search for the Ancient Novel.*

The University of Chicago Press, Chicago 60637

The University of Chicago Press, Ltd., London

© 2003 by The University of Chicago

All rights reserved. Published 2003

Printed in the United States of America

12 11 10 09 08 07 06 05 04 03   1 2 3 4 5

ISBN: 0-226-78993-4 (cloth)

Library of Congress Cataloging-in-Publication Data

Tatum, James.
    The mourner's song : war and remembrance from the Iliad to Vietnam / James Tatum.
        p. cm.
    Includes bibliographical references and index.
    ISBN 0-226-78993-4 (alk. paper)
        1. American literature—History and criticism.   2. War in literature.   3. Vietnamese
Conflict, 1961–1975—Literature and the conflict.   4. War poetry, American—History and
criticism.   5. Epic poetry, Greek—History and criticism.   6. Trojan War—Literature and
the war.   7. War poetry—History and criticism.   8. Mourning customs in literature.
9. Memory in literature.   10. Homer—Influence.   11. Homer. Iliad.   I. Title.
PS169.W27 T38 2003
810.9'358—dc21

2002009356

FOR BILL NOBLE

CONTENTS

ILLUSTRATIONS

INTRODUCTION

The *Iliad* speaks to the way we think about war, because the one impulse that has proved as enduring as human beings' urge to make wars is their need to make sense of them. The first step in making sense of any such loss is to mourn the dead. Nothing is more crucial to approaching Homer and the arts that come from war than thinking back on loss. Bereavement and mourning are things we come to know firsthand in life, sooner or later. Perhaps we learn them most efficiently through war. The *Iliad* has death and mourning in abundance, and the poetry it offers is the only enduring consolation. Homer finds significance in his war, as later poets would in theirs, by moving from the present moment to other points in time, juxtaposing the here and now with the past and the future. This reach to a distant moment gives the *Iliad* some of its most inspiring lines.[1] To think with Homer about war is to learn to compare and to juxtapose. It comes to seem natural to extend our imagination beyond the *Iliad,* to other wars and other poets. If Achilles was in Vietnam, as the psychiatrist and antiwar activist Jonathan Shay has argued, he was also in Okinawa, Battery Wagner, and the Somme.[2] This urge to trace connections between the war at Troy and later wars is inspired by the story and the poetry of the *Iliad.*

The dead of the Trojan War appear at the beginning of the poem and are never far away from us thereafter. Guided by the story of the *Iliad* at every point, this book begins and ends with mourners, their monuments, and their songs. It is no great thing now to be alert to such a somber design. Mourning and memorials are a preoccupation of our times, caught as we are in a postwar generation that is also a prewar generation, even a generation already at war. We think about wars through their mourners and monuments as much as any earlier age did. This memorial impulse is the point of departure for *The Mourner's Song* (chapter 1).

More enduring than any monument are songs created through the inspiration of the daughters of Memory and Zeus, the Muses. The third word of the *Iliad* is *thea*, the goddess whom Homer commands to sing of the rage of Achilles, but she and her sister Muses tend to be neglected in modern assessments of both Homer's poem and monuments generally. The Muses are the true inspiration for those following the path of mourning through poetry. Read as history, the *Iliad* seems a fragment of its war; at the same time, it seems to say everything there is to say about war. This compression of many stories is one of the most powerful effects of its poetry, and one of the many gifts of the Muses. With the deaths of Patroclus and Hector and the funeral rites that end the poem, with the nearing death of Achilles and fall of Troy, the *Iliad's* unfinished war is forever imminent, forever menacing. Those who know the *Iliad* cannot fail to wonder if its plot might not also be an anticipation of their own (chapter 2).[3]

Achilles' rage takes us into what the historian Gerald Linderman has termed the world within war and warriors' "abandonment of invulnerability. 'It can't happen to me' becomes perforce 'It *can* happen to me.'"[4] The quarrel between Agamemnon and Achilles and all its consequences are a spectacular example of military incompetence at the highest levels of command.[5] In the end Agamemnon's cause will prevail, Troy will fall, and for that reason alone the *Iliad* has always been as much a commander's story as a hero's tale. In this it is a prelude to the memoirs of Ulysses S. Grant. Both Homer and Grant give us much insight into what John Keegan has called the Mask of Command (chapter 3).

Commanders' quarrels come and go; war resumes. It is fought before the walls of Troy at some points, but mostly before a great defensive wall that the Achaeans build to defend themselves after Achilles, the best of the Achaeans, has withdrawn to his tent. This tale once annoyed Homer's more literal-minded critics for its improbable inversion of chronology, to say nothing of its bad tactics. Why did the Greeks get around to building a defensive wall only after ten years of war? It is a practical question any sensible strategist, but no poet, would ask. The site of war over which men struggle will prove as evanescent as the lives lost in the war itself. Even as the wall is built we learn a future the Greeks cannot yet know: once Troy has fallen and they have sailed away, the Achaean wall will be destroyed by the vengeful gods Apollo and Poseidon. In the indifferent face of nature and the obliteration of passing time is born the impulse to preserve the memories of the war dead, however and wherever that can be done.

I rehearse the story of the Achaean wall not only for itself, but for the reading it gives us of one of the famous episodes of the American Civil War. The sea at Morris Island south of Charleston Harbor obliterates the site of a battle in 1863 whose memory both sculpture and poetry have sought to preserve. Battery Wagner seems to have been made out of Homer's poetry. The fort itself has vanished, but it inspired both sculpture and poetry: Augustus Saint-Gaudens's Shaw Memorial in Boston, and Robert Lowell's poem "For the Union Dead" (chapter 4).

The further we go into the center of the *Iliad*, which is not accidentally the center of war itself, the more clearly we realize that there are two distinct directions in which human love can go, and that the *Iliad* interweaves both: love for those at home, and love for those at war. There is a proximity of hearth and battlefield, a juxtaposition of these loves, in the beloved companion of Achilles, Patroclus, and Andromache, the wife of Hector. We see human love and longing in an equipoise typical of war: the warrior's love at home and the warrior's love in the field. In their grief the survivors Andromache and Achilles reach a level of misery where heroic warrior is indistinguishable from widowed mother and future slave woman (chapter 5).

Were such love understood as fully before it is lost in war as it so often is afterward, would war become less popular? Never, the poets suggest. In war it becomes impossible to separate love from hate, or killing. These extremes of human emotion are interwoven and inextricable, especially in the central figures fighting the battles of the poem. Roughly half of the *Iliad*'s more than seventeen thousand lines are devoted to battle scenes; these proportions reflect the actual energies of war itself. The ferocity that drives these relentlessly brutal scenes is shaped by the very love that the peacetime imagination fondly sees as war's antithesis. As Glenn Gray puts it, love is at once war's ally and foe (chapter 6).[6]

If what war does to people can be alluring, what it looks like can have even more enduring appeal. As the source of the greatest of all spectacles in the *Iliad*'s war, the shield and the shining arms of Achilles enable him to unleash a destructive power that is as palpable as an aerial bombardment. Homer makes the most frightening objects of war into his most beautiful poetry. The making of Achilles' armor is the ultimate war fantasy for mortal men who fight war, who have no choice but to be mesmerized by the poet's translation of the arts of the divine craftsman of the gods into the poetry that we know as the shield of Achilles. I will focus particularly on the uses to which these gifts from Hephaestus are put. The armor of Achilles is dazzling and deadly. Technological triumphs of twentieth-century warfare such as the development of air power and the atomic bomb have at last enabled us to create weapons that rival the fiery arts of Hephaestus. The corpse-choked rivers of Troy found their realization in the teeming tributaries of the Ota River in Hiroshima, on August 6, 1945 (chapter 7).

The *Iliad* ends by confounding the waging of war with war's memorialization. The distance between warrior and civilian and the living and the dead collapses. So too do optimistic notions of war and peace. Our lasting memory of the end of the *Iliad* is not only of the imminent fall of Troy, or of the victory of Agamemnon, or even of Achilles and his approaching death, but of the burial and tomb of Hector, and of the final speeches of his wife and mother, and of Helen, each mourning Hector in her own way. The *Iliad* stops when the devastations of war are plain, yet we have a clear sense that much more is to come. The poem's counterpoint between individual grief and communal mourning is devastating, the whys and wherefores of war itself as unanswered at the end of the *Iliad* as they were at its beginning. The book ends by closing the circle of mourning that the *Iliad* begins, with Oguma Hideo's 1937 lament for the captive old women of Korea, "Long, Long Autumn Nights" (chapter 8).

My view of Homer and war poetry reflects the experience of the generation of Americans that came of age during the Vietnam War. The fate of belonging to that era is sometimes noted with glee when American classicists are criticized for not realizing what an effect that war had on their interpretation of ancient culture. There is nothing that can be done about this. So far as the reading of poetry goes, there is nothing that should be done. Ancient no less than modern poetry must be read in whatever world we live in and think we know. The Vietnam generation has been the subject of more than its share of thoughtfully self-regarding books. The best to date is Tom Engelhardt's *End of Victory Culture*.

Aside from my belonging to the culture Engelhardt describes, my initial inspiration for reading the *Iliad* as a war poem came not from muses, heavenly or otherwise, but from two mortal women: the French intellectual and activist Simone Weil, who died during World War II, exiled in England, and the American architect Maya Lin. I have probably read and taught the *Iliad* more than any other poem, even more than the classicist's other bible, the *Aeneid*, but I came later than I could have wished to Weil's *"Iliad"; or, The Poem of Force*, an essay she published first in Vichy France in 1940 under the solemn anagram of "Emile Novalis."[7] Weil's essay should speak directly to anyone who loses family and friends to death; most saliently, for me at that time, it spoke to the loss of a childhood friend killed in Vietnam in June 1966. His name is inscribed on the Vietnam Veterans Memorial in Washington, D.C., a monument dedicated in November 1981.[8] By coincidence, Weil died the same year my friend was born, 1943.

> The true hero, the true subject, the center of the *Iliad* is force. Force employed by man, force that enslaves man, force before which man's flesh shrinks away. In this work, at all times, the human spirit is shown as modified by its relations with force, as swept away, blinded, by the very force it

imagined it could handle, as deformed by the weight of the force it submits to. For those dreamers who considered that force, thanks to progress, would soon be a thing of the past, the *Iliad* could appear as an historical document; for others, whose powers of recognition are more acute and who perceive force, today as yesterday, at the very center of human history, the *Iliad* is the purest and loveliest of mirrors.[9]

Under the spell of Weil's essay, the two strands of Homer's poetry and Maya Lin's monument became intertwined, so that the *Iliad* and mourning became, for me, inseparable.

This was an ironic turn for someone in the optimistic business of showing others how vital the poetry of this purest and loveliest of mirrors could be: such vitality, yet such loss. If the monument in Washington was but one of countless examples that exemplify the role of force in human history, reading Weil's essay in company with that particular war memorial turned the *Iliad* itself into a tomb in verse from a vanished civilization.

Read as a monumental poem in an almost literal sense, one saturated with war and its consequences from opening line to last, the *Iliad* seemed to me to chart the course of any war, not just the one in Vietnam. It became a poem that followed the relentless progress toward the memorials that all wars now demand for their dead. Although Maya Lin's prize-winning design was first and foremost a national monument, and although it was scarcely unpatriotic, it emphasized death and loss to a degree unprecedented in official American war commemorations. Like the *Iliad*, the Vietnam Veterans Memorial makes mourning its destination. Its design pulls us down into it, drawing us to the level that mourners are drawn to at the end of the *Iliad*. What people in all wars share is not the infinitely varying causes of war, nor their battles, but the mourning for the dead that follows. The sorrows of wars today are no distance at all from the mourning at Troy, nor are their mourners' songs.

A NOTE ON READING HOMER

Readers of Homer in English have a long tradition of translation to draw on, and it is worth sampling every part of it. George Steiner's recent Penguin collection of English versions from the beginnings of the modern language to the present is an indispensable guide to anyone who wants to know more about the subject.[1] Throughout this book I will alternate between Richmond Lattimore (1951) and Robert Fagles (1990), but at points I will also turn to Robert Graves (1959), Martin Hammond (1987), Stanley Lombardo (1997), and Christopher Logue (1981, 1991), as well as to Homer's more distant translators, such as Keats's Chapman (1598–1611) and, above all, Alexander Pope (1715–20). His *Iliad* is available in many different editions, including paperback. Ideally it should be read in the magisterial edition of Maynard Mack.[2]

Urging Homer's readers to go to Pope is not an invitation to antiquarianism. In my experience the greatest drawback to reading him is not his present status as an antique and a classic, but his chosen form of heroic couplets. Rhyming iambic pentameters are not the way of contemporary translators or their audiences.

> Man, supposing you and I, escaping this battle,
> would be able to live on forever, ageless, immortal,
> so neither would I myself go on fighting in the foremost
> nor would I urge you into the fighting where men win glory.
>> (12.322–25, Lattimore)

> Ah my friend, if you and I could escape this fray
> and live forever, never a trace of age, immortal,
> I would never fight on the front lines again,
> or command you to the field where men win fame.
>> (Fagles)

Pope's heroic couplets seem as remote and artificial as Homer's own oral verse-making and traditional formulas.

> Cou'd all our Care elude the greedy Grave,
> Which claims no less the Fearful than the Brave,
> For Lust of Fame I shou'd not vainly dare
> In fighting Fields, nor urge thy Soul to War.

And that, as Mack observes, is exactly the point. Heroic couplets were not just appropriate for English readers in 1725; in a way Pope would not have foreseen but might have applauded, they now recapture something like the experience of a performance of Homer in Greek. Pope's artifices are closer to Homer's traditional poetry than any other verse form in English that has been used since: "Though neither the conventions nor the locutions were very close to Homer's they did, and still do, convey a sense of a 'made' language, a cunning artifice of meaning and sound, sound often tailored to fortify meaning, which is at its best a possible counterpart to, even if it is not an accurate reflection of the 'made' language of Homer." Translators like Lattimore have been alive to Homer's made language, but of poet-translators since Pope, Christopher Logue has done the most to turn the *Iliad* into a contemporary poem. To adapt Mack's words about Pope, Logue's accomplishment is remarkable for its irradiation of poetry by poetry.[3] Logue has translated only certain books of the *Iliad*, but he appears in the following pages wherever his "accounts" are available.

Two further comments. The first has to do with my frequent choice of Lattimore, or of Fagles, and what guides me in choosing one or the other. The choice is always to some degree a matter of taste, but it is not entirely a matter of which side of the bed you get up on.

The important thing to keep in mind about Lattimore's translation of 1951 is how fully it realizes the precepts of Matthew Arnold's lectures of 1861, "On Translating Homer." Arnold's ideal judges of translation were not Homer's readers, but the classicists in his audiences at Oxford.

> I must repeat what I said in beginning, that the translator of Homer ought steadily to keep in mind where lies the real test of the success of his translation, what judges he is to try to satisfy. He is to try to satisfy *scholars*, because scholars alone have the means of really judging him. . . . This, then, remains the one proper aim of the translator: to reproduce on the intelligent scholar, as nearly as possible, the general effect of Homer.[4]

Lattimore himself was a celebrated Hellenist as well as a poet, and his gift for getting every word and every nuance into a six-beat line that nearly always follows Homer's lines is one of the great success stories in modern translation. Teachers have so loved Lattimore that he turned into a classical version of Borges's ingenious Pierre Menard, author of the *Quixote*. For many, Richmond Lattimore actually became the author of the *Iliad*.

Now the kind of adoration that Arnold and Lattimore require is in increasingly short supply. Scrupulous fidelity to the formulaic diction of Homer's oral verse and a line-for-line rendering win high marks from Greek scholars, but take away the requisite piety and these same lines can become merely boring. The language is weirdly stilted and not like any poetry anyone has heard in English. Lattimore's dedication to literalism extends to the famous names of myth and history. In what at the time must have seemed a commendable effort to erase Rome and the Latinization of Hellenic culture, *Achilles* and *Athena* became *Achilleus* and *Athene*. I have never heard an English-speaking classicist say anything but "Achilles" and "Athena," but I have heard plenty of students and other first-time readers of Homer stumble over "Ahll-kill-youse" and "Atheen."

Why should such things have happened to "the finest translation of Homer ever made into the English language," as William Arrowsmith greeted it when it appeared? Aside from the probability that it wasn't—Pope still holds that particular crown of leaves—and aside from the inevitable tendency of any translation to go out of date, I have one comment that might explain why such a great version of the *Iliad* is at once so satisfying in detail and so increasingly tedious to read.

Lattimore excels in capturing the words and the lines of Homer, with an excellent ear and with a philological precision that makes his verse translation helpful in construing Homer's Greek. This is why it is so tempting to quote him whenever it is the detail and the exactness of something in Homer that you want to convey; Homer's words are nearly always there, as Arnold said they should be. The problem is that what works for the short run does not work for the long. A few lines may not be challenging for the reader, but hundreds of them, and then hundreds of pages of this carefully crafted, deliberately formulaic verse, are not something less pious readers can stand. They want poetry in English. Thus other versions, most recently Robert Fagles's, have become more popular, simply because they are more readable—and, with audiotapes, listenable. For the same reason that Fagles is so welcome, he can wear his welcome out. Sublime moments suddenly go informal and colloquial on you, punctuated in a jazzy way that overdetermines how they are to be read. Fagles's translations are at their best in the recordings of Ian McKellan (*Odyssey*) and Derek Jacobi (*Iliad*). Anything that moves Homer's audiences away from the sullen, silent reading of yesterday is to be encouraged.

In the meantime, I think readers should be aware of the variety of Homers there are available to read and hear in English. There is something to be gained from nearly all of them, which is why I vary the voices through which Homer comes to us.

The other point I would make about reading Homer in English concerns what is available for reading Homer beyond a translation of his lines. Pope's *Iliad* is a great translation not only for the quality of the poetry, but for the immense learning he brings to bear in his supplementary notes and essays. He strives to bring his readers the best that could be known and thought about Homer, as of his day, and if much of what he could find out has been superseded by the revolutionary work of Milman Parry and modern Homeric scholarship, the range of his critical insight remains breathtaking. Some of Pope's essays remain as alive and provocative as ever (on "Batels" or battle scenes, for example, and the notoriously dull catalogue of ships). No translator has ever taken his readers so seriously.

Anyone who wants to know more about Homer's poetry should go directly to the six volumes of the Cambridge commentary on the *Iliad* edited by Geoffrey Kirk. There will be points of interest only to those concerned with Greek, but readers will also find the riches of a field of scholarship that has consistently attracted some of the brightest talents in classics, all brought together in a highly compressed and accessible commentary in which it is possible to engage at almost any level with the poetry of Homer. The volumes by Richard Janko (volume 4, on books 13–16) and Mark W. Edwards (volume 5, on books 17–20) are particularly alive to the poetry they discuss. Janko on the *Patrokleia* (book 16) and Edwards on the shield of Achilles (book 18) offer readable distillations of great learning and critical acumen.

One MOURNERS AND MONUMENTS

Only the mourning and the mourned recall
The wars we lose, the wars we win;
And the world is—what it has been.
    Randall Jarrell, "The Range in the Desert"

Mourning inspires the poetry of war as surely as its monuments. The *Iliad* opens with the rage of Achilles that brings pains thousandfold upon the Achaeans and closes with the funeral rites of Hector, tamer of horses. It reduces the arc of a long war to bare outline: from the murderous rage required for killing, to funeral rites, whatever form they take. This is a concise, minimal statement of what war achieves. The *Iliad's* song connects the plot of war with the plot of life, so that its war becomes an accelerated, condensed version of life itself.[1]

The *Iliad* and many of the works we shall encounter are autopsies of their wars. The notion is not gratuitous. Reflect on what it is we are considering: the wounding and killing and dying on the massive scale that wars typically require; and then, the reasons, political as well as personal, that lead people to do these things. Just as an autopsy takes the end of life as its beginning, trying to deduce what in the life led to the end of it, so is it possible to contemplate the *Iliad* and every other kind of art made from war, starting from their endings.[2]

Death in war is not an easy thing to think about. As the American correspondent Michael Herr observes in *Dispatches*, death was what the Vietnam War was all about, yet none of the correspondents he was with could write about it. In Herr's terms, all war stories that are true to their inspiration should be autopsies. The closer a poet or writer or thinker gets to war, the less pressing it seems to be to follow a chronological order. In between, it is not chronology or the sequence of events that is driving the creation of the story, but urgency, and mortality. Consider what happened to the Vietnamese writer Bao Ninh in *The Sorrow of War*. He tells of a North Vietnamese veteran who tries to find a plot for his story. The veteran begins by assembling the pages of a manuscript that seem to have no coherent order.

It was during this period that I was attracted by this eccentric character. That's why I tried reading his long stories, although it was difficult. At first I tried to rearrange the manuscript pages into chronological order, to make the manuscript read like the sort of book I was familiar with. But it was useless. There was no chronological order at all. Any page seemed like the first, any page could have been the last. Even if the manuscript had been numbered, even if no pages had been burned, or moth-eaten, or withheld by the author, if by chance they were all there, this novel would still be a work created by turbulent, even manic inspirations.

One became immersed in each sequence, each page. Sometimes the descriptions were compelling. The long-forgotten name of a once-familiar battlefield moved me. The close-up fighting, the small details of the soldiers' lives. The images of former colleagues appearing for just a moment, yet so clearly. The flow of the story continually changed. From beginning to end the novel consisted of blocks of images. A certain cluster of events, then disruptions, some event wiped off the page as if it had fallen into a hole in time. Many would say this was a disruption of the plot, a disconnection, a loss of perspective. They'd say this style proved the writer's inherent weakness: his spirit was willing but his flesh wasn't. . . . All I knew was that the author had written because he had to write, not because he had to publish. He had to think on paper. Then of all things, he delivered everything to a lonely, mute woman, who could easily have destroyed his turbulent revelations.[3]

This riff is as old as fiction itself; recall the Arabic translation and edition from which *Don Quixote* is alleged to have come, or the scratches of a reed pen on papyrus from which begins an ancient novel like *The Golden Ass*.[4] But more than the cleverness of a good storyteller is on display in *The Sorrow of War*. Primo Levi discovered the same disorder when he came to write the first of his memoirs about the Holocaust, *If This Is a Man*.[5]

I recognize, and ask indulgence for, the structural defects of the book. Its origins go back, not indeed in practice, but as an idea, an intention, to the days in the Lager. The need to tell our story to "the rest," to make "the rest" participate in it, had taken on for us, before our liberation and after, the character of an immediate and violent impulse, to the point of competing with our other elementary needs. The book has been written to satisfy this need: first and foremost, therefore, as an interior liberation. Hence its fragmentary character: the chapters have been written not in logical succession, but in order of urgency. The work of tightening up is more studied, and more recent.

And none of the facts is invented.[6]

For all its directness, the plot of the *Iliad* has a strong affinity with the seemingly chaotic narratives of Bao Ninh and Primo Levi. Tidy notions of sequence and logic are not what guide those telling true war stories.

INTO THE MIDDLE OF THE STORY

> The purpose of the monument is to insert a dead and vanished past into the living present.
> Anne Carson, *Economy of the Unlost*

A monument would seem to be the very last thing to know about a war. Certainly it cannot be built until the requisite number of people have been lost. If the story of the *Iliad* is to be trusted, however, funeral rites are perhaps the first thing of all we should think of.

The Vietnam Veterans Memorial on the Mall in Washington looms larger in the imagination than it first appears when actually seen.[7] From a distance, as visitors walk into it, the memorial becomes all-embracing, dwarfing everything in sight once they are at its center. And then as they walk out of it, its simplicity and its scale reassert themselves, and it becomes once again the modest, low-lying site on the Mall it first seemed. My own explanation for this persistent telescoping of the mind's eye is that it is really the experience of visiting the memorial we are recalling, not the dimensions of the monument itself. And as countless visitors and a number of critics have made clear, it is the siting of the monument and the names of the war dead that combine to create the peculiar power the memorial has.[8] Maya Lin published her own conception of the work only recently.

> On a personal level, I wanted to focus on the nature of accepting and coming to terms with a loved one's death. Simple as it may seem, I remember feeling that accepting a person's death is the first step in being able to overcome that loss.
>
> I felt that as a culture we were extremely youth-oriented and not willing or able to accept death or dying as a part of life. The rites of mourning, which in more primitive and older cultures were very much a part of life, have been suppressed in our modern times. In the design of the memorial, a fundamental goal was to be honest about death, since we must accept that loss in order to begin to overcome it.
>
> The pain of the loss will always be there, it will always hurt, but we must acknowledge the death in order to move on.
>
> What then would bring back the memory of a person? A specific object or image would be limiting. A realistic sculpture would be only one interpretation of that time. I wanted something that all people could relate to on a personal level. At this time I had as yet no form, no specific artistic image.

The use of names was a way to bring back everything someone could remember about a person. The strength in a name is something that has always made me wonder at the "abstraction" of the design; the ability of a
name to bring back every single memory you have of that person is far more
realistic and specific and much more comprehensive than a still photograph,
which captures a specific moment in time or a single event or a generalized
image that may or may not be moving for all who have connections to that
time.[9]

The architect's conception of mourning intersects with the poet's. Names do
have the power to sum up the whole life of a person. When Andromache
mourns Hector, she says everything she could say in the single vocative *aner*,
"my husband."

> And white-armed Andromache led their songs of sorrow,
> cradling the head of Hector, man-killing Hector
> gently in her arms: "O my husband . . .
> cut off from life so young. You leave me a widow,
> lost in the royal halls—and the boy only a baby,
> the son we bore together, you and I so doomed.
> I cannot think he will ever come to manhood."
>   (*Iliad* 24.723–28; 24.850–56, Fagles)[10]

The Vietnam Veterans Memorial gives an official list of the names of
Americans who died in Vietnam between 1959 and 1975. There were
57,939 listed at the dedication in 1982; more recently the number was
58,196, with no final count likely.[11] The memorial concentrates starkly on
mortality and nothing else. Each name is a terse summation of the main business of war, one that visitors are reminded of on sunny days when they can
see their reflections imposed on the names of the dead. The east and west
wings of the memorial plunge them in medias res, a spatial and geographic
equivalent of Horace's account of the *Iliad*'s effect on its readers. Homer has-
tens into the outcome of the story; he pulls his listeners into the middle of
things as if they already knew the story (*Ars Poetica*, 148–49). The declining
walkway of the memorial pulls its visitors downward to its center. As they
go, a list of full names begins on the black marble wall rising from the
ground, at first one name per line, then two, then many more, until a dot
marks off units of ten. At first one thinks that the names on the low wall are
for the earliest deaths in the war, beginning with a trickle in 1959–63, rising
to a crescendo in 1964–69 at the center of the memorial and bottom of the
walkway, where thousands of names tower ten feet overhead, then falling
away to ever lower levels during the period of "Vietnamization" in 1970–75.

At the center, we think, we are at the moment when the killing and the dying were at their worst.

More nearly the opposite is the case. At the cardinal point where the two wings of the memorial meet, at a 125-degree angle, in alignment with the Washington Monument to the east (fig. 1) and the Lincoln Memorial to the west (fig. 2), the bottom left panel has "1975" and the top at the beginning of the right wing "1959" (fig. 3). Visitors then realize that the first names they see at either entrance are not the first to die, but those who died in the statistical middle of the war's casualties. Death, not date, creates this design. The names on the western wing of the wall date from May 25, 1968, to May 15, 1975, at the bottom of the western wing. The eastern wall begins at the top of the eastern wing and records the casualties from July 8, 1959, to May 25, 1968, narrowing down to the single name of Jessie C. Alba (fig. 4). Drawing on the military's concept of a "casualty day," the memorial lists each person killed or missing within a single day, in alphabetic order for that day, so that John H. Anderson Jr. begins the right wall by following Jessie Charles Alba for the casualty day of May 25, 1968.

To advance from either the left or the right wall to the center of the memorial is to enter a space where the war's deepening ferocity and destruction seem to be reflected in a descent and ascent: the greater the number of dead, the more earth and wall are required to cover them. But once again there is a counterpoint between our everyday ways of reckoning history and time and the reckoning the wall imposes. A drama of the total casualties of the war is being enacted by revealing their sheer volume, along with the actual, day-to-day loss. No single death is now any more or any less significant than any other. Just as Maya Lin predicted, visitors who come looking for one name are made witnesses to the sum total of all the deaths recorded there.

The juxtaposition of the names of the last and first Americans to die creates a narrative like the ring composition of archaic poetry and storytelling: start at point A, go as far afield in your storytelling as you please, but end by coming back to point A. The Trojan ally Glaucus begins a speech to the Greek Diomedes,

> High-hearted son of Tydeus, why ask of my generation?
> As is the generation of leaves, so is that of humanity.
> The wind scatters the leaves on the ground, but the live
>   timber
> burgeons with leaves again in the season of spring returning.
> So one generation of men will grow while another dies.
>   (*Iliad* 6.145–49, Lattimore)

Figure 1. Maya Lin, Vietnam Veterans Memorial, east wall (All photos are by the author unless otherwise indicated.)

Figure 2. Vietnam Veterans Memorial, west wall

Figure 3. Ring composition: the center of the Vietnam Veterans Memorial

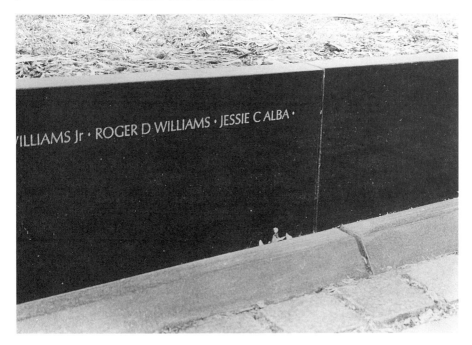

Figure 4. In medias res: the east wall of the Vietnam Veterans Memorial

Glaucus ends many lines later, with "Such is my generation and the blood I claim to be born from" (*Iliad* 6.211). As we visit the memorial, we follow a linear and chronological sequence, reckoning our lives by day and year, by the time of day, by our own age. But as we do so, we move in counterpoint to the way the memorial itself is working. While we progress in our living, straight lines, the dead we visit are in a chronological circle that has no beginning or end. As Maya Lin puts it, "the chronological sequence began and ended at the apex so that the time line would circle back to itself and close the sequence. A progression in time is memorialized. The design is not just a list of the dead. To find one name, chances are you will see the others close by, and you will see yourself reflected through them."[12] The two walls of the monument are tilted at an angle that causes them to rise from the earth on the left as we enter, then descend into the earth on the right as we leave. The effect of this rise and decline is not so much a Christian resurrection as an insurrection of the dead. As in Glaucus's simultaneously linear and circular patterns of the generations of men, the line of a single human life is set within the larger recurring pattern of all life, and death.

THE MISSING OF THE SOMME

Sir Thomas Browne states: "But to subsist in bones, and be but Pyramidically
extant, is a fallacy in duration." The ancients may have been as much aware
of this fallacy as Sir Thomas; those who have a well-grounded belief in
immortality need not be driven to such poor stuff.
Richmond Lattimore, *Themes in Greek and Latin Epitaphs*

The peculiar power of the Vietnam Veterans Memorial can be measured not
just by the poets, but by works that inspired the memorial, and works that
the memorial inspired in turn. Maya Lin was in an architectural design course
at Yale when she learned about Sir Edwin Lutyens's gigantic four-faced arch
on a hilltop overlooking the valley at Thiepval, in northern France in the
Department of the Somme. It lists all the names that could be recorded of
British and French soldiers whose remains could not be recovered or identi-
fied (fig. 5).[13] The success of Lutyens's 1919 cenotaph at Whitehall led to a
commission for a memorial to the missing of the battles of the Somme (July
1915 to March 1918). No two monuments could be more different, for-
mally. What they share with the *Iliad* is a way of giving monumental expression to death.

Sited directly on the battlefield, Lutyens's Memorial to the Missing of the
Somme offers an experience very different from the gentle, unobtrusive
Vietnam Veterans Memorial (fig. 6).[14] It sits on a ridge of the British and
French lines of the 1916 battle, facing north toward the German lines. One
of Maya Lin's teachers, Vincent Scully, brings the monument to life as a nov-
elist might, by imagining the war that gave birth to it.

As always, the infantry was heading for the high ground. We can follow
their track across the open fields today. Lutyens' memorial looms indis-
tinctly far ahead of us on the height. We move toward it. There is no cover.
We imagine the machine guns sweeping the gentle slopes. We turn toward
the little folds in the earth that open to left and right of the road and seem
to offer a refuge from that fire: it is made apparent to us that the infantry did
exactly the same before us. They are still there, many of them, laid out
neatly in small cemeteries where the artillery found them. We arrive at the
height, the objective. The monument looms over us, stepping mountain-
ously up and back in brick and white trim like one of the American sky-
scrapers of the 1920s. All at once we see that it is in fact an enormous
monster. The tight circles of its tondi become demonic eyes; its high arch
screams. It is the open mouth of death that will consume us all.[15]

Scully wants us to imagine what the battle was like that produced this monument. He is not writing history, but trying to use the monument's design to

Figure 5. Names on the Memorial to the Missing of the Somme, by Sir Edwin Lutyens, Thiepval, France

Figure 6. Memorial to the Missing of the Somme, frontal view

translate his present audience back to the carnage that created the missing of the Somme.[16]

As one approaches the northern front of the memorial, the angle of vision from below is so steep that the large central arch does loom overhead, as Scully's "open mouth of death." The Thiepval memorial is set into a sloping hillside, so that its front, northern-facing side looks toward the German lines. It seems, at that angle, at the foot of the memorial, to be springing out of the ground. Its heavy mass recalls the ruins and the exposed cross vault of the pilgrimage church of Notre Dame de Brebières, in the town of Albert in the valley below.[17] Its heavy mass also suggests a Roman triumphal arch in a far-from-triumphant setting. In his personal memoir of his grandfather's generation in the Great War, *The Missing of the Somme*, Geoff Dyer makes a practical point about Lutyens's work. It is not easily comprehended, in any ordinary sense. The monument is almost impossible to photograph adequately from any angle at ground level.[18]

Immediately in front of the monument is a field of white tombstones and crosses, which march in orderly rows up to the elevated platform of the memorial. Before, around, and inside, the 73,077 names are inscribed on the sixteen piers of the arches. Outside on the south-facing attic story of the memorial is carved "THE MISSING 1914–1918 OF THE SOMME"; at the center of the monument, underneath the arches, is the Great War Stone, with an inscription drawn from Ecclesiasticus, "THEIR NAME LIVETH FOR EVERMORE." Dyer's assessment sums up the effect on the visitor's eye. As a maker of war memorials, Lutyens is as allusive to traditional designs as his follower Maya Lin.

> Permanent, built to last, the monument has none of the vulnerability of the human body, none of its terrible propensity for harm. Its predominant relation is to the earth—not, as is the case with a cathedral, to the sky. A cathedral reaches up, defies gravity effortlessly, its effect is entirely vertiginous. And unlike a cathedral which is so graceful (full of grace) that, after a point, it disappears, becomes ethereal, the Thiepval Memorial, after a point, simply refuses to go any higher. It is stubborn, stoical. Like the deadlocked armies of the war, it stands its ground.
>
> The contrast with a cathedral is telling in another, broader sense. In keeping with Lutyens' general preference, the Memorial is stripped of Christian symbolism; there was, he felt, no need for it. For many men who survived, the Battle of the Somme (which, in memory, represents the core experience and expression of the Great War) put an end to the consoling power of religion. "From that moment," a soldier has said of the first day's fighting, "all my religion died. All my teaching and beliefs in God had left me, never to return." In some ways, then, the Thiepval Memorial is a memorial if not to death, then certainly to the superfluousness of God.[19]

If Lutyens's design itself is uncompromising about human mortality, the vague but unmistakably biblical promise of names living for evermore is one step toward the consolation of religion. Another counter to seeing the Missing of the Somme as a memorial to death and to the superfluousness of God could be found by going out the north arch and seeing the crosses on the graves in the field below the north face of the monument. There is all a Christian would need to find a promise of life eternal, even in the midst of death. Like the conventional memorial of Frederic Hart that was added to Maya Lin's original design, these additions offer consolation to those who want to find it. But the overwhelming experience is not one of consolation.

Thiepval's 73,077 names do more than put the Vietnam Veterans Memorial's record of American losses into numerical perspective (fig. 6). The evocation of Lutyens's work links America's own war with a battle and a war notorious for their senseless waste of life. The connections are particularly striking in Maya Lin's use of the Somme memorial's rising angle out of the ground (fig. 7); in Washington that is recalled by the rising two wings of the

Figure 7. Memorial to the Missing of the Somme, foundation wall

Vietnam Veterans Memorial directed toward the Washington Monument and the Lincoln Memorial, symbols of national foundation and struggle. As one draws closer to the Somme memorial, the imaginary connection between the two becomes even more compelling (fig. 8).

HERE ARE RECORDED
NAMES OF OFFICERS
AND MEN OF THE
BRITISH ARMIES WHO FELL
ON THE SOMME BATTLEFIELDS
JULY 1915–FEBRUARY 1918
THE FORTUNES OF WAR
DENIED THE KNOWN
AND HONOURED BURIAL
GIVEN TO THEIR
COMRADES IN DEATH

The further one pulls away from a war, the more prominent the cost in suffering and loss may seem; the political and strategic calculations that lay be-

Figure 8. Thiepval through the Vietnam Veterans eye (Photo by William Noble)

hind can take on a different order. Visitors' comments in the official register offer the same sentiments that are left at the Vietnam Veterans Memorial in Washington.

No words can convey the feelings I have. *Never* forgotten. (Grandson of Albert Dinnage/Killed 21.3.18)

The start of a new world, a new century. A tragedy. Rest in peace.

I came to see my granddad and I was moved.

They are not forgotten. We must never forget. We owe them so much.

So difficult, even now, not to feel so very sad and proud. I never want this to happen again.

A very fitting memorial to such brave men. They shall grow not old.

I am more than thankful to have survived 6^1/$_2$ years during 1939–1945. What a scale of sacrifice.

Found reference to a long-lost unknown uncle at last. So sad. RIP xxx

We owe it to our brave lads never to forget but to learn.

RIP Great Uncle Bruce Clark.

We came to pay our respects to great granddad Herbert Davis, missing on the Somme—Peace.

Bien entretenu

I hope I never have to weep for my son the way your mother wept for you . . . Words fail me.

Un grand merci pour vôtre aide

I cannot understand how this was allowed to happen. The futility of war is plain to see. May we never experience it. And for what? A bloody waste and a bloody shame.[20]

The names of the dead still draw mourners to these monuments, and their sheer numbers overwhelm us again.

As Dyer observes, there is something peculiarly prophetic about Lutyens's design: "Thiepval is not simply a site of commemoration but of prophecy, of birth as well as of death: a memorial to the future, to what the century had in store for those who were left, whom age would weary."[21] Another thing that gives Thiepval such power is the knowledge of how close it comes to proclaiming something very different from the kind of humane sentiment that inspired Maya Lin and Geoff Dyer. Little change would be required in the compass coordinates of human affection to make any monument to a war's dead the staging ground for the next war. The warring nature of monuments and memorials can be seen by referring to some work that is definitely related to what we have been considering, but morally and spiritually at opposite ends of the scale.

WAR BY OTHER MEANS

At the same time that Sir Edwin Lutyens was working out his design for the Thiepval memorial (1924), Adolf Hitler was sketching a similar *Triumphbogen*, or Arch of Triumph, in Berlin. Elias Canetti quotes Albert Speer's recollection of Hitler's comments: it would be 120 meters high, twice the size of Napoleon's Arc de Triomphe in Paris. In Hitler's words, "That will at least be a worthy monument to our dead in the World War. The name of every one of our 1,800,000 casualties will be carved in granite!"[22] As Canetti observes of Hitler's 1925 sketch, if so many names actually could be carved on a monument, they would be closer together than they ever could be in a crowd—for example, in a rally at Nuremberg: "not yet the corpses of his new war, planned and desired by him, they are the casualties of the first war, in which he served like anyone else." But Hitler plainly conceived of his memorial to the dead of the Great War as a way to lead the German nation into the next. As Canetti says, "Without the dead of World War I, he [Hitler] would never have existed."[23] And even if so many names could be inscribed—twenty times the names of Lutyens's memorial, nearly forty times the names of Maya Lin's—they would in truth be ignored, because this would be *his* Arch of Triumph.[24]

It is not necessary to go back to Assyrian reliefs or Roman triumphal sculpture to find Hitlerian fantasy made fact. The Iraqi writer and political exile Samir al-Khalil has shown that something very close to Hitler's Arch of Triumph in spirit and purpose, if not design, was realized in Saddam Hussein's Victory Monument, dedicated on August 8, 1989.[25] The "design idea" was spelled out in an invitation card to the dedication:

> The ground bursts open and from it springs the arm that represents power and determination, carrying the sword of Qadisiyya. It is the arm of the Leader-President, Saddam Husain himself (God preserve and watch over him) enlarged forty times. It springs out to announce the good news of victory to all Iraqis, and it pulls in its wake a net that has been filled with the helmets of the enemy soldiers, some of them scattering into the wasteland.[26]

For al-Khalil the art of Saddam Hussein's monument is the most vulgar kind of kitsch, but too horrifying to ignore.

> To look at the helmets in the knowledge that their scratches, dents and bullet holes were made by real bullets, that actual skulls might have exploded inside, is just as awe-inspiring as the knowledge that these are not anybody's arms, but the President's own. Or, for that matter, that not any old steel was used in the sword blades, but only that taken from Iraqi "martyrs."[27]

Grotesque as these triumphal imaginings are, they follow a venerable tradition of far longer duration than the memorials to humanity that began to appear in the twentieth century.

At the other end of the moral scale from Hitler and Hussein's works lie the Holocaust memorials dedicated to the memory of Jewish victims of the Nazis' genocidal program. Even these monuments are not immune from opposing interpretations and unsympathetic uses. In the view of Palestinians, such memorials are part of a program to legitimize Israel, and even a pretext for a war. In *The Texture of Memory*, James Young recounts how during the Intifada in 1988 in Gaza and the West Bank, a delegation of Palestinians laid a wreath at Nathaniel Rappoport's Warsaw Ghetto Monument, with an inscription in Polish "to those who perished in the Ghetto Uprising from those who perished in the Palestinian Uprising." This followed an earlier visit by a PLO delegate to the same memorial, who laid a wreath and declared that "as the Jews were then justified to rise up against their Nazi murderers, so now are the Palestinians justified in their own struggle with the Zionists."[28] From out of their own struggles the Palestinians were able to channel the traditional Jewish injunction to remember in a way that Rappoport himself could not anticipate. The same fate befalls the work of Maya Lin.

A VIETNAM WALL EXPERIENCE

War memorials are the trademarks of ownership.
Edward Bond, "Notes on Imagination"

The "Moving Wall" reproduces the original memorial in Washington in seventy-four hinged panels of Plexiglas mounted on wood frames. In the words of one of its original organizers, John Devitt, "The Moving Wall is just like the 'Wall' in Washington except for size. The mood, the emotions, the tears and the love are the same size."[29] It travels the country on a flatbed truck, typically spending a week at each site. "That is to give people time to come back. Most people come several times, because for veterans and parents, the first time is hard." As if made to exemplify some theory about the variability of interpretation, the Moving Wall takes on meanings that can change from one site it visits to the next. It could be set up in the middle of a town square or village green, or any other peaceful civic space. In November 1996, however, this reproduction of Maya Lin's work was exhibited at a military academy dedicated to the education of the next generation of officers, for the next war.

"The Vietnam Wall Experience at Norwich University (The oldest private military college in the nation)," in Northfield, Vermont, presented the names of twenty-two graduates of the university, joining five Northfield residents and more than one hundred servicemen and women from Vermont "who never returned." As the official program explained,

> The replica of "The Wall" (the Vietnam Veterans Memorial in Washington), produced by Habitat of Tempe, Arizona, has a simulated granite surface that looks and feels like the black Indiana granite used in the memorial in Washington. The process of inscribing the more than 58,000 names is the same sandblasting process used to create the original. Special care has been taken to be sure that the names are accurate and up to date.
>
> Constructed as a traveling memorial, the 240-foot replica, and the ceremonies that have taken place all around the country, have helped our nation reach a reconciliation with its history.

The traveling wall's simulated black granite walls are two-thirds the size of the original. The 125-degree angle of the two walls' intersection is maintained. The names from the original monument are all there, but the outer parts of each wall had to be cut up into sections. Transport and assembly dictate everything. If the long walls in Washington that gradually narrow down to a single name had been reproduced exactly, the traveling wall might take too much space. The effect of the gradual decline from ground level to ten feet and more below would be prohibitively expensive to reproduce. So the

Figure 9. The Vietnam Wall Experience, Northfield, Vermont

traveling wall is all at ground level, without the declining walkway (fig. 9). The names at the end of the tapering walls are grouped together in a squared end. The ensemble turns the three-dimensional experience of the original design into a two-dimensional cutout.

Practitioners of what Jessica Mitford calls the "American way of death" sponsored this appearance of the Moving Wall.[30] The sponsorship is of some relevance. To create a pleasing and comforting setting for a farewell to the dead, in the modern American funeral "home," evisceration, embalming, and cosmetology are all raised to a high art to guarantee that the realities of death remain unseen, for the brief space of time needed, and that what is seen appears in a reassuring light. (Appropriate indirect lighting is part of the effect.) In their own way, American funeral customs are no less strange than the well-documented mummification techniques of the ancient Egyptians, or the morbid science that is the subject of Ilya Zbarsky's strangely moving memoir of his father's lifework (preserving Lenin's corpse), *Lenin's Embalmers*.[31] This level of discretion, entirely typical of American ways of dealing with death (and not dealing with it), was particularly effective in the military setting of Norwich University. At this visit it seemed as if West Point and Forest Lawn were in collaboration.

Figure 10. Sacred ground, the Vietnam Wall Experience

In Northfield, Vermont, the only available site large enough to display the memorial was the university's parade ground and sports field. Tanks, portable outdoor toilets, and pieces of athletic equipment were moved to one side. A sign affixed to a trash can at the entrance warned visitors to observe an appropriate level of decorum (fig. 10). Women and men from the university's Corps of Cadets served as a twenty-four-hour honor guard. Dressed in parade uniforms, with rifles and fixed bayonets, they marched and paused at each turn of the watch, as if guarding a tomb—which they indeed were. Along with the flags and the assembled local veterans and visitors, the honor guard maintained a far stricter control over its memorial than is kept over the original in Washington.

Anyone who lived through the American war in Vietnam in the United States will find this escalation in control familiar. Maya Lin's design is made to mean the opposite of what she had envisioned; mourning the dead of one war becomes training for cadets who will fight the next. Yet this experience was no less real for those who visited the Moving Wall than a trip to Washington is for those who see the original memorial; as the traveling wall's sponsors noted, the tears and the sorrow are just as real. Millions of Americans never visit Washington, so, as the veterans and funeral directors and

Figure 11. Tracing names, the Vietnam Wall Experience

others who sponsored the experience had wanted, the Vietnam Veterans Memorial came to them.

As at Thiepval or Washington, the essence of the wall experience is best savored in details. The surface of the traveling wall is a thinly coated metal sheet a few millimeters thick. Slips of paper were handed out to encourage schoolchildren to do an exercise in rubbing with pencils, which provided a souvenir of their excursion to the exhibit (fig. 11). In several sections the frequent rubbing has begun to wear some of the names away.[32]

A view behind the scenes shows how the stage was set. The panels are metal sheets propped up with metal poles that fix the Moving Wall to a metal base (fig. 12). The ensemble has to be securely held down by additional ropes tied to stakes, since a strong wind could easily blow the exhibition down. The wall experience is most like being at the memorial in Washington at its center, though, again, there is a significant difference. The ensemble is foursquare, and on a level plane, with a wooden walkway in place of the descending and ascending stone walkways in Washington. The honor guard cadets are ever present, their fixed bayonets reminding you what the purpose of this Vietnam veterans memorial is, and what you should and should not remember.

Figure 12. Behind the scene, the Vietnam Wall Experience

AN AMERICA WAR EXPERIENCE

>Do they think of me now
>in those strange Asian villages
>where nothing ever seemed
>quite human
>but myself
>and my few grim friends
>moving through them
>hunched
>in lines?
>When they tell stories to their children
>of the evil
>that awaits misbehavior,
>is it me they conjure?
>W. D. Ehrhart, "Making the Children Brave"

Winners get to name their wars; the Trojan War will forever be the Trojan, not the Greek, War. But the *Iliad* and much other art from war enables us to enter as intimately into the mourning of an enemy as of a friend. It has never required a great leap of the imagination to see Homer's Trojan War as also the Trojans' Greek War. What Americans call "the Vietnam War" was in this sense obviously "the America War" for the Vietnamese. There is perhaps even more reason today to think of this conflict as the America War, since it was the Vietnamese of the north and of the Viet Cong, and not the Americans and their allies in the south, who eventually won it.

The Vietnam Wall Experience at Norwich University was a highly disciplined guide to what its war was supposed to mean. In this respect it was far more typical than Maya Lin's original of what such monuments are designed to accomplish, so far as governments are concerned. But as with all such conflicts that continue to live in our imagination, the American Vietnam War does not yet reduce to such a single meaning, however ardently the teachers of cadets might wish it.

Knowing that no such official war monument could help but omit as much as it commemorates, the antiwar activist and artist Chris Burden took Maya Lin's design and used it to unheal memory's wounds. A preliminary sketch of his *Other Vietnam Memorial* foresaw a "list of three million Vietnamese killed during the US involvement in Vietnam"; it would be on "Copper pages, hinged on [a] central pole," and could be turned by viewers.[33] In the catalogue prepared for a 1992 exhibition of *The Other Vietnam Memorial* at the Museum of Modern Art, Burden is quoted as saying, "I just thought somewhere there should be a memorial to the Vietnamese that were killed in the war. So I wanted to make this book, sort of like Moses' tablet, that would be an official record of all these three million names. I would suspect that we will be lucky if we get twenty-five percent of the names; other ones would be nameless, basically faceless, bodies. . . . I want the size of the sculpture . . . to reflect the enormity of the horror."[34]

The result is a memorial statistically impressive in its numbers, at the cost of making actual sense. In order to register three million casualties, Burden took a catalogue that contained four thousand Vietnamese names, transformed them into verbal integers, and designed a computer-generated permutation of them. As the exhibition's curator, Robert Storr, observed, "A degree of abstraction necessarily persists. Even so, the war that so many want to consign to the past has never been more actual, with the enormity of the bloodletting at last represented *in toto*. Reckoning the gross facts of history in terms of the fate of individuals, Burden's 'Other Vietnam Memorial' thus partially retrieves the Vietnamese dead from statistical purgatory and so from a double disappearance: the 3,000,000 it symbolically lists are the displaced persons of the American conscience."[35] *The Other Vietnam Memorial* is not only marked by a degree of abstraction. The aim is to exhaust the very idea of an American Vietnam War memorial.

Nations rarely build war memorials to their enemy dead, and when they do, as in Atatürk's monument to the British and Commonwealth dead at

Figure 13. Victory billboard, Ap Bac, Vietnam

Gallipoli (and to their mothers), postwar politics usually inspire the gesture.[36] Unlike Burden's *Other Vietnam Memorial,* war monuments and memorials in Vietnam are never conceived as counterparts to anything in the United States. They are uniformly the nation's commemoration of its dead and its celebration of victory in a war for independence. The Vietnam Wall Experience at Norwich University is closer to these America War monuments than any other Vietnam War memorial.[37] Their themes are as far from Burden's abstraction as can be imagined. Trophies and other souvenirs are prominent, as in the billboard on the highway in the Mekong Delta celebrating a victory at Ap Bac over the Americans and their helicopters in January 1963 (fig. 13). Throughout Vietnam the random names generated for Burden's *Other Vietnam Memorial* turn into documented lists of civilians and soldiers who are martyrs who died to win independence from foreign rule. To commemorate the 1972 Christmas bombing, the remains of an American B-52 have been left where they fell in Huu Tiep Lake in the village of Ngoc Ha in the northwestern part of Hanoi. A plaque at the site reads: "At 22:00 hours on December 27, 1972, the capital's anti-aircraft forces shot down this B-52 in the area of Ngoc Ha Village. This is one out of 23 B-52s shot down from Hanoi's skies. The strategic surprise attack against Hanoi by the B-52s of the Ameri-

Figure 14. Wreckage of an American B-52, Hanoi

can Empire was destroyed" (fig. 14). An easier stop for Americans than this gruesome souvenir is the crumbling concrete monument to a pilot who parachuted into a small lake in the northern sector of Hanoi and was captured and beaten by local farmers. As the inscription reads, "On September 26, 1967, on the Chapai Lake, Vietnamese people and army in Hanoi captured the American pilot Major John Sney McGan of the United States Air Force, who flew an A-4 fighter. This was the eighty-first fighter and it was shot down near the Yen Phu City electric plant. It was also one of ten American fighters shot down on the same day" (fig. 15). "John Sney McGan" is a garbled version of the name of John McCain, the U.S. senator, then the son of one of the top American commanders in the war and for that reason one of North Vietnam's prize American captives.

Outside the cities, the sites of some of the most ferocious battles of the war have long since been overgrown with tropical forestation. There are some locations that seem to preserve exactly the devastation of war while, perversely, they do nothing of the kind. At the remote site of Khe Sanh, in the central highlands near the Laotian border, there are traces of tunnels and bunkers, but most of the deep holes and earthworks that I could see in March 1994 were the work of dealers in scrap metal who scavenged the battlefields

Figure 15. McGan (McCain) monument, Hanoi

long after the war was over (fig. 16). A waving stone flag, a monument set in the middle of what used to be the marines' landing strip at Khe Sanh, recalls the war's rhetoric. It presents this inscription:

> The area of Tacon point was built by the Americans and their Saigon pup-pets. Built in 1968 including an airport and a steady defense system with 10,000 occupying soldiers and thousands of assault troops from the Ameri-cans and the Saigon puppet regime, in order to stop assistance from the north to the battle of the three countries of Indochina.
>
> After 170 days of offensives and siege, on July 7, 1968, Tacon Khe Sanh was liberated. We destroyed the enemy and his strategic systems, to the west of National Road No. 9, killing and capturing 11,900 enemy soldiers and shooting down 197 aircraft and also destroying much other war mater-ial of the Americans and their puppet regime.
>
> Khe Sanh became a Dien Bien Phu for America.

American air and firepower guaranteed that there would be no replay of the French defeat of 1954, however. General Giap never intended the siege at Khe Sanh to be a Dien Bien Phu for the Americans, but a diversion from the main event he was planning for 1968, the Tet offensive. When Khe Sanh's

Figure 16. Scrap metal excavation holes, DMZ

strategic uselessness for even a war of attrition was at last obvious to the
American commanding generals—it had been obvious to the marines from
the beginning—they evacuated the position and took everything with them
that could conceivably be used as a war trophy, or as material for propa-
ganda, not reckoning on the value scrap metal would have for a poor economy.

For Americans, the memorial to the victims of the 1968 massacre at Son
My (My Lai) will have more resonance than any other site in Vietnam. Over
its entrance are Ho Chi Minh's words, always inscribed at Vietnamese war
cemeteries: "There is nothing compared to freedom and independence."
The site of the massacre is documented by both art and the famous pho-
tographs seen around the world after My Lai was discovered. The museum
has in large letters over its front: "Never Forget Our Anger against the US
Oppressive Imperialists." Sculpture groups are scattered throughout the site,
all of them executed by Thu Ho, whose wife, Vu Thi Lien, was a young girl
who survived the massacre in the village and became its chief international
witness after 1968 (fig. 17).

My Lai is a reality that Burden's *Other Vietnam Memorial* seeks to evoke, but
it is no neutral record, either. The documentation of American war atrocities

Figure 17. Memorial sculpture, My Lai

is as scrupulous as possible; wherever the names or locations of victims could not be determined, the blank spaces themselves became a matter of record. Memorial stones mark the places where houses once stood, in which the owners and their families were killed. The museum's official casualty list (literally, "Name List of All of the People Who Were Killed at That Time") says that 182 women were killed (17 of them pregnant), 173 children (56 of them unnamed), and thirty-seven men over the age of sixty. The site where the most people were herded together and shot is now a drainage ditch marked with a memorial in English as well as Vietnamese (fig. 18).

Even as the American Vietnam War was being fought, there was also a civil war between the North and South Vietnamese. This led to memorials of a war that still seems under way, even as we visit it years later. During the war the South Vietnamese took Arlington National Cemetery for their model and with American advisors began construction in the late 1960s of a national cemetery for the soldiers of the Army of the Republic of Vietnam (ARVN, in American parlance). With the acceleration of the American withdrawal from the war (what the Americans termed "Vietnamization"), the casualties of the ARVN increased exponentially. By the end of the war in 1975 there was a huge but unfinished cemetery; as of 1994 its dilapida-

Figure 18. Execution ditch, My Lai

Figure 19. ARVN cemetery, Bien Hoa

tion had progressed at a steady rate. Some families paid villagers nearby to tend the graves, but for the most part the graves were abandoned and the tombstones defaced. Goats grazed in the weeds that grew among the graves (fig. 19).

In his memoir of a return to Vietnam after the America War was long over, Neil Sheehan observes, "In Washington, the names of each of our Vietnam dead were inscribed on a memorial near the hallowed temple to Abraham Lincoln. No one accepted responsibility for these dead ARVN soldiers. . . . In death they were discarded." Sheehan's Vietnamese guide, Mr. Tien, himself a veteran of the war who fought against the ARVN, was moved to say, "This should not happen to anyone."[38] The comparison with the Vietnam Veterans Memorial in Washington is quite apt. Sometimes war memorials are constructed too long after a war is over, as American vets argued when they pressed for what eventually became the Vietnam Veterans Memorial in Washington. The ARVN cemetery at Bien Hoa shows that they can sometimes be built too soon. In the accompanying photograph (fig. 20), for example, the name of the Buddhist sergeant Le Dinh Suong is preserved, as well as his branch of service (marines) and the date of his death (May 13, 1969),

Figure 20. The tombstone of Le Dinh Suong, Bien Hoa

but his picture has been chiseled out. Of all the monuments one could imagine, none expresses more directly the arbitrary way time has of dealing with the war dead than the poor traces of memorials that survive at Bien Hoa.

Pilgrimages to such memory places have become one of the preoccupations of our time. Proust is an eloquent witness to what can be recovered by such travel to these sites of memory.

> These are most hazardous pilgrimages, which end as often in disappointment as in success. It is in ourselves that we should rather seek to find those fixed places, contemporaneous with different years. . . . There is no need to travel in order to see it again; we must dig down inwardly to discover it. What once covered the earth is no longer above but beneath it; a mere excursion does not suffice for a visit to the dead city: excavation is necessary also. But we shall see how certain fugitive and fortuitous impressions carry us back even more effectively to the past, with a more delicate precision, with a more light-winged, more immaterial, more headlong, more unerring, more immortal flight, than these organic dislocations.[39]

A pilgrimage to the monuments of Thiepval, Norwich, or Bien Hoa is the kind of organic dislocation Proust describes. It leaves us more than ever in need of that delicate precision of thought, that light-winged, immaterial, immortal flight. We need the songs that the Muses inspire.

Two THE DAUGHTERS OF MEMORY

> The history of modern poetry is that of the continuous dichotomy of the
> poet, torn between the modern conception of the world and the sometimes
> intolerable presence of inspiration.
>
> Octavio Paz, *The Bow and the Lyre* ("Inspiration")

The theme of the *Iliad,* announced in the first word of the first line, is the rage
(*mēnis*) of Achilles. Many subsequent artists get down to business with equal directness. But today the goddess (*thea*) whom Homer calls on to sing this song of
Achilles' rage is passed over quickly. This move into the passing lane makes a
lot of sense for modern readers. Muses seem a most dispensable part of ancient
poetry. Far more dignified than muses, we think, is the veneration of *memory.*

From the standpoint of a traditional poem like the *Iliad* our solemn obses-
sion with memory is a serious mythological transgression.[1] The monuments
and the songs of war are created through the inspiration of the Muses, the
daughters of Zeus and Mnemosyne (Memory, or Remembering), whose duties are most fully described in Hesiod's hymn to them at the beginning of
the *Theogony.* When we make Memory our theme rather than her daughters,
more than divine dignity is lost. The modern insistence on memory as a construction—as opposed to the retrieval of facts—is but a rediscovery of the
inspiration of the Muses, translated into the abstractions of psychology,
rather than the delightful language of poetry and myth.

A modern command like Nabokov's memoir, *Speak, Memory,* summons the
wrong goddess. She is the mother of the nine Muses, the inspiring beings
who help mortal poets shape their imagination of war and all else.

> And then again the Olympian Muses and daughters of aegis-
> bearing Zeus
> hymn the races of men and of the brawny giants,
> and thrill the heart of Zeus in the realm of Olympos.
> Mnemosyne, mistress of Eleutherian hills,
> lay with father Zeus and in Pieria gave birth to the Muses
> who soothe men's troubles and make them forget their sorrows.
>
> (*Theogony* 50–55, Athanassakis)

We now like to say that our memories are constructed, fictions in the sense of the Latin *ficta*, things fashioned, made up. How would Memory or her daughters respond to our present orthodoxy? The one time they spoke to Hesiod directly, they were far from timid creatures.

> Listen, you country bumpkins, you swag-bellied yahoos,
> We know how to tell many lies that pass for truth,
> And we know, when we wish, to tell the truth itself.
> (*Theogony* 26–28, Athanassakis)

Memory herself never speaks in Homer or Hesiod, but her daughters might have reacted in a similar fashion to our current orthodoxies.

> Theorists and psychologists, mere grants and contracts,
> You proudly make memory a matter of the moment,
> Forgetting all the while the muse you should command.

As Octavio Paz observes in *The Bow and the Lyre*, inspiration still happens, and it matters. Randall Jarrell is at least as substantial a "war poet" as Wilfred Owen or any other soldier-poet of modern wars who fought and died in the trenches, yet he never saw a day of combat.[2] It is this inspiration that Odysseus praises so highly in the blind singer of tales who never went to Troy.

> Demodokos, accept my utmost praise.
> The Muse, daughter of Zeus in radiance,
> or else Apollo gave you skill to shape
> with such great style your songs of the Akhaians—
> their hard lot, how they fought and suffered war.
> You shared it, one would say, or heard it all.
> (*Odyssey* 8.487–92; 8.520–25, Fitzgerald)

Muses are not an archaic and irrelevant feature of ancient war stories, but crucial for the artist who would create something about war (war poetry being only one of the things a muse can inspire). The abandonment of muses, while generally a sound move in human progress, left those who would turn war into art perennially challenged. Let us see what happens when they try to work without these daughters of memory.

THE NEED FOR DISTANCE

What Homer relates to us is not a datable past and, strictly speaking, not even a past; it is a temporal category that floats, so to speak, above time, always avid to be present. It is something that happens again as soon as two lips utter the old hexameters, something that is always beginning and that does not cease to manifest itself. History is the place where the poetic word is incarnated.
Octavio Paz, *The Bow and the Lyre* ("The Consecration of the Instant")

An ordinary mortal's need for distance is well articulated by Proust's narrator in *Sodom and Gomorrah* (known in English by the prissy circumlocution *Cities of the Plain*), who suddenly recaptures with stunning power the reality of a past event. He has returned to the seaside resort at Balbec where his grandmother had taken him as a child, and as he bends over to unlace his shoes, an unexpected scene from the past comes back to him.

> I had just perceived, in my memory, stooping over my fatigue, the tender, preoccupied, disappointed face of my grandmother, as she had been on that first evening of our arrival, the face not of that grandmother whom I had been astonished and remorseful at having so little missed, and who had nothing in common with her save her name, but of my real grandmother, of whom, for the first time since the afternoon of her stroke in the Champs-Elysées, I now recaptured the living reality in a complete and involuntary recollection. This reality does not exist for us so long as it has not been recreated by our thought (otherwise men who have been engaged in a titanic struggle would all of them be great epic poets); and thus, in my wild desire to fling myself into her arms, it was only at that moment—more than a year after her burial, because of the anachronism which so often prevents the calendar of facts from corresponding to the calendar of feelings—that I became conscious that she was dead.[3]

The past becomes more powerful an experience in his memory than the original experience itself.

Distance enables even those who have no direct experience of war to create works of astounding power about it. This can be more than a temporal dislocation, as Stephen Crane discovered when he wrote *The Red Badge of Courage* from Civil War narratives, many of which were written before he was born. It was not immortality through song that Crane wished to create, but the distance from the present that ancient myth and legend have for modern writers. His solution came as he was revising *The Red Badge of Courage*, when he decided to make his story one about general types, not specific characters.[4] His revisions followed closely on reading a prodigious number of Civil War stories such as Grant's *Personal Memoirs* and back issues of *Century Magazine*. He also knew Tolstoy's short story "The Raid" and his collected war correspondence, "The Sebastopol Sketches,"[5] both of which came directly out of Tolstoy's experience in fighting and observing the Crimean War.

There is no record that Crane had any interest in working closely with Homer. He had probably read the *Iliad*, as so many have, early in his education, and not looked at it since. What Crane wanted to achieve was to remove his story from any connection to history.[6] This move into the timeless creates the mythlike quality of Crane's story.

Fittingly for Crane's young Henry Fleming, literature of any kind is a remote notion, a realm where Greek and Roman heroes easily blend into medieval gestes and fairy tales with their knights and castles. Henry gathers all such past wars into the dimmest recollection, a vague childhood memory. A purple patch sums up the distance from the *Iliad* that Henry thinks he enjoys.

> But awake he had regarded battles as crimson blotches on the pages of the past. He had put them as things of the bygone with his thought-images of heavy crowns and high castles. . . . He had long despaired of witnessing a Greek-like struggle. Such would be no more, he had said. Men were better, or, more timid. Secular and religious education had effaced the throat-grappling instinct, or, else, firm finance held in check the passions. . . . Tales of great movements shook the land. They might not be distinctly Homeric, but there seemed to be much glory in them.[7]

This has the irony of Socrates at his worst moments.[8] By the time Henry Fleming's battles are over, they are every bit as throat-grappling and Greek-like as any reader of Homer could desire. Crane's deceptively low-key "episode from the Civil War" emerges as a precocious war epic in miniature.

Anything but naive and artless, *The Red Badge* bears up quite well when played against the classical epic forms from which it so ironically distances its hero. In relation to nearly all the long American war novels and memoirs that were to follow it, the hundred pages of *The Red Badge of Courage* feel like the modern equivalent of the so-called *epyllion*, or "little epic" of Hellenistic Greek literature, a learned tradition best represented for us now by the Roman Catullus's masterpiece, poem 64. This is a highly compressed interweaving of heroic Greek myths, each set into a complex of interlocking tales of such epic-making events as the voyage of the *Argo* and the beginning of the love of Jason and Medea, the wedding of Achilles' parents Peleus and Thetis, Ariadne's abandonment by Theseus, and the song of the Fates at the birth of Achilles.

In the space of not much more than a hundred pages, Crane's "episode" quickly threatened to eclipse every other Civil War story. He was able to achieve an effect of timelessness that accords well with modern readers' sense of a seeming timelessness in ancient epic poetry. He creates his own equivalent of Homeric epic's effect on readers: of being of its time, and not of its time at all. *The Red Badge* is set in the American Civil War, as recognizable an epoch as any in history, yet any traces that would render a specific time, date, and place in the war have been polished away.[9] Crane's most recent biographer, Linda Davis, gives a sample of the revisions of his final draft, each of which tends to make his story seem timeless and mythical. When the first character is introduced in the second paragraph, he had first written, "Once, Jim Conklin developed virtues," but he canceled the name and wrote above it "a certain soldier"; then he inserted with a caret the additional epithet *tall*: "Once, a certain tall soldier developed virtues . . ." (fig. 21). Further down, we read of "the youth" instead of Henry Fleming and "his comrade" for "young Wilson." Along with his predilection for vivid, color-coded descriptions of nature, Crane's eccentric preference for types over names was so striking that Frank Norris found the style easy to parody. "A Mere Boy stood on a pile of blue stones. His attitude was regardant. The day was seal brown. There was a vermilion valley containing a church. . . . The Mere Boy was a brilliant blue color. The effect of the scene was not unkaleidoscopic. After a certain appreciable duration of time the Mere Boy abandoned his regardant demeanor."[10]

Crane aimed to move from history to fiction, from specific historical and geographical locations to types, as in his ambition to make his battles themselves "types." In his desire to create a "psychological portrait of fear," he wanted to shift the focus from generals to the privates who do the killing and the dying in modern warfare. The preference for type marks character and place and event for their exemplary qualities rather than particular ones. It is as if Crane had taken to heart Aristotle's influential ninth chapter in the *Poetics*, to move from the particulars of a unique historical person and event to the universals of poetry and philosophy. As *type*'s etymology in the Greek *typos* and its verb *tuptein* suggests ("to strike," "to brand," "to mark," "to imprint a sign"), a type is something one stamps or imprints, as on a coin type, rather than something one inherits. Crane's conception of types of character for his war narrative is thus exactly the opposite of a Greek, and specifically Homeric, way of thinking about the nature of men in battle. There the *hērōs* and *hērōes* generally have a *horos* or finite term to their season and are explicitly linked to the *hōrē* or actual season of other growing and living things. In his speech to the Greek hero Diomedes the Trojan ally Glaucus plays on this connection between heroic identity and the passing seasons of the year: as is the generation of leaves, so are the generations of humanity.[11]

The title of *The Red Badge of Courage* evolved just as the text itself did, away from the explicit and literal, toward the timeless and metaphorical. As his final draft was on its way to the printers, Crane's working title was "Private Fleming: His various battles." On the same first page of the final manuscript, the working title is scratched out and the one that was published appears in a large hand. The title *Red Badge of Courage* offers not just a theme but a metaphor, and one appropriate both for the color-saturated world of the novel and for the turning point in Henry Fleming's fortunes, when he gets his red badge of courage. Crane's last-minute inspiration is sometimes disparaged by those who do not know his work, as if he were as gushing and

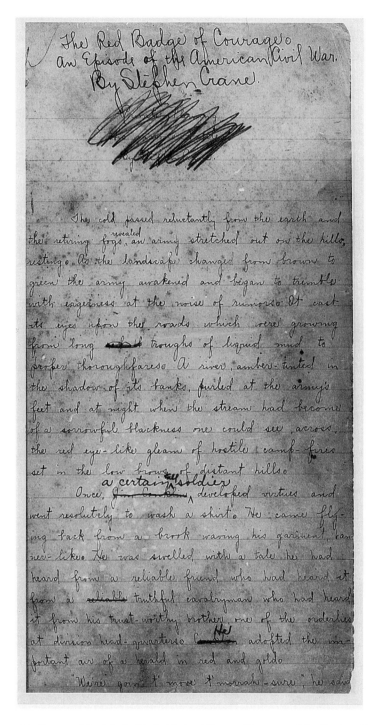

Figure 21. Corrected final draft, *The Red Badge of Courage* (Courtesy of the Stephen Crane Collection, #5505, Clifton Waller Barrett Library, The Albert and Shirley Small Special Collections Library, University of Virginia Library.)

naive as the title itself. In fact, it is an inspired lifting of the thoughts of Henry Fleming, the youth who "wished that he, too, had a wound, a red badge of courage."[12] Although *The Red Badge* came in for mockery and parody as soon as it was published—"The Blue Blotch of Cowardice," "The Red Badge of Hysteria"[13]—the origin of this overheated metaphor is as ironic as everything else Crane's youth says or thinks. *The Red Badge of Courage* is true to the story Crane begins in the way that Homer's *mēnis* or anger of Achilles is to his.[14]

At the same time *The Red Badge* is remote from the *Iliad*'s way of seeing things. When Crane removed the unique identity typical of both history and ancient heroic poetry (Henry Fleming becoming "the Youth," Jim Conklin, "a certain soldier"), he eliminated what Homer most wanted to create, the immortality of a name like Hector, Helen, or Achilles. His procedure is the reverse of creating immortality through song, yet to his readers the tale does indeed suggest ancient Greek-like struggles and Homeric movements. Even though these are utterly different kinds of wars, worlds, and works, by aiming for "types" Crane has managed to bring them together. The types of *The Red Badge of Courage* give it an Iliadic, Homeric quality—distancing Henry's war and making myth of it so that it seems as remote from us as the *Iliad*.

THE COMPRESSION OF OPPOSITES

It was not dying: everybody died.
It was not dying: we had died before
In the routine crashes—and our fields
Called up the papers, wrote home to our folks,
And the rates rose, all because of us.
We died on the wrong page of the almanac,
Scattered on mountains fifty miles away;
Diving on haystacks, fighting with a friend,
We bladed up on the line we never saw.
We died like aunts or pets or foreigners.
(When we left high school nothing else had died
For us to figure we had died like.)
Randall Jarrell, "Losses"

According to traditional theories of poetry, no skill is more important for a poet than a facility for metaphor. Aristotle points out in the *Poetics* that this is a skill that cannot be taught, because it depends on an ability to perceive similarities in dissimilars, the likeness in unlike things.[15] The *Iliad* and most war poetry abound with examples of this unteachable art.[16] Consider the moment when Menelaus is wounded by an arrow from the Trojan Pandarus in book 4. It is an infamous deed, since it breaks a truce and plunges both sides back into battle. It is also the occasion for one of the most famous similes in the *Iliad*, and one of the most puzzling.[17] Perceptions and things are juxtaposed that are otherwise never proximate in time and space.

> The bitter arrow was driven against the joining of the war belt
> and passed clean through the war belt elaborately woven;
> into the elaborately wrought corselet the shaft was driven
> and the guard which he wore to protect his skin and keep the
>   spears off,
> which guarded him best, yet the arrow plunged even through
>   this also
> and with the very tip of its point it grazed the man's skin
> and straightway from the cut there gushed a cloud of dark
>   blood.
> As when some Maionian woman or Karian with purple
> colors ivory, to make it a cheek piece for horses;
> it lies away in an inner room, and many a rider
> longs to have it, but it is laid up to be a king's treasure,
> two things, to be the beauty of the horse, the pride of the
>   horseman:
> so, Menelaos, your shapely thighs were stained with the color
> of blood, and your legs also and the ankles beneath them.
>   (4.134–47, Lattimore)

This is a stunning evocation of what it may be like to be hit by a weapon in war, and not know at first what has happened to you. The simile also pushes us far beyond that immediate impact of war, to thoughts of artisan women at work. We already know that this is not going to be a mortal wound.

> Still the blessed gods immortal did not forget you,
> Menelaos, and first among them Zeus' daughter, the spoiler,
> who standing in front of you fended aside the tearing arrow.
> She brushed it away from his skin as lightly as when a mother
> brushes a fly away from her child who is lying in sweet sleep,
> steering herself the arrow's course straight to where the
>   golden
> belt buckles joined and the halves of his corselet were fitted
>   together.
>   (4.127–33, Lattimore)

The homely domestic image of a mother brushing a fly away from a sleeping child turns Menelaus into a distant object unaware of both his beauty and the danger that threatens him. He is already regarded at a distance, as a thing to contemplate, a lovely vision.

What we see here as well is a conflation of scenes of war and peace, a perception that neither Menelaus nor Agamemnon may understand, but something the enemy archer Pandarus could view with detachment: a deadly arrow shot in war creates a wound that is beautiful. The delicate task of staining the white surface of ivory yields an artifact, and so does the arrow from Pandarus's bow working on Menelaus's body. There are erotic overtones for Menelaus, the cuckolded husband and king: his shapely thigh running with blood suggests a kind of martial Adonis. The arrow's progress through his armor and the grazing of his flesh inspire the simile, which turns on the precision of the Maionian women's art. The spreading stain from the dye shows how close he comes to turning into a lovely artifact of battle; the bloodied thigh of the warrior even suggests the flowing blood of a menstruating woman.

Such perceptions are typical of war. In his World War II memoir, *The Warriors*, the philosopher Glenn Gray says that "War compresses the greatest opposites into the smallest space and the shortest time."[18] The density of the war experience is like the poet's compression of opposites into a new unity that often defies comprehension.[19] In *Bloods*, Wallace Terry's oral history of African Americans who served in the Vietnam War, Heywood T. Kirkland recalls what happened to a fellow soldier:

> He went down to the water hole to fill up his canteen. On his way back, he stepped on a 500-pound bomb that was laid in a tank track.
>
> You don't walk in no tank tracks, because that's where the bombs are usually. Charlie would use the rationale that most tanks would follow their tracks, and they would booby-trap tank tracks.
>
> We didn't see that white brother anymore. All we saw was a big crater, maybe six feet deep. And some remains. You know, guts and stuff. And the dirt had just enveloped the stuff. It looked like batter on fish and batter on chicken pieces. His body looked like that.[20]

There is no report of the explosion, only the aftermath; a deep crater and some dust-covered remains. The precision of the observation in Kirkland's simile brings the silent memory to life through its confusion of images drawn from food and war.

This imaginary fusion of opposites attempts to give a name to nameless feelings and perceptions. It is difficult to say which image haunts us more, the pain and death that such similes describe or the homely pleasures of cooking and craftsmanship that now seem much less innocuous, much less comforting.

The figurative thinking that war inspires can also be found in the art of war photographers, who are no more simply reporting the facts of war's

mayhem than Homer. In the civil war in El Salvador in the 1980s, a rebel soldier fighting against the Salvadorean army knew the little figurines of *calaveras,* or skeletons, made for El Día de los Muertos, the Day of the Dead,
mementos mori that are among the most familiar icons in a culture that does
not shrink from mortality. The Mexican artist Felipe Linares's seething cauldron of calaveras in *Pantéon de Diablito Rojo* (or *Pantheon of the Little Red Devil*)
(fig. 22) shows policemen, generals, politicians, and other oppressors of the
people getting their fit punishment.[21] The rebel turned the artistry and hu-
mor of these traditional figures back into fact. The war photographer James
Nachtwey's picture of a mutilated corpse from that civil war shows a victim
of terrorism whose skull has been treated like a work of art (fig. 23). What
experience in game hunting or in the art of cooking did that unknown warrior have, to strip the flesh so carefully from the skull as to resemble the *figura
descarneada* or defleshed body of the Day of the Dead? The framing of
Nachtwey's picture suggests a Goyaesque deposition from the cross, fully
comparable to the brilliantly drawn horrors of *The Disasters of War.*[22] This fusion of opposites leads to a mental confusion not unlike the confusions of
war itself.

The handiwork of the anonymous Salvadorean rebel is shaped by the
same unteachable art that fashions metaphor and simile, though it is art per-
verted to a debased level. Homer turns a war wound into an aesthetic moment, distancing us from the blood running down the white thighs of
Menelaus so that we can think of such oddly dispassionate parallels in the
crafts of war and the crafts of women, even as both Menelaus and his brother
Agamemnon look at this wounding by Pandaros's arrow in fear and trem-
bling. In El Salvador, the folk artist's talent for creating a figure for human
mortality is turned into an instrument of terror in war. The same careful
technique of carving figurines is transferred from wood or ivory to actual human flesh. This half-finished anatomy lesson is an act of sadism typical of the
killing and mutilating in war, with a clear message to those who discover it:
This is what we can do to you, and it is more than just kill you.

Nachtwey's photograph works on us like Homer's similes. Perhaps the
most salient is this one describing the struggle of Greeks and Trojans over
the naked body of Patroclus, which is treated here like the by-products of a
slaughterhouse.

> As when a man gives the hide of a great ox, a bullock,
> drenched first deep in fat, to all his people to stretch out;
> the people take it from him and stand in a circle about it
> and pull, and presently the moisture goes and the fat sinks

Figure 22. Felipe Linares, a cauldron of *calaveras*, detail from *Pantéon de Diablito Rojo* (Courtesy of Fowler Museum of Cultural History, UCLA. Photo by Denis J. Nervig.)

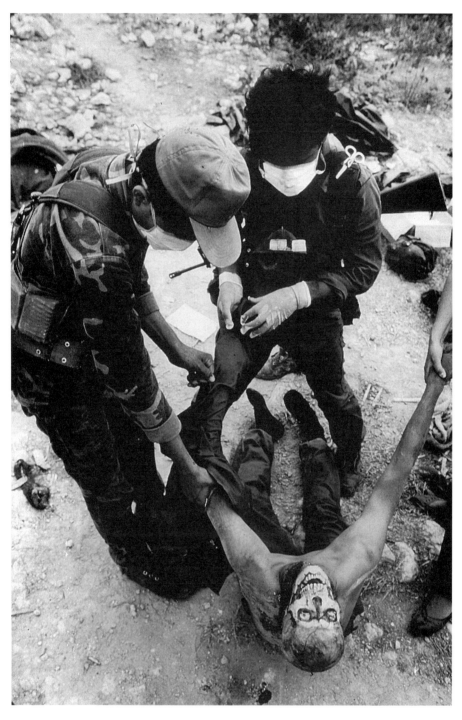

Figure 23. James Nachtwey, *Army Soldier Killed in Rebel Attack*, Tejutepque, El Salvador, 1984 (Used with permission of Magnum Photos, Inc.)

> in, with so many pulling, and the bull's hide is stretched out
>   level;
> so the men of both sides in a cramped space tugged at the
>   body
> in both directions; and the hearts of the Trojans were hopeful
> to drag him away to Ilion, those of the Achaeans
> to get him back to the hollow ships.
>   (17.389–97, Lattimore)

At first the distance between skinned ox-hide and warrior's corpse seems vast, and the association, bizarre. The people working together on the hide are the opposite of the warriors locked in struggle. Not alike in one way, they are entirely alike in another. The difference between a man's body and an animal's recedes; it is tanning and stretching skin that we are witnessing, nothing more. This sets human slaughter and animal slaughter at the same level, where dignity vanishes, where tugging leads to a slaughtered man and a slaughtered ox-hide becoming, in a matter-of-fact way, one and the same thing.[23]

This is not the worst thing that could have happened to the body of Patroclus.

> But Hector, when he had stripped from Patroclus the glorious
>   armour,
> dragged at him, meaning to cut his head from his shoulders
>   with the sharp bronze,
> to haul off the body and give it to the dogs of Troy.
>   (17.125–27, Lattimore)

As for that ox-hide: modern students of violence often say that one of our innovations in organized violence has been the application of industrial technologies to the extermination of human beings.[24] But this application of state-of-the-art technology to killing in war is the oldest of moves. War and its effect on human imagination suggest that it is more the particular objects than the mode of thinking that have changed. Works of war always come from the works of peace, where technology, which is never innocent, continues to play its role. When Simoeisios is slain by Ajax with a spear thrust through the right breast and shoulder, he falls

>   like some black poplar,
> which in the land low-lying about a great marsh grows
> smooth trimmed yet with branches growing at the uttermost
>   tree-top:
> one whom a man, a maker of chariots, fells with the shining

> iron, to bend it into a wheel for a fine-wrought chariot,
> and the tree lies hardening by the banks of a river.
> Such was Simoeisios, whom illustrious
> Ajax killed.
> (4.482–89, Lattimore)

Simoeisios ("born of the river Simois") lives up to his name: he falls like a poplar in a marsh, cut down and bent into a wheel for a chariot. Simoeisios now lies hardening anonymously by a riverbank—a stripling cut down and processed in war.[25]

War charges mundane tasks and objects in peacetime with unexpected meanings: pieces of chicken and fish in batter for deep-fat frying, little skeletons for the celebration of El Día de los Muertos, a precious piece of ivory carved and stained to adorn some nameless nobleman's horse, a communal tanning of a fat-soaked ox-hide, a pliant tree cut down and bent to a circle to season by a riverbank. Each of these artifacts appears in a continuum of poetry made from war, one that ranges from Homer's *Iliad* to an African American veteran's recollections for an oral history of the American Vietnam War, to anonymous folk art and its perversion in El Salvador, to the photographer whose work memorialized both. By ordinary calculations in history, geography, or politics these would be discontinuous artifacts; they share no theme save the imagination of war that gives them birth. Each draws a connection between the familiar, everyday experiences of the world outside war and the unfamiliar experience of the world within war. Each of them illustrates the range of creativity that the poetry of war can achieve.

Artists play on this continuity between the destructive and the creative impulse, over and over again; the combination of destructiveness and creativity animates everything they do. We imagine that this is a unity of opposites that can happen only in a work of art, and then war makes us see these contrary elements all about us, even in peacetime. Poetry of war moves on a continuum from literal fact to the most fanciful kinds of likeness and unlikeness imaginable. It is a dynamic process, moving from one extreme to another, a space where Glenn Gray's compression of opposites always exists. However beautiful it may be, the poetry that comes out of war never loses the essential tension implicit in its origins.

There is much pleasure to be had in this compression of opposites. Captured weapons, uniforms, battle standards, and civilian booty have always furnished toys for children and trophies for grown-ups, whether they be images on an Assyrian relief, Roman triumphal arches, the columns of Trajan and Marcus Aurelius, or Saddam Hussein's victory monument in Baghdad created out of the helmets taken from thousands of captured or dead Iranian soldiers. In World War II an American soldier sent a letter opener carved out of a Japanese soldier's bone to the president of the United States. Roosevelt declined the souvenir, and the story was widely broadcast in Japan as an example of American racism and inhumanity.[26]

An artifact that appears early in the *Iliad* conveys a similar tension, a piece of war booty casually mentioned in the sweep of the narrative, and not at all like the gruesome images from El Salvador or World War II. We see Achilles in book 9, for the first time after his great quarrel with Agamemnon, as he is visited by Agamemnon's representatives, Phoenix, Odysseus, and Ajax:

> Now they came beside the shelters and ships of the
>   Myrmidons
> and they found Achilles delighting his heart in a lyre, clear-
>   sounding,
> splendid and carefully wrought, with a bridge of silver upon it,
> which he won out of the spoils when he ruined Eëtion's city.
> With this he was pleasuring his heart, and singing of men's
>   fame,
> as Patroklus was sitting over against him, alone, in silence,
> watching Aiakides and the time he would leave off singing.
>   (9.185–91, Lattimore)

The lyre from Eëtion's city is a beautiful artifact, typical of the spoils that men go to war to claim. Nothing would seem less sinister. As he regularly does with significant objects, the poet goes into some detail to make us see as well as hear the pleasure that it brings.[27] The lyre is not armor or weaponry. It seems especially civilized when we recall Andromache's earlier account of the death of her father, Eëtion.

> It was brilliant Achilles who slew my father, Eëtion,
> when he stormed the strong-founded citadel of the Kilikians,
> Thebe of the towering gates. He killed Eëtion
> but did not strip his armor, for his heart respected the dead
>   man,
> but burned the body in all its elaborate war-gear
> and piled a grave mound over it, and the nymphs of the
>   mountains,
> daughters of Zeus of the aegis, planted elm trees about it.
>   (6.414–20, Lattimore)

Distant as it seems from the stark images of tanning, ivory carving, and cooking that we have seen invoked, the lyre from Eëtion's city would necessarily convey a completely opposite meaning to Andromache. If we recall it, our awareness of her story might give a poignant twist to the sentiment of this moment, perhaps even a bitterer edge to Achilles' play with the spoils of war. The song of men's fame that Achilles sings so movingly to himself depends for its accompaniment on an instrument that was captured from her father. The music of his heroic song has in it a tension that vibrates from the strings of his lyre, with overtones hinting at moments far different from this seemingly civilized pause in a war. Just so does the *Iliad* open, not with the twang of strings on Apollo's lyre, but with the twang of his bowstring, in the plague he sends on the Achaeans.[28]

Yet the lyre from Eëtion's town is different in style but not in substance from the bloodiest spoils of war. In Michael Lynn-George's words, "The lyre itself tells a story, one in which every possession is also a tale of plunder."[29] Achilles sings of men's fame—the general theme of epic poetry, though not the theme of the *Iliad*—and he performs this song with spoils taken from a slain enemy's city. What would be a heartbreaking reminder to Andromache, memories of a father and home and way of life lost, is for her father's killer something to be admired, a lovely instrument to accompany a warrior's song.

Three RAGE FOR ORDER

Oh! Blessed rage for order, Pale Ramon,
The maker's rage to order words of the sea.
    Wallace Stevens, "The Idea of Order at Key West"

Before the first poet made the first song about war and before the first veteran told his story, war already had its poets. The commanders of war are its first poets; in the root sense of the word, they are its first makers. Homer's story of the rage of Achilles and his quarrel with Agamemnon in the opening books of the *Iliad* reflects a keen understanding of the structures of command that create a world of war.

Today the commander's story is often passed over for individual accounts of ordinary soldiers. Sometimes those who lead wars seem as remote from those they lead as the Olympian gods themselves. The *Iliad* suggests that nothing could be more shortsighted than such a disconnect. It is against a commander's vision that Achilles so famously rebels. The entire poem is the consequence of that challenge. Agamemnon and what in a modern army would be called his lieutenants barely turn back the dissolution of the Greek army that Achilles sets in motion. Their war resumes its course in a book whose greatest poetry has lamentably become nothing but a time-bound burst of Panhellenic pride, the so-called catalogue of ships. The second book of the *Iliad* is a commander's song. To appreciate the arts of Agamemnon and his successors, we will need to draw on the clarity and directness of Ulysses S. Grant and other commanders. They make strategies that those they command must be ready to die for.

RAGE WITHIN THE WORLD OF WAR

> There is, I believe, something useful to be gained from a study of war
> and violence in Homer.
> Hans van Wees, *Status Warriors*

Only in the last few years have classicists begun to read the *Iliad* as a war poem.[1] There have been studies of parts of it as specimens of war, especially the tactics of Homeric warfare and the poet's narrative techniques in orchesating battle scenes.[2] These are recent developments. As Hans van Wees bserves, though the *Iliad* may seem to be synonymous in our minds with var, neither *war* nor *battle* rated so much as an entry in the index to one of the najor resources for Homeric studies of the twentieth century, the 1962 edition of Wace and Stubbings's *Companion to Homer*.[3] Van Wees's own book *Status Warriors* begins with a more precise formulation than the generic word *war* itself could convey. For him, the story of the anger of Achilles is primarily concerned with "ethical, psychological and practical problems associated with anger and revenge, rather than with alienation, death or justice—subjects with which modern interpretations tend to be preoccupied"; the Homeric poems "reflect ideals of social stratification in Homer's own time. By presenting these ideals of stratification as the reality of the past, the epics indirectly legitimise the reality of stratification in the present."[4] The *Iliad* spoke directly to the men who ran the world—a reasonable observation, given the nature of the society that it portrays.[5] But van Wees also links violence in the Homeric world with the violence of contemporary Western culture, ranging from that perpetrated by nations, to the violence of street gangs and criminals.

Classicists had some reason not to read the *Iliad* this way. It was not so much oversight as it was the consequence of inheriting a view of Homer as *the* poet of the classical tradition, a view originating in ancient Greece, restated by classicists ever since, and now the bedrock position of general courses in humanities, especially the American "great books" course.[6] This veneration has contributed to the view of the *Iliad* as pure poetry, rather than pure poetry that also happens to be about war. In his Vanier Lectures of 1970, *War as a Way of Life in Classical Culture*, Eric Havelock observed that the more the *Iliad* was admired as a literary masterpiece, the more remote it became from everyday life: "This remoteness, which becomes an ingredient, perhaps an essential one, in Homer's sublimity, began to be visible in antiquity."[7] While the *Iliad* itself became more purely poetic, and divorced from the daily concerns of European life, its ideological framework, which put war at the center of human history, was inherited by both Herodotus and Thucydides. Dedicating his book to the memory of Ernest Wilfred Havelock, killed on the Somme in 1916, and speaking in October 1970 at a Canadian university during the American Vietnam War, Havelock was thinking of much more than classical studies. He argued that European culture has been living with this heritage from Homer and especially the historians of Greece ever since. "Neither of them [Herodotus and Thucydides] could evade that general view of the human condition which in Homer places warfare at the center of man's activities. This, rather than the events of their epoch as such, supplied that secret dynamic which made both of them into historians of war."[8]

Classicists read Homer with a clear focus on his Greek, especially Achilles' rage (*mēnis*) and its consequences. This focus on rage was not only good philology, it is also a view of war that modern historians have come to articulate with more precision. If we are interested in the stories of individuals, *war* does not tell us as much as *rage* does. To focus on rage and emotions is now our way of understanding the world within war, a world that is increasingly understood as an expression of human psychology as much as an event in political policy and military strategy. As Jill Lepore puts it at the beginning of her book on King Philip's War (1675–76),

> Words about war are slippery, and "war" itself may be the slipperiest of all. War is hell, we say, and war's a game. War is a contagion, the universal perversion. War is politics by other means, at best barbarism, a mean, contemptible thing. We say many things about war, not all of them profound, and few as pithy as these. Eminently quotable remarks aside, war is perhaps best understood as a violent contest for territory, resources, and political allegiances, and, no less fiercely, a contest for meaning. At first, the pain and violence of war are so extraordinary that language fails us: we cannot name our suffering and, without words to describe it, reality itself becomes confused, even unreal. But we do not remain at a loss for words for long. Out of the chaos we soon make new meanings of our world, finding words to make reality real again, usually words like "atrocity" and "betrayal."[9]

Although there are as many different ways to describe war as there are writers, one thing all agree on is its indescribability. These abstractions are all we have, and they never seem to be adequate.

Homer's theme of the rage of Achilles goes to the heart of what it is that makes wars happen: the desire to kill, whether calculated and ritualized or unchanneled and uncontrollable. In *The Face of Battle* John Keegan similarly directs his war story away from political history, toward psychological rather than historical themes.[10] In this sense *war* and the war story are always an experience and a narrative waiting to happen, an entry word to a more particular experience. The proem of the *Iliad* compresses awareness of the issues that both Keegan and Lepore raise about describing war in history.

The *Iliad*'s concentration of war into Achilles' rage once seemed to separate it from history, both ancient and modern. The Great War veteran and military historian Basil H. Liddell-Hart introduces his memoir *The Real War, 1914–1918* in a way that would exclude just this kind of concentration.

Some may say that the war depicted here is not "the real war"—that this is to be discovered in the torn bodies and minds of individuals. It is far from my purpose to ignore or deny this aspect of the truth. But for anyone who seeks, as I seek here, to view the war as an episode in human history, it is a secondary aspect. Because the war affected individual lives so greatly, because these individuals were numbered by millions, because the roots of their fate lay so deep in the past, it is all the more necessary to see the war in perspective, and to disentangle its main threads from the accidents of human misery. Perhaps this attempt is all the more desirable by reason of the trend of recent war literature, which is not merely individualistic, but focuses attention on the thoughts and feelings of some of the pawns of war. The war was, it is true, waged and decided in the minds of individuals more than in the physical clash of forces. But these decisive impressions were received and made in the cabinets and in the military headquarters, not in the ranks of the infantry or in the solitude of stricken homes.[11]

Liddell-Hart's focus on larger themes is no evasion, though those who are well read in Graves, Owen, Remarque, and other Great War writers might be tempted to think so. A combat veteran himself, Liddell-Hart knew at first hand what the poets of the Great War were attempting to convey. That is not his theme: he wants the commander's vision, not the vision of the commanded. Now we have largely separate traditions of the soldier's memoir and of the commander's story. What the *Iliad* does for us, schooled as we are in those traditions, is show how to bring together war stories that Liddell-Hart would keep apart.

In the first book of the *Iliad*, Achilles is like one of Linderman's American soldiers of World War II, without a past or future world outside war to flee to, so caught up is he in the world created by fighting and killing and dying. No matter what the reasons were for starting his war, no matter how good they seemed at the time, others far more compelling now supersede the original purpose, and they have been generated within the war itself.

> I for my part did not come here for the sake of the Trojan
> spearmen to fight against them, since to me they have done
> nothing.
> Never yet have they driven away my cattle or my horses,
> never in Phthia where the soil is rich and men grow great did
> they
> spoil my harvest, since indeed there is much that lies between
> us,
> the shadowy mountains and the echoing sea; but for your
> sake,

> O great shamelessness, we followed, to do you favour,
> you with the dog's eyes, to win your honour and Menelaos'
> from the Trojans. You forget all this or else you care nothing.
>   (1.152–60, Lattimore)

Such discoveries are not confined to the poets and their heroes. What Lincoln said at his second inaugural in 1865 is a concise commentary on the war we see at the opening of the *Iliad*: "Neither part expected for the war the magnitude, or the duration, which it has already attained. Neither anticipated that the cause of the conflict might cease with, or even before, the conflict itself should cease. Each looked for an easier triumph, and a result less fundamental and astounding." His own war would soon lead to results equally fundamental and astounding for Lincoln himself, results that he had already foreseen.

But Achilles is not just addressing the war aims of Agamemnon. There is also a complaint against personal injustice and hypocrisy, and a sense that he is fighting a war for others whose interests scarcely coincide with his own. In this respect the *Iliad*'s opening puts it in line with the experience of any warrior who finds himself enlisted in a cause for which he has no sympathy. It became a familiar story in twentieth-century war literature, where men are often found fighting for a cause they have no part of. Yeats's "An Irish Airman Foresees His Death" makes Achilles' complaint with exceptional pathos.[12]

> I know that I shall meet my fate
> Somewhere among the clouds above;
> Those that I fight I do not hate,
> Those that I guard I do not love;
> My country is Kiltartan Cross,
> My countrymen Kiltartan's poor,
> No likely end could bring them loss
> Or leave them happier than before.
> Nor law, nor duty bade me fight,
> Nor public men, nor cheering crowds,
> A lonely impulse of delight
> Drove to this tumult in the clouds;
> I balanced all, brought all to mind,
> The years to come seemed waste of breath,
> A waste of breath the years behind
> In balance with this life, this death.[13]

The political status of the Irish in the British Empire's Great War has its direct parallel in African American literature of the nineteenth and twentieth enturies.[14] In John Oliver Killens's *And Then We Heard the Thunder,* a 1954 novel about African American soldiers in the Pacific war, the hero of the story, Solly, is walking up the gangway of his troop ship. Hearing the navy band playing "God Bless America," he thinks of his wife, Millie, whom he's leaving behind.

> He hoped she could hear the band playing and that she would know how much it helped him to understand why Americans, no matter their color or condition, had to go to fight for their country so many thousands of miles away from home. "God bless America . . . God bless America" . . . *I love this land* . . . He really loved this land.
>
> They stopped in the middle of the block and stood waiting until the last white regiment was all aboard. He wanted to look back for one last glimpse of Millie.
>
> *I love you, Millie—I love this land—*
>
> He wanted desperately to look back, but he would not let himself. Then they started again, marching toward the ship, and it hit him like a vicious kick in the solar plexus, as suddenly the band stopped playing "God Bless America" and jumped into another tune—"The Darktown Strutters' Ball."
>
> He didn't want to believe his ears. He looked up heatedly at the ship and saw some of the white soldiers on deck, waving and smiling innocently and friendly-like at the Negro soldiers below, and yelling "Yeah, man!" and popping their pinky-White fingers. A taste of gall crept from his stomach up into his mouth. . . .
>
> . . . He just felt his anger mounting and he wished he could walk right out of the line and to hell with everything. Nothing had changed though. He would still do what he had to do. He would take care of himself, he would get ahead in the Army, he would come home safe and sound to Millie. He would hate it and at the same time take advantage of it. There was nothing else that he could do. His face filled up, his eyes were warm and misty too. With "The Darktown Strutters' Ball" ringing in his ears he put up his head and threw his shoulders back, and he kept on marching toward the big white boat.[15]

Killens offers us a crash course, in one easy lesson, about going to war for racist America in World War II. As with Yeats's Irish airman and as with Achilles, Solly's bitter discoveries change nothing in the ongoing, overarching reality of the war being fought, but they do show how the world before war affects the way it is waged. Homer's critics never tire of telling us how marvelous the design of his poem is: leaving out the origins of war, not trying to tell the whole story. Perhaps the *Iliad*'s design is compelling because it comes from the poet's perception of what war actually means, both to those who are in it, and to those who survive it.

MUDDLING THROUGH

For their part, the Greeks knew Homer and all the ironies of his poem, and then went forward to war anyway. This is what people in wars do. In his last speech to the Athenians, as reported by Thucydides, Pericles is a candid critic of the vagaries of civilian opinion in war. He speaks for the abiding presence of commanders throughout military and political history, especially in democracies. These may not be the leaders we want, but they are the ones we will always turn to.

> For going to war is great folly for those whose general good fortune gave them a choice; but when it was necessary either to become the subjects of others by yielding or to prevail by taking risks, the one who shuns danger deserves condemnation more than the one confronting it. I am the same, my position unchanged; it is you who have shifted, because it developed that you were persuaded when unharmed and regretted it when injured, and in your weakened state of mind my policy appears wrong (because there is grief felt by each of you right now, but realization of the benefits is still a long way off for one and all), and since a great reversal has befallen you, and that with little warning, your attitude is too feeble to persevere in what you resolved. (Thucydides, *The Peloponnesian War* 2.61, Lattimore)

The opening books of the *Iliad* are an analysis—if you will, a demolition and reconstruction—of John Keegan's mask of command.[16] There are two being worn here: Agamemnon, the king whose rule is sanctioned by Zeus, and Achilles, who has a plan of his own to wreck Agamemnon's war. When Achilles quits the scene, he sets in motion a destabilizing challenge to Agamemnon's war.

> Once the two had fought it out with words,
> battling face-to-face, both sprang to their feet
> and broke up the muster beside the Argive squadrons.
> Achilles strode off to his trim ships and shelters,
> back to his friend Patroclus and their comrades.
> (1.304–7; 356–60, Fagles)

The *Iliad* builds on the conflict between what war leaders desire and the unforeseen twists and turns that every war takes. It anticipates the thinking of Clausewitz, Grant, and other, later military leaders and theorists of war, through the vicissitudes of Agamemnon. He has received bad press in myth and poetry, not only for his treatment of Achilles, but for the sacrifice to Artemis of his daughter Iphigenia. That notorious crime, suppressed in Homer's poems, moves to center stage in Aeschylus's *Oresteia*. Even so, it is not hard to believe Homer's Agamemnon capable of such enormities; he has a deplorably casual attitude toward his marriage and family, and one altogether typical of his culture.[17] He also has enough talent to marshal the Greeks and make them fight his war for him.

To appreciate Agamemnon as a commander, one needs to think like a general. This will not appeal to some civilians, but the aim is not to translate Homer into a handbook for would-be generals—no commander in his right mind would want Agamemnon for a model. We need only realize that he is like other commanders in war, whose purpose is quite distinct from that of the soldiers whose stories modern readers find so much more congenial. Nothing could be more misguided than to withdraw with Achilles into his tent and sulk at Agamemnon as well. To do that is to miss an essential, bitter realization: all that happens to Achilles and everyone else at Troy is framed by the overarching plan of Zeus, and that plan leads to Agamemnon's ultimate success. What matters to Achilles is that Agamemnon and the Achaeans be punished for not honoring him. They are punished, terribly, but what matters to Agamemnon is that Hector be slain and Troy be taken. The sufferings of the Achaeans and possibly even Patroclus's death are matters of some regret—he says—but if the overall aims of his war are served by these casualties, so be it. Near the end of the poem (book 23), Agamemnon will take part in the funeral rites and games, compliantly doing whatever Achilles bids be done, and he never speaks. At that point Agamemnon can afford to be silent.

Those who fight wars are always going to be the leading figures in their war story, whether it is the status-seeking heroes of ancient epic poetry or, as Samuel Hynes shows, the soldiers of modern armies.[18] The further we go from the center of war in a modern war story, where the soldiers are, the more attenuated the audience: strategists talk to strategists, generals to generals, presidents to presidents, tyrants to tyrants. The present divide between the story of the commander and the story of those he commands is exemplified by the administrative delusions in the top levels of American government in the 1960s, analyzed in David Halberstam's *The Best and the Brightest*, and by some of the consequences of those errors, described in Neil Sheehan's memoir of ground-level reporting from Vietnam, *A Bright Shining Lie*. The *Iliad* shows a totality of the war experience, from high to low, from war's organizers, to war's killers and their victims, to war's survivors.

In comparison to a talent inspired by the Muses, the military imagination and particularly the mind of a commander run on one track, and necessarily so. In order to command and to lead armies into action, there must be that clarity of the moment which permits decisions, then action. The *Iliad* begins after one such decision, to bring the Greeks to Troy, when the consequences of that powerful but single-minded action are plain to see. Achilles' plea to Thetis to get Zeus to make the war go in favor of the Trojans, to punish Agamemnon for dishonoring the best of the Achaeans, is the next move, with consequences no one but Zeus could foresee. Both Achilles and Agamemnon have flawed visions of what war can be. As strategists both reach a level of military incompetence that is not so celebrated as it might be.

From years of clinical observation and a series of case studies of British blunders in war and military disasters, from the Crimean War, through the Somme, to Arnhem in 1944, the British military psychologist Norman Dixon concluded that military life enables certain kinds of leaders in war to inflict on their fellow soldiers "depths of misery and pain virtually unknown in other walks of life."

> There is no reason to suppose that incompetence occurs more frequently in military subcultures than it does in politics, commerce or the universities. There are, however, apart from the heavy cost of military disasters, special reasons for studying cases of military ineptitude. The first is that military organizations may have a particular propensity for attracting a minority of individuals who might prove a menace at high levels of command, and the second is that the nature of militarism serves to accentuate those very traits which may ultimately prove disastrous.[19]

The military incompetence of commanders is often responsible for cataclysmic events far out of proportion to anything those responsible for them contemplated. As Dixon observes, in war, the commanders are far less likely to be held accountable for them.

> In the Vietnam War alone, military commanders were responsible for executing policies that cost the United States 300 billion dollars. They were responsible for releasing thirteen million tons of high explosives (more than six times the weight of bombs dropped by the U.S.A. in all theatres during the whole of the Second World War). They were responsible for the delivery of 90,000 tons of gas and herbicides. And they were responsible for the deaths of between one and two million people. These are great responsibilities. Errors of generalship on this scale would be very costly.[20]

The *myr'i Achaiois algea* or pains thousandfold that the Achaeans suffer as a consequence of Achilles' rage (line 2 of the poem) are a fine example of Dixon's theory of military incompetence in action. In the *Iliad*, military incompetence, not war in a general sense, nor the transgressions of Helen and Paris, is what causes so much suffering and dying.

It takes kings and heroes to achieve pains thousandfold. On one side there is Agamemnon's mishandling of Achilles, Achilles' narcissism and total lack of interest in everything about his fellow soldiers except their regard for him, and Nestor's guileful persuasion of a well-meaning but gullible Patroclus. On the other, there is Paris's flagrant refusal to return Helen, and Priam's fatal acquiescence, in a debate at Troy in book 7 (344–80). Priam and the Trojans' decision seemed so improbable that Herodotus concluded Homer was uninterested in plausibility, but was rather bent on showing that crime does not pay.[21]

Of course, Agamemnon's incompetence is an embarrassment to anyone looking for an ideal commander. At the opening of book 2 he is inspired by a dream sent from Zeus to test the resolve of an army that has been at war for ten years at Troy. Agamemnon spontaneously proposes to break camp and sail home, and the army immediately runs for the ships. To Olympian observers this is an unacceptable turn of the mortal plot they interfere with from time to time.

> And now they might have won their journey home,
> the men of Argos fighting the will of fate, yes,
> if Hera had not alerted Athena: "Inconceivable!
> Child of Zeus whose battle-shield is thunder,
> tireless one, Athena—what, is *this* the way?
> All the Argives flying home to their fatherland,
> sailing over the sea's broad back? leaving Priam
> and all the men of Troy a trophy to glory over,
> Helen of Argos, Helen for whom so many Argives
> lost their lives in Troy, far from native land."
> (2.155–62; 2.181–90, Fagles)

Agamemnon's bright idea creates a farce of the highest order. As Dixon observes, a good general is like a good comedian: he needs to have a fine sense of timing. Nothing could be more ill timed than Agamemnon's scheme to test the mettle of his men. The *Iliad's* war progresses the way most wars progress, in a manner so flawed and accidental that it seems a miracle the war ever gets won. The profound disorder at the center of the world of the *Iliad* is the disorder at the heart of war. Achilles' revolt leads to an ever-greater disorder that is the result of Achilles' own spectacular version of military incompetence, as well as of the plan of Zeus.

The difference between Achilles and later warriors who must confront

their own versions of Agamemnon is that he is more perceptive, more articulate, and more consequential in his rebellion than ordinary warriors on a
battlefield could ever be. He has analytical powers, in the literal sense; he
dissects the society of war, with no thought of the consequences for anyone
but himself. The aim of a commander in a war is different. He wants to win
it, and for that purpose he needs to get men to die for him. Robert E. Lee's order for a frontal assault on the entrenched Union lines on the third day of
the battle of Gettysburg led to the near annihilation of George Pickett's
brigade, a command decision that led to consequences as dire as any slaughter we see in the *Iliad*.[22] But Lee remains forever the revered commander in
Southern accounts of the war in no small part because James Longstreet and
other lieutenants could never be enough like Achilles to oppose Lee force-
fully enough, either in person or in print.

   Achilles' status as the greatest of heroes seems to make him too remote
from later warriors to be of much relevance. But this is to rush past what is
genuinely important about him in assessing later soldiers' stories. It is precisely his parentage and its implications that play so significant a role;
Achilles owes not a little of his military incompetence to his immortal
mother, Thetis.[23] According to prophecy, if Thetis had a son by either Poseidon or Zeus he would grow up to create a third act in the father-and-son
family drama that began with Zeus's grandfather Ouranos (Sky). Hesiod's
Theogony tells us how Ouranos's son Kronos overthrew him by castrating
him, and then how Zeus in turn overthrew Kronos by outwitting him and
his plan to devour all his children as they were born. Thetis's son by an immortal would overthrow Zeus. Thus Thetis is forced to mate with the mortal father of Achilles, Peleus; she is quite explicit about her unhappiness with
Zeus's arrangements in book 18. Her son is destined to live a short life, not
only because he is a mortal, but because his death in war would put an end to
her potential challenge to Zeus's power. Thetis is the original mother of all
incompetents who stands behind those who would devise strategies for ad-
vancing themselves through war.[24]

   One of the great heroes of Dixon's *Military Incompetence* is Douglas Haig,
the strategist of the Somme in 1916 and many other bloodbaths for the
British in the Great War. Haig's mother seems to have played a major role in
seeing that her son advanced to that dubious eminence. A good deal of what
Dixon terms "pathological achievement-motivation" appears in Agamemnon, the son of a mother convicted of adultery with his uncle Thyestes, but
even more so can it be seen in the enraged hero Achilles, the best of the
Achaeans, with whom he quarrels. Both heroes' stories resonate throughout
the career of General Haig.

The evidence suggests that Haig's burning ambition to succeed overlay a pronounced fear of failure, itself a product of childhood. Since he was devoted to his mother it is reasonable to suppose that her bitter disappointment over his intellectual backwardness caused him considerable anguish. He felt perhaps that he had failed her, and particularly after her death, worked towards proving himself. He was an ardent seeker of social approval, particularly from the King. He disliked publicity and nursed an unreasoning dislike of newspaper reporters. He preferred the company of his inferiors to that of his equals. Though professing a great belief in the value of loyalty, he rarely had a good word to say of his military contemporaries and was quite ruthless in his machinations against his erstwhile chief, Sir John French.

Finally, he showed a predisposition towards persisting in tasks that were so difficult that failure seemed excusable. As Liddell-Hart wrote of Third Ypres, he chose a spot "most difficult for himself and least vital to the enemy."

It seems, then, that Haig possessed more than his fair share of traits associated with authoritarianism. He was conventional, conservative, unimaginative and rigid. He had a "closed" mind, was pathologically ambitious, anti-intraceptive and punitive. He was superstitious, militaristic, obsessive and devoid of real compassion. Finally, and not very surprisingly in view of his other attributes, he was never popular. He commanded respect and adulation but lacked that warmth which elicits affection from one's fellow men.[25]

Agamemnon and Achilles are at once van Wees's status warriors and Dixon's military incompetents. Thanks to his divine mother Thetis, and to his own heroic temper, Achilles' quarrel with Agamemnon constitutes a dialectical examination of the mask of command. He changes nothing in Agamemnon's mind, nor does Agamemnon in his, but in their struggle the two of them reveal much about those who seek to direct the fragile military society that exists within war. Their quarrel is a perennial story waiting to be retold. Nearly any famous commander we can name would have hated Achilles as much as Agamemnon does. Any soldier, the more nameless the better, would feel the same about Agamemnon. The difference is that in less epic armies, where heroes are in short supply, such a cosmic rebellion would be dealt with by quicker discipline, up to and including summary execution.[26]

The great quarrel of the *Iliad* dramatizes what Karl von Clausewitz has to say about policy and violence in war, in a passage that is generally misrepresented by the often-quoted aphorism "War is politics by other means."[27] This is a simplification that the most famous Western theorist of war anticipated and tried to avert.

War is simply a continuation of political intercourse, with the addition of other means. We deliberately use the phrase, "with the addition of other means" because we also want to make it clear that war in itself does not suspend political intercourse or change it into something entirely different. In essentials that intercourse continues, irrespective of the means it employs. The main lines along which military events progress, and to which they are restricted, are political lines that continue throughout the war into the subsequent peace. How could it be otherwise? Do political relations between peoples and between their governments stop when diplomatic notes are no longer exchanged? Is war not just another expression of their thoughts, another form of speech or writing? Its grammar, indeed, may be its own, but not its logic.

If that is so, then war cannot be divorced from political life; and whenever this occurs in our thinking about war, the many links that connect the two elements are destroyed and what we are left with is something pointless and devoid of sense.[28]

For Achilles, as for Yeats's Irish airman and Killens's Solly, war becomes a Clausewitzian *sinn- und zweckloses Ding*, something pointless and devoid of sense. The contradiction Clausewitz warns of emerges in wars whose political aims are not reconciled with military objectives; that is the lesson, for example, in Robert McNamara's conclusion to the first volume of memoirs about his role in the American Vietnam War.

Finally, we must recognize that the consequences of large-scale military operations—particularly in this age of highly sophisticated and destructive weapons, are inherently difficult to predict and control. Therefore, they must be avoided, excepting only when our nation's security is clearly directly threatened. These are the lessons of Vietnam. Pray God we learn them.

In the end, we must confront the fate of those Americans who served in Vietnam and never returned. Does the unwisdom of our intervention nullify their effort and their loss? I think not. They did not make the decisions. They answered their nation's call to service. They went in harm's way on its behalf. And they gave their lives for their country and its ideals. That our effort in Vietnam proved unwise does not make their sacrifice less noble. It endures for all to see. Let us learn from their sacrifice and, by doing so, validate and honor it.[29]

McNamara served as secretary of defense in the Kennedy and Johnson administrations and was one of the principal architects of that war. The contradictory aims that informed American leadership in the war carry straight into his memoirs of it thirty years later, a confusion that both generals and the political leaders they serve can easily confront if they have not understood clearly enough the nature of war.

Even with the greatest clarity in command, war's outcome is bound to be messy and unpredictable. Closer to the clearly focused wars of U. S. Grant or of William Westmoreland's nemesis, Nguyen Giap, Agamemnon's success can be measured by the sheer amount of bloodshed his command engenders, bloodshed that Clausewitz says is of the essence in fighting a war. "We are not interested in generals who win victories without bloodshed. The fact that slaughter is a horrifying spectacle must make us take war more seriously, but not provide an excuse for gradually blunting our swords in the name of humanity. Sooner or later someone will come along with a sharp sword and hack off our arms."[30] By this measure Agamemnon does very well.

NOT A SOLDIER, BUT WAR

> I propose to move immediately upon your works.
> Ulysses S. Grant, Fort Donelson, Tennessee, 1862

Ulysses S. Grant did even better.

The strategic point of view, Agamemnon's point of view, is indispensable to war's progress. Successful wars' commanders cannot be distracted by what Liddell-Hart terms "the accidents of human misery." Of Grant, Gertrude Stein observes in *Wars I Have Seen* that "war is soldiers and soldiers have not to be war but they have to be soldiers. Which is a nice thing. . . . And it is like the wars now they are not soldiers they are war. Veterans always feel it is soldiers even though they know that it is war. Somehow General Grant was not a solider he was war and that is the reason I liked him."[31] The war that Stein sees Grant personify accounts for the confidence of his famous exchange with General Buckner, the commander of the Confederate forces at Fort Donelson, Tennessee, in February 1862. Buckner started negotiations for surrender with all the face-saving he could muster.

> Sir:—In consideration of all the circumstances governing the present situation of affairs at this station, I propose to the Commanding Officer of the Federal forces the appointment of Commissioners to agree upon terms of capitulation of the forces and fort under my command, and in that view suggest an armistice until 12 o'clock today.

To this Grant sent the terse reply that turned him into "Unconditional Surrender Grant."

> Sir:—Yours of this date, proposing armistice and appointment of Commissioners to settle terms of capitulation, is just received. No terms except an unconditional and immediate surrender can be accepted.
>
> I propose to move immediately upon your works.

The phrase about unconditional surrender is famous, but what is less often heard in the folklore of this exchange is that deadly last sentence: "I propose to move immediately upon your works." Buckner's feeble reply is all moonlight and magnolias.

> Sir:—The distribution of the forces under my command, incident to an unexpected change of commanders, and the overwhelming force under your command, compel me, notwithstanding the brilliant success of the Confederate arms yesterday, to accept the ungenerous and unchivalrous terms which you propose.[32]

Mark Twain charged the whole Civil War to the South's passion for the novels of Sir Walter Scott. It is as if Buckner had stepped from the pages of *Ivanhoe* and were surprised to find himself in the wrong kind of war. Grant records this reply in his memoirs without comment.

There is little evidence that Grant or other commanders in the Civil War had read Clausewitz's work, but he exhibits the same preference for pragmatic and simple instruction over academic and philosophical debates about it. It is ironic that Clausewitz's name is now synonymous with theories, because he himself had no use for them. "They aim at fixed values. But in war everything is uncertain. . . . War is dangerous—so dangerous that no one who has not taken part in it can conceive of what it was like."[33] In war, "the light of reason is refracted in a manner quite different from what is normal in academic speculation."[34]

The *Personal Memoirs* are a commander's bible and they open with a biblical genealogy: "My family is American, and has been for generations, in all its branches, direct and collateral. . . . Matthew Grant the founder of the branch in America, of which I am a descendant, reached Dorchester, Massachusetts, in May 1630. . . . I am of the eighth generation from Matthew Grant, and seventh from Samuel."[35] This takes a long view of the war, deliberately homespun for a nation recreated by Abraham Lincoln, just as Charles de Gaulle's celebrated opening of his memoirs sets the stage for the story of a war that opens with France's total defeat and ends with France's triumph: "Toute ma vie, je me suis fait une certaine idée de la France."

> All my life I have thought of France in a certain way. This is inspired by sentiment as much as by reason. The emotional side of me tends to imagine France, like the princess in the fairy stories or the Madonna in the frescoes, as dedicated to an exalted and exceptional destiny. Instinctively I have the feeling that Providence has created her either for complete successes or for exemplary misfortunes. If, in spite of this, mediocrity shows in her acts and deeds, it strikes me as an absurd anomaly, to be imputed to the faults of Frenchmen, not to the genius of the land. But the positive side of my mind

also assures me that France is not really herself unless she is in the front rank; that only vast enterprises are capable of counter-balancing the ferments of disintegration inherent in her people; that our country, as it is, surrounded by the others, as they are, must aim high and hold itself straight, on pain of mortal danger. In short, to my mind, France cannot be France without greatness.[36]

De Gaulle is constrained to live up to his name and to assert the identity of France's original imperial identity in the Roman Empire: Gallia, Caesar's Gaul. De Gaulle, what was once Gaul and is now France, and France's grandeur all mingle in a way diametrically opposed to the plain genealogy of the *Personal Memoirs*. Madonnas and princesses suggest the mythical and historical model de Gaulle manages to invoke: nothing less than a Joan of Arc who would lead the French against their latest foreign invaders. Yet contrary as their rhetoric may be, the aim of both generals is to make their wars fit into a larger pattern. If this requires de Gaulle to play down inconvenient facts of history—the collaboration of the French with the German occupation, the vexed alliance with the English and Americans—so be it.

De Gaulle was aiming to return to power and did so within a few years of the completion of his work. Grant was dying as he wrote his memoirs, in hope of supporting his family. At the end he takes a more detached and less self-serving view than most such memoirists do.

I feel that we are on the eve of a new era, when there is to be a great harmony between the Federal and Confederate. I cannot stay to be a living witness to the correctness of this prophecy; but I feel it within me that it is to be so. The universally kind feeling expressed for me at a time when it was supposed that each day would prove my last, seemed to me the beginning of the answer to "Let us have peace."

The expressions of these kindly feelings were not restricted to a section of the country, or to a division of the people. They came from individual citizens of all nationalities; from all denominations—the Protestant, the Catholic, and the Jew; and from the various societies of the land—scientific, educational, religious, or otherwise. Politics did not enter into the matter at all.

I am not egotist enough to suppose all this significance should be given because I was the object of it. But the War Between the States was a very bloody and a very costly war. One side or the other had to yield principles they deemed dearer than life before it could be brought to an end. I commanded the whole of the mighty host engaged on the victorious side. I was, no matter whether deservedly so or not, a representative of that side of the controversy. It is a significant and gratifying fact that Confederates should

have joined heartily in this spontaneous move. I hope the good feeling inau-
gurated may continue to the end.[37]

Addressing a war that at the time and for long after seemed to have ended
much less ambiguously than de Gaulle's, the *Personal Memoirs of U. S. Grant*
conveys something of what that martial intelligence must have been like in
action; in John Keegan's estimation, Grant's memoirs are "perhaps the most
revealing autobiography of high command to exist in any language."[38] Not
even de Gaulle can surpass Grant for cool detachment from the bloody war
he helped bring to an end.

> It is probably well that we had the war when we did. We are better off now
> than we would have been without it, and have made more rapid progress
> than we otherwise should have made. The civilized nations of Europe have
> been stimulated into unusual activity, so that commerce, trade, travel, and
> thorough acquaintance among people of different nationalities, has become
> common; whereas, before, it was but the few who had ever had the privilege
> of going beyond the limits of their own country or who knew anything
> about other people. Then, too, our republican institutions were regarded
> as experiments up to the breaking out of the rebellion, and monarchical
> Europe generally believed that our republic was a rope of sand that would
> part the moment the slightest strain was brought upon it. Now it has shown
> itself capable of dealing with one of the greatest wars that was ever made,
> and our people have proved themselves to be the most formidable in war of
> any nationality.[39]

But Grant was never a General Haig. When serving as a young officer in
Mexico he was repelled by the spectacle of the bullfights, because of the
needless suffering. "Every Sunday there was a bull fight for the amusement of
those who would pay their fifty cents. I attended one of them—just one—
not wishing to leave the country without having witnessed the national
sport. The sight to me was sickening. I could not see how human beings
could enjoy the sufferings of beasts, and often of men, as they seemed to do
on those occasions."[40] Much as he deplored it, the war of 1848 with Mexico
was invaluable preparation for the war of 1861–65.

> My experience in the Mexican war was of great advantage to me afterwards.
> Besides the many practical lessons it taught, the war brought nearly all the
> officers of the regular army together so as to make them personally ac-
> quainted. It also brought them in contact with volunteers, many of whom
> served in the war of the rebellion afterwards. . . . The acquaintance thus
> formed was of immense service to me in the war of the rebellion—I mean
> what I learned of the characters of those to whom I was afterwards opposed.

I do not pretend to say that all movements, or even many of them, were made with special reference to the characteristics of the commander against whom they were directed. But my appreciation of my enemies was certainly affected by this knowledge. The natural disposition of most people is to clothe a commander of a large army whom they do not know, with almost superhuman abilities. A large part of the National army, for instance, and most of the press of the country, clothed General Lee with just such qualities, but I had known him personally, and knew that he was mortal; and it was just as well that I felt this.[41]

One of Grant's personal officers complements this perception of Lee in his own memoirs. Horace Porter's *Campaigning with Grant* was published in 1897, the same year in which Grant's Tomb was completed, and conveys something of what Grant was like to deal with from a soldier's and officer's perspective.[42] Porter is an ardent defender of his subject, as in his comments on the notoriously bloody frontal assault at Cold Harbor. Grant is quoted by Porter as saying, "I regret this assault more than any one I have ever ordered. I regarded it as a stern necessity, and believed that it would bring compensating results; but, as it has proved, no advantages have been gained sufficient to justify the heavy losses suffered."[43] Grant had come close to pressing Lee to the breaking point, as was later learned. "There were critics who were severe in their condemnation of what Grant called 'hammering' and Sherman called 'pounding'; but they were found principally among the stay-at-homes, and especially the men who sympathized with the enemy."[44]

Porter was moved by Grant's generalship to do more than describe the famous meeting that marked the end of the war. His description of Lee's surrender at Appomattox in the parlor of the McLean House is complemented by drawings: "The sofa in the McLean House," "Table at which Lee sat," "Chair in which Lee sat," "Chair in which Grant sat," and "Table on which Grant wrote the articles of surrender."[45] His illustrations are like Grant's own effort to set his generalship within a larger pattern of American history (fig. 24). The homey detail suggests that in ending their war Lee and Grant were returning to the civil space whence they came.

CATALOGUE ARIA

> The unanimity of men at war is like that of a school of fish, which will swerve,
> simultaneously and apparently without leadership, when the shadow of an
> enemy appears, or like a sky-darkening flight of grasshoppers, which, also all
> compelled by one impulse, will descend to consume the crops.
> Edmund Wilson, *Patriotic Gore*

One thing all commanders love is a good parade. Herodotus reports that as King Xerxes was poised on the shores of Asia before crossing into Greece cock had come, but was apprehensive that hostilities might begin in the mean time, upon the termination of the temporary truce, and asked Babcock to write a line to Meade informing him of the situation. Babcock wrote accordingly, requesting Meade to maintain the truce until positive orders from Grant could be received. To save time, it was arranged that a Union officer, accompanied by one of Lee's officers, should carry this letter through the enemy's lines. This route made the distance to Meade nearly ten miles shorter than by the roundabout way of the Union lines. Lee now mounted his horse, and directed Colonel Marshall to accompany him. They started for Appomattox Court-house in company with Babcock, followed by a mounted orderly.

When the party reached the village they met one of its residents, named Wilmer McLean, who was told that General Lee wished to oc-

THE SOFA IN THE McLEAN HOUSE.

cupy a convenient room in some house in the town. McLean ushered them into the sitting-room of one of the first houses he came to; but upon looking about, and seeing that it was small and unfurnished, Lee proposed finding something more commodious and better fitted for the occasion. McLean then conducted the party to his own house, about the best one in the town, where they awaited General Grant's arrival.

The house had a comfortable wooden porch with seven steps leading up to it. A hall ran through the middle from front to back, and upon each side was a room having two windows, one in front and one in rear. Each room had two doors opening into the hall. The build-

Figure 24. The sofa in the McLean House, Appomattox. Line drawing from Horace Porter, *Campaigning with Grant,* 471. (Photo by Mark Austin-Washburn.)

with the Persian army and fleet, he decided to hold a review of his entire fleet and army in a single view. This account comes as close as anything in ancient literature to expressing the exaltation that attends the great invasion fleets of history, particularly the Allied landing at Normandy in 1944—and also some of the dread.

> And when he saw the whole Hellespont hidden by ships, and all the beaches and plains of Abydos filled with men, he called himself happy— and the moment after burst into tears. Artabanus his uncle, the man who in the first instance had spoken his mind so freely in trying to dissuade Xerxes from undertaking the campaign, was by his side; and when he saw how Xerxes wept, he said to him: "My lord, surely there is a strange contradiction in what you do now and what you did a moment ago. Then you called yourself a happy man—and now you weep."
>
> "I was thinking," Xerxes replied; "and it came into my mind how pitifully short human life is—for of all these thousands of men not one will be alive in a hundred years' time."[46]

Appropriately for the self-interested thinking of a monarch, Xerxes' moving moment has entirely to do with the impact on him of the disappearance of his host; it is a visible sign of the evanescence of his own power. The tactical review and deployment of forces in war puts all the commander's cards on the table. It is meant to be encouraging, strengthening the resolve of both the men they command and the commanders themselves. But as Xerxes' sentimental reading of his great invasion force suggests, this kind of moment serves a commander's eye above all others.

So do the official songs that commanders and their forces use in war. At about the same time Walt Whitman was serving as a volunteer nurse in Washington and putting together *Specimen Days* and other poems from the Civil War, one of General William Tecumseh Sherman's men composed a song about his famous march in 1864 from Atlanta to the sea. Adjutant Byers was a prisoner of the Confederates when he wrote it, and in one of the more civil moments of an increasingly uncivil war, performed it to an appreciative audience of Confederate ladies.

> Then forward, boys! forward to battle!
>   We marched on our wearisome way,
> We stormed the wild hills of Resaca—
>   God bless those who fell on that day!
> Then Kenesaw frowned in its glory,
>   Frowned down on the flag of the free;
> But the East and the West bore our standard,
>   And Sherman marched on to the sea!

Chorus
Then sang we a song of our chieftain,
   That echoed over river and lea;
And the stars of our banner shone brighter
   When Sherman marched down to the sea![47]

Sherman records the entire song in his memoirs. As Charles Royster observes in *The Destructive War,* North and South entertained contradictory myths of nation-making that could be resolved only by the destruction of one or the other.[48] Sherman foresaw what was to come in 1861, even as the war began, and his war music has never been mistaken for something one could sing to audiences of Confederate ladies. "You people of the South don't know what you are doing. You think you can tear to pieces this great Union without war. But I tell you there will be blood-shed, and plenty of it. And god only knows how it will end."[49]

There are Greek poets soon after Homer such as Callinus and Tyrtaeus who are as dedicated to making war songs as Adjutant Byers; as poets they offer something more than words to march to. With the invocation to the Muses and the marshaling of Greek forces that ends book 2 of the *Iliad,* however, we are dealing with a war song of a different order.

Although it does not now have the reputation for being in any sense musical, Homer's long account of Greek forces, the so-called catalogue of ships that concludes book 2, is one long song of military organization. At this point it will doubtless seem pedantic to try to enforce a more accurate label, but it must be tried. This is not the list or register of names and information that it has become.[50] For those who need to catch up with the story of the Trojan War, it might be a useful rehearsal of the hosts of Greeks and Trojan allies who came to Troy. But as it happens in the poem, the point is neither to play catch-up for the newcomer to the Trojan War nor to flatter the pride of those who already know the story. The real show is the reintegration and redirection of the commander's instrument of war that Achilles' revolt comes perilously close to destroying. The poem turns into a celebration of a commander's powers.

Today this song is little more than a guidebook in hexameters to archaic Greece, not at all the inspired song from the Muses that Homer and his audiences knew. The last English translator who took Homer's song of the Greeks at Troy as seriously as the poetry demands was Pope. His version of 1725 is a classic epic poem in its own right and shows what a great translator could do to rescue what had long been an infamously dull stretch of ancient poetry.

To make Homer's song live again, Pope does not hesitate to give us every-

thing that appears in Homer's poetry, and more. There is glossing information that has absolutely no parallel in Homer—who in the *Iliad*'s first audiences needed to be told about the nine Muses and their duties?—and he
makes every turn of Homer's verse completely clear. The Muses invoked are
also reminiscent of the heavenly Muse invoked at the beginning of *Paradise
Lost*, one who can illuminate Hell itself with her light.

> Say, Virgins, seated round the Throne Divine,
> all-knowing *Goddesses*! immortal Nine!
> Since Earth's wide Regions, Heav'n's unmeasur'd Height,
> And Hell's Abyss hide nothing from your sight,
> (We, wretched Mortals! lost in Doubts below,
> But guess by Rumour, and but boast we know)
> Oh say what Heroes, fir'd by Thirst of Fame,
> Or urg'd by Wrongs, To *Troy*'s Destruction came?
> To count them all, demands a thousand Tongues,
> A Throat of Brass, and Adamantine Lungs.
> Daughters of *Jove* assist! inspir'd by You
> The mighty labour dauntless I pursue:
> What crowded Armies, from what Climes they bring,
> Their Names, their Numbers, and their Chiefs I sing.[51]

The scrupulously literal version of a modern classic like Richmond Lattimore's translation seeks to remove all the traces of the intervening centuries
that Pope took for granted as part of his task.

> Tell me now, you Muses who have your homes on Olympos.
> For you, who are goddesses, are there, and you know all
>   things,
> and we have heard only the rumour of it and know nothing.
> Who then of those were the chief men and the lords of the
>   Danaans?
> I could not tell over the multitude of them nor name them,
> not if I had ten tongues and ten mouths, not if I had
> a voice never to be broken, and a heart of bronze within me,
> not unless the Muses of Olympia, daughters of Zeus of the
>   aegis,
> remembered all those who came beneath Ilion.
> (2.484–92, Lattimore)

By contrast, Pope would use anything and everything to make sure his version re-created for his readers what he imagined Homer's audiences might

have known. The notion that it is enough to translate literally what Homer created was alien to him.

Pope does one other thing that separates him from his successors. His Muses are no tedious business that we have to get through, somehow. (In *Kings*, his "account" of books 1 and 2, Homer's best translator today, Christopher Logue, omits the Muses and their song entirely.) Having already supplied in the verse all his readers need to know, Pope is free to underscore the critical interpretation this passage demands, as well as any translator since:

> It is hard to conceive any Address more solemn, any Opening to a Subject more noble and magnificent, than this Invocation of Homer before his Catalogue. That Omnipresence he gives to the Muses, their Post in the highest Heaven, their comprehensive Survey thro' the whole Extent of the Creation, are Circumstances greatly imagined. Nor is anything more perfectly fine or exquisitely moral, than the Opposition of the extensive Knowledge of the Divinities on the one side, to the Blindness and Ignorance of Mankind on the other. The Greatness and Importance of his Subject is highly rais'd by his exalted manner of declaring the Difficulty of it, *Not tho' my Lungs were Brass*, &c. and by the Air he gives as if what follows were immediately inspir'd, and no less than the joint Labour of all the Muses.[52]

The Muses and their song mark a crucial stage in the transformation of war into poetry. Here as elsewhere, these archaic creatures are as relevant to later texts as any other part of the *Iliad*.

As performed, the Muses' song requires far more energy and inspiration than the opening invocation to the Muse to sing of the rage of Achilles. As a commander's song it celebrates the restoration of a martial society. It gives the Greeks a tactical structure for the whole series of battles that follows, as the invocation to the Muses and the marshaling of the ships are introduced by a series of five similes that will not have their equal until the catastrophic dissolution of this Greek army as it retreats from battle with the naked corpse of Patroclus in book 17 (735–59).[53] The poet moves us from elemental forces in nature to ever more structured images of human beings' exerting their control over nature, and to pastoral scenes.[54]

> As obliterating fire lights up a vast forest
> along the crests of a mountain, and the flare shows far off,
> so as they marched, from the magnificent bronze the gleam
>   went
> dazzling all but through the upper air to the heaven.
> These, as the multitudinous nations of birds winged,

of geese, and of cranes, and of swans long-throated
in the Asian meadow beside the Kaystrian waters
this way and that way make their flights in the pride of their
    wings, then
settle in clashing swarms and the whole meadow echoes with
    them,
so of these the multitudinous tribes form the ships and
shelters poured to the plain of Skamandros, and the earth
    beneath their
feet and under the feet of their horses thundered horribly.
They took position in the blossoming meadow of
    Skamandros,
thousands of them, as leaves and flowers appear in their
    season.
Like the multitudinous nations of swarming insects
who drive hither and thither about the stalls of the sheepfold
in the season of spring when the milk splashes in the milk
    pails:
in such numbers the flowing-haired Achaians stood up
through the plain against the Trojan, hearts burning to break
    them.
These, as men who are goatherds among the wide goatflocks
easily separate them in order as they take to the pasture,
thus the leaders separated them this way and that way
toward the encounter, and among them powerful
    Agamemnon,
with eyes and head like Zeus who delights in thunder,
like Ares in girth, and with the chest of Poseidon;
like some ox of the herd pre-eminent among the others,
a bull, who stands conspicuous in the huddling cattle;
such was the son of Atreus as Zeus made him that day,
conspicuous among men, and foremost among the fighters.
    (2.455–83, Lattimore)

The imagined scenes move from fire and birds, leaves and flowers, swarming insects, finally to goatherds and their goat flocks, so that Agamemnon emerges in the last simile as the climax of the whole series. He is completely reestablished and the war resumes as soon as his command does. The catalogue follows this remarkable crescendo in similes.[55] They point us toward their strategic significance, the reintegration of the army under Agamemnon's command that Achilles, and more recently, Agamemnon's own folly and the war-weariness of his men had come close to destroying. It was a danger that Thersites had seen and come even closer to articulating than Achilles himself.

> How shameful for you, the high and mighty commander,
> to lead the sons of Achaea into bloody slaughter!
> Sons? No, my soft friends, wretched excuses—
> women, not men of Achaea! Home we go in our ships!
> Abandon him here in Troy to wallow in all his prizes—
> he'll see if the likes of us have propped him up or not.
> Look—now it's Achilles, a greater man he disgraces,
> seizes and keeps his prize, tears her away himself.
> But no gall in Achilles. Achilles lets it go.
> If not, Atrides, that outrage would have been your last.
>   (2.233–42; 2.272–81, Fagles)

Thersites sounds like a parody of Achilles, who hates him as much as Agamemnon or Odysseus or the rest of the Greeks do—as does the poet himself, who does not refrain from a uniquely ad hominem attack. Thersites is the ugliest man in the Greek army at Troy, who also speaks the ugliest thoughts, thoughts all the more unwelcome to Agamemnon because they are so close to the thoughts and language of Achilles.

> But Odysseus stepped in quickly, faced him down
> with a dark glance and threats to break his nerve:
> "What a flood of abuse, Thersites! Even for you,
> fluent and flowing as you are. Keep quiet.
> Who are *you* to wrangle with kings, you alone?
> No one, I say—no one alive less soldierly than you,
> none in the ranks that came to Troy with Agamemnon.
> So stop your babbling, mouthing the names of kings,
> flinging indecencies in their teeth, your eyes
> peeled for a chance to cut and run for home.
> We can have no idea, no clear idea at all
> how the long campaign will end . . .
> whether Achaea's sons will make it home unharmed
> or slink back in disgrace."
>   (2.246–53; 2.282–96, Fagles)

Odysseus's intervention checks this rebellion by seizing on the comic potential of Thersites, already a man who would seem worse than any other man there. Odysseus is punishing him for what he looks like as much as for what he says. As would happen in any comedy, the purpose of this little episode is to flatter everyone but the victim. Odysseus takes the scenario away from Thersites and turns him into an instrument of command. The men laugh at him, and that laughter seals Agamemnon's return to power.

The strategic purpose of the catalogue that follows this birth of comedy is not incompatible with poetry, as Pope explains: "the admirable Judgment wherewith he introduces this whole Catalogue, just at a Time when the Posture of Affairs in the Army render'd such a Review of absolute Necessity to the Greeks; and in a Pause of Action, while each was refreshing himself to prepare for the ensuing Battles."[56] This is an acute comment on the posture of affairs. Because of the opening book's account of the superheated quarrel with Achilles, we might well overlook the hosts of other men and heroes that surround Agamemnon. Why would Achilles have served Agamemnon so long and so loyally, and only now be rebelling against that service? Thucydides suggests that the whole Greek force may have been at Troy not because of some abstract principle of fair play, or out of loyalty to Agamemnon's oath to Helen's father Tyndareus to safeguard the marriage of Helen and Menelaus, but because of the sheer power he commanded.

> Agamemnon, as I see it, assembled his force more by surpassing his contemporaries in power than by leading suitors bound by the oaths to Tyndareus. . . . I think that Agamemnon, combining this inheritance [from his grandfather Pelops] with greater naval strength than anyone else, assembled and launched the expedition less because of good will than because he was feared. For he obviously brought with him the greatest number of ships and in addition supplied the Arkadians, as Homer, if he is good enough evidence, has stated clearly. And he says further, in the "Transmission of the Scepter," that "he was lord over many islands and all Argos"; now as a mainlander he wouldn't have ruled any but offshore islands (and these wouldn't be "many") unless he had possessed a navy. It is this campaign that must be used to gauge what earlier ones were like. (Thucydides, *The Peloponnesian War*, 1.9, Lattimore)

The catalogue is an aria of the power Agamemnon marshaled for war. Its strategic and poetic visions are inseparable.

THE OLD MAN'S STRATEGY

> The persuasion of a companion is a strong thing.
> Nestor to Patroclus, *Iliad* 11.793 (Lattimore)

Even in the comparatively simpler world of the status warriors of the *Iliad*, a commander like Agamemnon cannot direct every moment of the war; the point loses its abstraction when he is wounded in book 11 and forced to withdraw from battle. He needs to be able to pass along his orders to lieutenants who will carry out his designs effectively. Above all, the art of waging war demands improvisatory skills of the highest order. It often happens that a crucial turn in a battle's fortunes depends on a strategy a commander hits on almost by chance.

In the *Iliad* this improvisation comes from Nestor, the elder king of the Greek army whose reputation for long-winded speeches obscures his effectiveness as a strategist in the service of Agamemnon's army. Patroclus is the pivotal figure in this war story, a hero whose death precipitates Achilles' ferocious return to battle, the death of Hector, and the imminent fall of Troy. Nestor is the counselor who sees the way out of the Greeks' dilemma, and he seizes it. What he manages to accomplish will once again take us deeply inside the world within war.

The old are often the victims of war, not its agents. Priam of Troy is famously so. But old men can also be like Nestor. He makes no secret of his preference for the heroic achievements of his generation, over the achievements of the present one. He seems an early version of Polonius to many now, with our well-developed tendency to marginalize the old. But Nestor is far more formidable than he at first appears. He is the single most effective war strategist in the *Iliad*. Rhetorical triumphs with war-weary men or a clown like Thersites are one thing, success with Achilles quite another. In their efforts to keep him in the war, through the famous embassy of Phoenix, Ajax, and Odysseus in book 9, Odysseus is a distinct failure, a would-be persuader whose flattery and rhetorical stratagems Achilles sees through instantly.[57]

Nestor is a different kind of commander, an adversary Achilles never confronts as he does Agamemnon or Odysseus. Whereas Agamemnon relies on sheer power and position to enforce his command, and Odysseus seeks to persuade with flattering words, Nestor sees that the way to Achilles' heart lies through Patroclus and the feelings he has for him. His strategy to get Achilles back into the war is determined by his age; his son Antilochus and others are the generation that now has to do the fighting. Living in the past as much as the present, the past that old men always find more congenial, he can work his will only through a distillation of his powers of observation and experience. He is sophisticated in his understanding of how to play on the emotions generated by war, because he has to be. His strategic skills are manifest when we compare him to Agamemnon and Odysseus, and even more so if we recall the other old man of the *Iliad*, the king of Troy.

As an elder statesman Nestor is of a completely different order from Priam. He gets young men to do his fighting and dying for him through acute observation of his audiences and the speeches he gives them. These are never the wandering exercises in nostalgia they too easily seem to us, but acts of persuasion, shaped in performance, to address his present audience and turn it to his point of view.[58] He does not go on the famous embassy to Achilles, but this elderly stay-at-home selects the cast of characters and gives them their script.

> First of all let Phoenix, beloved of Zeus, be their leader,
> and after him take Aias the great, and brilliant Odysseus.
> . . . .
> And the Gerenian horseman Nestor gave them much
>   instruction,
> looking eagerly at each, and most of all at Odysseus,
> to try hard, so that they might win over the blameless Peleion.
> (9.168–81, Lattimore)

They come close to winning him over, but not close enough.

On his own, with Patroclus alone and away from Achilles' company, Nestor has more success. His account of how he served under aged King Neleus is exemplary.

> Now Neleus would not
> let me be armed among them, and had hidden away my horses
> because he thought I was not yet skilled in the work of
>   warfare.
> (11.717–19; 11.716–18, Lattimore)

But Nestor did fight and win great honor:

> There the Achaeans
> steered back from Bouprasion to Pylos their fast-running
>   horses,
> and all glorified Zeus among the gods, but among men
>   Nestor.
> (11.759–61; 11.758–60, Lattimore)

Nestor reminds Patroclus that he was present with Odysseus when Menoitios, Patroclus's father, sent him away from Phthia to Agamemnon.[59]

> And Peleus the aged was telling his own son, Achilles,
> to be always best in battle and pre-eminent beyond all others,
> but for you, Menoitios, Aktor's son, had this to say to you:
> "My child, by right of blood Achilles is higher than you are,
> but you are the elder. Yet in strength he is far the greater.
> You must speak solid words to him, and give him good
>   counsel,

> and point his way. If he listens to you it will be for his own
>   good."
> That is what the old man told you, you have forgotten. Yet
>   even
> now you might speak to wise Achilles, he might be persuaded.
> Who knows if, with god helping, you might trouble his spirit
> by entreaty, since the persuasion of a friend is a strong thing.
>   (11.783–92; 11.782–92, Lattimore)

And then Nestor thinks of something new to add to the inspiring tale of his own past accomplishments, and that injunction from Menoitios:

> But if he is drawing back from some prophecy known in his
>   own heart
> and by Zeus' will his honored mother has told him of
>   something,
> let him send you out, at least, and the rest of the Myrmidon
>   people
> follow you and you may be a light given to the Danaans.
> And let him give you his splendid armor to wear to the
>   fighting,
> if perhaps the Trojans might think you are he, and give way
> from their attack, and the fighting sons of the Achaeans get
>   wind
> again after hard work. There is little breathing space in the
>   fighting.
> You, unwearied, might with a mere cry pile men wearied
> back upon their city, and away from the ships and the shelters.
>   (11.794–803; 11.793–802, Lattimore)

This idea seems to promise a risk-free appearance in war, almost as an observer, one who will be enough to turn the tide "easily . . . with a battle cry" (*breia . . . autēi*, 11.802). But for all his present role as a loyal companion, Patroclus is a warrior in his own right, and this prospect of a limited war arouses his own desire to fight. He speeds back, tending the wounded Eurypylos and Menoitios on his way.

> But when he saw the Trojans were sweeping over the rampart
> and the outcry and the noise of terror rose from the Danaans
> Patroclus groaned aloud then and struck himself on both
>   thighs
> with the flats of his hands and spoke a word of lamentation:
> "Eurypylos, much though you need me I cannot stay here

> longer with you. This is a big fight that has arisen.
> Now it is for your henchman to look after you, while I
> go in haste to Achilles, to stir him into the fighting.
> Who knows if, with god helping, I might trouble his spirit
> by entreaty, since the persuasion of a friend is a strong thing."
> (15.395–404; 15.397–406, Lattimore)

The last two lines are exactly what Nestor had said to Patroclus, save for one word: "you might trouble" (*orinais*, 11.792) in Lattimore's version changing to "I might trouble" (*orinō*, 15.403). This is not only a fine example of the subtle variations possible in sophisticated oral verse composition; from a commander's viewpoint, Nestor's calculated words turn into another man's impulse. Patroclus doesn't just recall the message that the old man has planted in his mind. It has become part of him, and he acts on it.[60]

Nestor plays on the emotions not of Achilles himself, but of his less wary companion. Nothing is accomplished by issuing direct orders to the greatest heroes fighting in this war, when they don't want to do what is needed.[61] What Patroclus says in his haste to Eurypylos repeats just the first part of Nestor's precept. The other part, the fatally specific part, emerges when he has returned to Achilles and says:

> But if you are drawing back from some prophecy known in
> your own heart
> and by Zeus' will your honored mother has told you of
> something,
> then send me out at least, let the rest of the Myrmidon people
> follow me, and I may be a light given to the Danaans.
> Give me your armour to wear on my shoulders into the
> fighting;
> so perhaps the Trojans might think I am you, and give way
> from their attack, and the fighting sons of the Achaeans get
> wind again
> after hard work. There is little breathing space in the fighting.
> We unwearied might with a mere cry pile men wearied
> back upon their city, and away from the ships and shelters.
> (16.36–45, Lattimore)

This again is a direct report of Nestor's words, though Patroclus does not acknowledge it. Homer brings out the specifically strategic aspect of this compassion for fellow warriors in the lovely simile at the opening of book 16.

> Meanwhile Patroclus came to the shepherd of the people,
> Achilles,

> and stood by him and wept warm tears, like a spring dark-
>   running
> that down the face of a rock impassable drips its dim water.
>   (16.2–4, Lattimore)

The slight change in the first half of the line reinforces the parallel, as the poet otherwise repeats verbatim a brief simile from book 9, when Agamemnon wept tears of frustration at his inability to get the Achilles problem resolved.

> They took their seats in assembly, dispirited, and Agamemnon
> stood up before them, shedding tears, like a spring dark-
>   running
> that down the face of a rock impassable drips its dim water.
>   (9.13–15, Lattimore)

Tears are the most visible and expressive sign of human feeling, just as an impassable rock is a metaphor for the most hardened kind of heart; the combination of these extremes of feeling in one person suggests the extremes Agamemnon must be feeling at this moment. At the same time he is the immovable rock and the weeping stream. In its exquisite details this seems to sum up Agamemnon's agonizing situation powerfully.

But in what sense is Agamemnon's simile appropriate to Patroclus's character? He is the opposite of Agamemnon. He has gone to the battle to find out for himself what is happening, and what he discovers moves him deeply. Among the many things this repeated simile can suggest to us, not the least is what it shows us about the qualitative difference between the commander and the commanded. While Patroclus is selfless in his weeping, pitying the suffering of his fellow warriors, Agamemnon's tears spring entirely from his self-absorption and humiliation at being defeated.[62]

And now his desire has been transmitted through a chain of command that only the poet and his Muses enable us to see. Agamemnon's dilemma is transformed so adroitly through Nestor's calculated play on Patroclus's compassion that Patroclus comes to feel about his companion's suffering the way Agamemnon felt about his own suffering—however that was. The simile suggests that at some level they are of like mind. So far as a commander's vision goes, they are. Patroclus will soon accomplish all that Agamemnon could desire, without even realizing it. The strategic implications of what he experiences as a personal, private moment add a level of pathos to mortal calculations that Homer intensifies with a rare intervention.

> So he spoke supplicating in his great innocence; this was
> his own death and evil destruction he was entreating.
>   (16.46–47, Lattimore)

This reach from Agamemnon's tears to Patroclus's brings together the war commander's plotting and the intensely personal, individual experience of the soldier. They are connected not just by actions and their consequences, but also by emotion.

Commanders in war count on such bonding in their soldiers. Next to the authority and the discipline they seek to impose, this loyalty of fighting men to one another is crucial. Comradeship has a strategic, calculated aspect that marches alongside the feelings many soldiers have for their comrades in battle. Writing of this bond in World War II, the military historian S. L. A. Marshall observes,

> I hold it to be one of the simplest truths of war that the thing which enables an infantry soldier to keep going with his weapons is the near presence or the presumed presence of a comrade. The warmth which derives from human companionship is as essential to his employment of the arms with which he fights as is the finger with which he pulls a trigger or the eye with which he aligns his sights. The other man may be almost beyond hailing or seeing distance, but he must be there somewhere within a man's consciousness or the onset of demoralization is almost immediate and very quickly the mind begins to despair or turns to thoughts of escape. In this condition he is no longer a fighting individual, and though he holds to his weapon, it is little better than a club.[63]

The most admirable and selfless instincts of soldiers in war can, if properly channeled, also serve the strategic interests of their commanders, as Patroclus's care for his fellow warriors does here.

But the tears of Patroclus and Agamemnon also suggest that the emotions a commander and his men share are at once the same and profoundly different. In the end there will be that distance that always exists between the commander who sends men into war to die and the men who die trying to do his bidding. The trickling stone face of a spring: the commander and those he commands are of like mind and heart as they confront the sorrows of war, and then they are not alike at all.

Four THE WORDS OF THE SEA

Marathon and Gettysburg are battlefields that have endured far longer than
the soldiers who fought on them. In sea warfare and in the air, by contrast,
no visible trace remains of the spaces that men fight and die for, and we think
of this vanishing as a matter of course. Yet the same thing can happen on
land, and for the poets of war this kind of obliteration has proven anything
but a matter of course. The evanescence of the *Iliad*'s landscape of war is foretold at the end of the first day of battle following Achilles' withdrawal. The
Greeks' situation at this moment seems bad enough, but it will prove to be
the easiest day of all. The sites of these epic struggles will disappear as surely
as the men who fought on them.

Such oblivion in the face of nature is not easy to comprehend when the
subject obliterated is, for example, you. Hector, ever observant of the conventions of war, trusts in the burial sign of the hero's tomb (*sēma*) to cover a
hero's body (*sōma*), and make it a thing of wonder for men of the future. The
man who dies by Hector's hand has much to look forward to.

> If I kill him, if Apollo gives me that glory,
> I will take his armor to holy Ilion
> And hang it in the temple of the Archer God.
> The corpse I will send back to your hollow ships
> So you long-haired Achaeans can give it burial
> And heap up a tomb by the broad Hellespont.
> So someone in generations yet to come
> Will say as he sails on by the darkening sea,
> "That is the tomb of a man long dead,
> Killed in his prime by glorious Hector."
> Someone will say that, and my fame will not die.
>
> (7.81–91; 7.84–94, Lombardo)

Hector's fame does not die, but survives because of Homer's immortal song, not because of any material relic. The irony is as blatant as it is sad. In this sense the battlefield of the Trojan War represents the eventual fate of all battlefields. Something like the *Iliad's* totally obliterated space confronts us in the empty sea at Morris Island off the coast of Charleston, South Carolina. This site of a famous battle in 1863 for the Confederate Battery Wagner is now completely submerged in the Atlantic. Never is the need for poetic witness more evident than when the landscapes of war themselves vanish.

THE TOMB AND THE WALL

When the war at Troy reaches its final year, the Greeks build a wall to defend themselves against the Trojan assault after Achilles' withdrawal. The wall becomes the focal point for most of the fighting in the poem. Like all battle-field sites, the Achaean wall is part of nature and destined to change. But the *Iliad* accelerates and compresses events; the telescoping experience of war is carried to its extreme here, as we learn something neither Greek nor Trojan can know. After Troy falls and the Greeks sail away, Poseidon and Apollo will level all their works, and it will be as if their battles had never taken place.

At the end of the first day of battle in the *Iliad*, the Achaeans are driven back to their ships by the Trojans and Hector. As he so often does throughout the poem, their elder statesman, Nestor, tells the Greeks what they must do next.

> And let us heap a single great barrow over the pyre,
> one great communal grave stretched out across the plain
> and fronting it throw up looming ramparts quickly,
> a landward wall for the ships and troops themselves.
> And amidst the wall build gateways fitted strong
> to open a clear path for driving chariots through.
> And just outside the wall we must dig a trench,
> a deep ditch in a broad sweeping ring
> to block their horse and men and break their charge—
> then these headlong Trojans can never rush our armies.
> (7.336–43; 7.386–95, Fagles)

For practical and humane reasons the dead must be removed from the field and buried. A truce enables this to happen.

> And hard as it was to recognize each man, each body,
> with clear water they washed the clotted blood away
> and lifted them down to ash and returned to sacred Troy.
> (7.424–26; 7.491–93, Fagles)

So the wall is built, but imperfectly. The Greeks forget to sacrifice to the gods. Why? The press of the moment? Carelessness? Poseidon is angry because they will have created something intended to last forever and make them forget the gods' due. Zeus assures him he will destroy it, robbing the men who build the wall of their glory.

> Come then! After once more the flowing-haired Achaeans
> are gone back with their ships to the beloved land of their
>   fathers,
> break their wall to pieces and scatter it into the salt sea
> and pile again the beach deep under the sands and cover it;
> so let the great wall of the Achaeans go down to destruction.
> (7.459–63, Lattimore)

This exchange frames the battles that resume in book 8. At this point, Zeus's promise is an assurance made by one Olympian god to another. The warriors can know nothing of what we and the gods know. All the war crafts of human beings will come to naught, and their war effort, like the city itself, will be obliterated, and the place where the wall was and the fighting around it will be smoothed away, as if the war and the wall had never been.

In book 12, after Achilles has refused to rejoin the battle and the Greeks have resumed fighting, their leaders are wounded and drop out of the battle one by one. At this point, the poet returns to the promise Zeus made to Poseidon and looks past the present battle to the time when Hector is dead and Achilles' rage is ended:

> So long as Hector was still alive, and Achilleus was angry,
> so long as the citadel of lord Priam was a city untaken,
> for this time the great wall of the Achaeans stood firm.
> But afterwards when all the bravest among the Trojans
> had died in the fighting, and many of the Argives had been
>   beaten down,
> and some left, when in the tenth year the city of Priam was
>   taken
> and the Argives gone in their ships to the beloved land of
>   their fathers,
> then at last Poseidon and Apollo took counsel
> to wreck the wall, letting loose the strength of rivers upon it.
> (12.10–18, Lattimore)

Then the battle comes to this same wall, and its assault and its defense are the center of action until Patroclus and Achilles appear. And yet its impermanence is what is fixed before these actions resume.

This is a future we can apprehend only through the song of the Muses. Not even this race of almost godlike men can elude oblivion. As E. T. Owen puts it,

> Our attention is fixed on the wall as the center of interest by the account of its subsequent destruction at the hands of Poseidon and Apollo, in accordance with the promise of Zeus to Poseidon at 7.459–463. Thus casually the poet wakens again the feeling that the earlier passage in its context aroused—the sense of the transitoriness of the interests for which men strive with such intensity—and its presence gives an ironic colouring at the outset to the picture of Hector's triumphs, which supports and enhances the note of menace running throughout the book.[1]

The Achaean wall is the counterpart of the walls of Troy itself. Walls are the sturdier, more literal realizations of the borders that mark off one side from another, one enemy from another, one nation from another.

The story of the Achaean wall shows that those who fight in wars always have a third opponent, one that deals with both sides with equal impartiality: the passing of time. The battlefield becomes a figurative ground for imagining mortality. Keith Stanley reads these walls as expressions of the folly of war: "The fortified city and the fortified camp are now immured equally in their delusions. . . . The Greek wall is thus a climactic symbol of the mutual self-confinement, stalemate, and futility that the poet sees at the heart of the ten-year war."[2] This is a seductive and Olympian view of the subject; Stanley shows how Homer's poetry carries us away from the present moment, to a remote time no actual mortal in war can know. The Greeks and Trojans may well be locked in a futile struggle, but they cannot know this; and even if they could, how could they act on it?

The same limitations can be charged to any mortal beings engaged in war, not least those who fought at Battery Wagner. Battery Wagner itself is now nothing but a memory whose actual site has ceased to exist. The wall of the Achaeans and Battery Wagner mark a change in the landscape of war, an obliteration by nature, that mirrors the obliteration of those who died there. Through poets and historians and artists we can only imagine men fighting and dying there, in the fiercest struggles. The *Iliad's* warriors and the soldiers of 1863 fought against the same fate, each of them vanishing into the elemental emptiness to live only in history and poetry.

Such are the shining consolations of the muses of which Octavio Paz speaks in *The Bow and the Lyre.*

> We are nothing in relation to so much existence turned in on itself. And from this feeling that we are nothing we proceed, if contemplation is pro-

longed and panic does not overtake us, to the opposite state: the rhythm of
the sea keeps time with that of our blood; the silence of the rocks is our own
silence; to walk among the sands is to walk through the span of our con-
sciousness, as boundless as they; the forest murmurs allude to us. We are
part of all. Being emerges from nothing. The same rhythm moves us, the
same silence surrounds us. . . .

Death is not a thing apart: it is, in an inexpressible way, life. The revelation of our nothingness leads us to the creation of being. Thrown into the
nothing, man creates himself in the face of it.[3]

One of Homer's most famous traditional verses plays upon the sounds of poetry that Paz would have us evoke: *para thina poluphloisboio thalassēs*, "along the
shore of the loud-crashing sea." Out of the barrenness of the most deserted
shore comes poetry to oppose that nothingness.

THE BATTLEFIELD VANISHES

> We try to discover in things, which become precious to us on that account,
> the reflection of what our soul has projected onto them; we are disillusioned
> when we find that they are in reality devoid of the charm which they owed, in
> our minds, to the association of certain ideas.
> Virginia Woolf, *To the Lighthouse*

Since records of tourism began, ambitious men have gone to Troy to measure themselves by its heroic landscape. There is nothing like having the *Iliad* on your mind and brooding about your destiny while looking out over
the landscapes of the Troad, to the south of the Dardanelles and the Helles-
pont. Alexander the Great is said to have taken Achilles as his personal
model and made the *Iliad* his bible on the art of war.[4] According to ancient
legend, his only regret was that he didn't have a Homer to celebrate his
deeds. A use of Homer more to modern scholarly tastes is the one Heinrich
Schliemann made in the 1870s. He turned the *Iliad* in the opposite direction
from Alexander and other ambitious kings, reading it not as a prophetic
poem of an ambitious man's future but as a historical record of a genuine
past. He thereby began modern Homeric archaeology with his first excava-
tions at Troy.[5]

Thus arose the modern historical and archaeological impulse that links
Homeric texts with sites. This scientific curiosity is so natural to us that we
forget how misguided it can be for the reading of poetry. Much of what we
readers of Homer want to see on the shores at Troy, the *Iliad* warns us, has
long since ceased to exist. Only the song endures. Reducing the landscape of
war to the seashore, sand, sky, and ocean is to bring it to such an elemental
level that one could as well be on any seashore anywhere. The poetry points

us to that place, and then beyond it; it uses the obliterated landscape as a figurative comment on the evanescence of the warriors who fought long ago.

If it is essential for historians to go to whatever site is in question, in poetry, today, something like the opposite may be the case. It becomes important that we not go to the actual site of Troy, that we make no attempt to
mesh its landscape with the one that the poem gives us. It becomes essential
to avoid reading Homer's verse against its actual settings. There can be field
trips for students of poetry and art—think of the cottage industries that surround the home turf of such poets and writers as Wordsworth, Proust, Frost,
and Tolstoy. War poetry takes us in another direction entirely, to other wars,
other seashores. This is a redirection of the documentary impulse, a personal
inspection not to uncover something in the past, but to find something in
the present already envisioned in the poetry of the past. This is a search for
the sacred ground of a battlefield that has ceased to exist, unlike the experience that Edward Linenthal describes in his book on patriotic American
landscapes, *Sacred Ground*: "Conspicuous by their presence on the martial
landscape are battlefields, prime examples of sacred patriotic space where
memories of the transformative power of war and the sacrificial heroism of
the warrior are preserved. These sites, symbolically transformed by the
events that took place there, are visited by those who seek environmental
intimacy in order to experience patriotic inspiration."[6]

Environmental intimacy is impossible at Battery Wagner. Today all you
can do at the site is sail over it. From land it is possible to drive from Charleston to Folly Island, the staging ground for the Union troops as they moved
against Wagner in the summer of 1863. Because of the erosion by the Atlantic and the movement of sandbars, you can see nothing from the north
shore of Folly Island but a lighthouse in the middle of the sea. The shore and
surf are exactly like any other. This view across the water to the left of the
lighthouse, between that and the diminished shore of Morris Island, is as
close as it is possible to get to a view of the site of the land battle. This is a
fate Virginia Woolf would envy (fig. 25).

In itself, the empty sea at Morris Island says nothing about the historical
significance of the battle of 1863. What the site does is enforce a gap between our desire to remember Battery Wagner and our realization of the terrible impersonality and indifference of passing time. The site of Battery
Wagner is as different from the sites of Gettysburg and Vicksburg as can be
imagined. Vast military parks meticulously document every stage of the decisive battle in Pennsylvania and siege in Mississippi; here, nothing remains
but the vestige of Morris Island, and the sea. History and poetry have to supply what landscape cannot.[7]

The Union's grand assault of July 18, 1863, followed many hours of bom-

Figure 25. Lighthouse and Morris Island, from Folly Island beach

bardment from both land and sea, beginning at 7:45 P.M. and ending at 1:00 A.M. The Fifty-fourth Massachusetts Regiment of 650 men led by Colonel Robert Gould Shaw bore the brunt of the casualties; one of its members, Sergeant William C. Carney, wounded four times, was the first African American to receive the Medal of Honor.[8] The effect of the concentrated artillery and musket fire on assault forces converging into such a confined space was devastating, as a contemporary chronicler, Robert C. Gilchrist, observed following the battle: "blood, mud, water, brains and human hair melted together; men lying in every possible attitude, with every conceivable expression on their countenances; their limbs bent into unnatural shapes by the fall of twenty or more feet; the fingers rigid and outstretched, as if they had clutched at the earth to save themselves; pale beseeching faces, looking out from among the ghastly corpses with moans and cries for help and water, and dying gasps and death struggles."[9]

The burial of Robert Shaw and his men may not have been so brutal as the Northern press made it out to be. John T. Luck, a Federal assistant surgeon who had been captured by the rebels and helped tend to the wounded after the battle, spoke with the commanding Confederate general Hagood about Shaw's body. Because Shaw had commanded black troops, Hagood said, "I shall bury him in the common grave with the Negroes that fell with him." In the Northern press this decorous sentence became "I buried him with his niggers." The Confederate commander of the Charleston defenses, P. G. T. Beauregard, had ordered the same care for black and white wounded, and there was no discrimination in death. The bodies of other white officers were returned; Shaw's was not. Shaw's family thought it the most glorious interment possible. According to Colonel George P. Harrison Jr., of the Georgia Thirty-second, "Shaw's body was laid 'without roughness and with respect'"; then the burial detail "placed on his body 20 of the dead Blacks whom he had commanded."

In the confusion of command, supporting columns that were supposed to follow the initial assault of the Massachusetts Fifty-fourth failed to attack, so the lives of Shaw and his men seemed at first wasted. But the assault electrified the North and earned Wagner as much fame as battles many times larger, with many more casualties. The Union nurse Clara Barton had watched Shaw's assault and the ensuing slaughter. In a letter from December 1863, some months after the campaign had moved on from Morris Island, she captures what the deaths and sacrifices she would later commemorate had already become, at the battle site itself. "We have captured one fort—Gregg—and one charnel house—Wagner—and we have built one cemetery, Morris Island. The thousand little sand-hills that in the pale moonlight are a thousand headstones, and the restless ocean waves that roll and break up on the whitened beach sing an eternal requiem to the toll-worn gallant dead who sleep below."[10]

THE POSEIDON OF MORRIS ISLAND
There were sound reasons in geology and engineering for the disappearance of Battery Wagner. It did not vanish because of the inadvertent omission of duties owed to any particular gods, but neither were the reasons for Wagner's disappearance mundane. To the extent that there was a god of commerce in nineteenth-century America, one might say that Battery Wagner was sacrificed on that god's altar.

The federal engineer Quincey A. Gillmore was the Poseidon of Morris Island. He had been part of the Union forces besieging Charleston during the war and was by a twist of fate one of the engineers most responsible for Charleston's revival as a port following the war. He was in charge of coastal defenses from Cape Fear to St. Augustine, but worked in the New York City office of the Corps of Engineers. In November 1875 he drew up plans for the improvement of Charleston Harbor, with the aid of South Carolina's congressional delegation, and received a two-hundred-thousand-dollar appropriation from Washington.[11] Gillmore's plan proposed to use the scouring power of the ebb tides to keep open a twenty-one-foot channel. The problem was an intricate one, as summarized in the official Corps of Engineers' modern history of the project.

> The problem was getting exactly the right tidal flow. If too much water were directed outward through a new channel, a new bar would form farther out from the entrance. If the flow of the flood tide were directed, both its scouring power and the movement of sand into the inner harbor would be increased. Extreme care had to be taken lest the prevailing northeast to southwest movement of sand on the Charleston bar cause a piling up in the new channel. Finally, the peculiar feature of Charleston Harbor required expert evaluation. The funnellike configuration of the Sullivan's and Morris Islands' shorelines forced the flood tides to pile up near the shore and then find their way into the harbor over the whole length of the bar in a quite even flow. What Gillmore had to do was to figure out how to harness and direct the natural flow of the ebb tide to a degree sufficient to maintain a channel of the desired depth while neither moving the Charleston bar nor interfering with the flow of the flood tide into the harbor.[12]

Gillmore's solution was to construct two parallel jetties into the Atlantic from the shores of the two islands flanking the Charleston Harbor entrance, the one on the south curving out from Morris Island (the site of Battery Wagner) to the one coming from the north, from Sullivan's Island. "At a point about 9,000 feet from Sullivan's Island and 14,000 feet from Morris Island, the jetties straightened to a parallel about 2,900 feet apart. The direction of their parallel pointed directly toward the city of Charleston." This plan was carried through after the construction of the jetties, and the port was opened up to commerce, which was from the beginning the aim of Gillmore's project. As reported in the *Charleston News and Courier* in 1878, "the commercial effect will undoubtedly be great. There will no longer be any doubt. . . . Charleston will soon become the receiving and distributing point for a vast section of the country now supplied by longer lines and at greater cost by Baltimore and New York. The field is open to Charleston." The shoreline of the northern counterpart to Morris Island, Sullivan's Island, held its configuration, and it is even possible that erosion slowed on the shore of Morris Island, whose beaches had withdrawn fifteen hundred feet since a coastal survey done in 1823–25. A preliminary sketch Gillmore made at the beginning of the project shows the way the prevailing tide and sand movement could be turned to Charleston Harbor's advantage (fig. 26). From an engineer's point of view, the site of Battery Wagner was, literally, a castle built on sand.

Gilmore turned natural forces to his own designs, just as Poseidon and

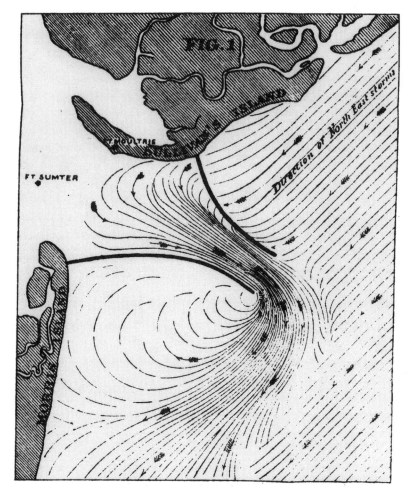

Figure 26. Quincey A. Gillmore, preliminary sketch for the Charleston Jetties Project. From *Annual Report of the Chief of Engineers,* 569, plate 2, fig. 1. (Photo by Mark Austin-Washburn.)

Apollo devised a way to wreck the great war works the Greeks left behind at Troy. Homer's technological details are formidable, fully as intricate as Gillmore's calculations for his jetties. To resume the story where we broke off above, which is where those modern readers who have little taste for technical descriptions in Homer also tend to stop:

> Then at last Poseidon and Apollo took counsel
> to wreck the wall, letting loose the strength of rivers upon it,
> all the rivers that run to the sea from the mountains of Ida,

Rhesos and Heptaporos, Karesos and Rhodios,
Grenikos and Aisepos, and immortal Skamandros,
and Simoeis, where much ox-hide armour and helmets were
    tumbled
in the river mud, and many of the race of the half-god mortals.
Phoibos Apollo turned the mouths of these waters together
and nine days long threw the flood against the wall, and Zeus
    rained
incessantly, to break the wall faster and wash it seaward.
And the shaker of the earth himself holding in his hands the
    trident
guided them, and hurled into the waves all the bastions'
    strengthening
of logs and stones the toiling Achaians had set in position
and made all smooth again by the hard-running passage of
    Helle
and once again piled the great beach under sand, having
    wrecked
the wall, and turned the rivers again to make their way down
the same channel where before they had run the bright stream
    of their water.
    (12.17–33, Lattimore)

Of the many differences that one could draw between Quincey Gillmore and Poseidon and Apollo, perhaps not the least important is that Gillmore had a genuine desire to improve his former enemies' lives by reshaping the seashore and the approaches to Charleston Harbor.

FOR THE UNION DEAD

The battle of July 1863 for Battery Wagner was commemorated most famously by the memorial Augustus Saint-Gaudens made in the 1890s to be set up opposite the State House in Boston (fig. 27). It is generally regarded as Saint-Gaudens's masterpiece. Its vitality is given a powerful reading by Robert Hughes in *American Visions*.

Stoic and resolute, the men march forward to the beat of a drummer boy in front. Their uniforms do not have the emblematic neatness a lesser sculptor might have given them. They are rumpled and creased, each in a different way, which goes with the individuation of the men's faces. They are not cogs in a machine but citizen soldiers, volunteers with free will—an essential part of the sculptor's message, reflecting the inscription on the Shaw Memorial that "they gave proof that Americans of African descent possess the pride, devotion and courage of the patriot soldier." The visual rhythm of the column is given by the barrels of the rifles carried at the slope, which divide the space vertically; and by the six spiral ends of the blanket rolls and the disks of the water bottles, which meter it horizontally. Every small form plays its part. This is the most intensely felt image of military commemoration made by an American.[13]

By the time Hughes was writing, the Shaw Memorial had been rescued for at least the time being from the terrible vulnerability of monuments. It had not always been so well read and valued. Robert Lowell's poem about the fate of this monument, "For the Union Dead," was composed in the 1950s and 1960s era of civil rights battles, at a point when construction of a new aquarium and a parking garage in the Boston Common required that the Shaw Memorial be temporarily removed and stored in a crate. Lowell's focus on a moment of memorialization is far less consoling than his friend and mentor Allen Tate's earlier "Ode to the Confederate Dead."[14] It is that ode in part which Lowell is answering.

In his poem from the 1930s, Allen Tate contemplates the graves of the dead soldiers, not just of a losing side in a war, but of a doomed slave society. At the end of his elegy he foresees much the same thing for the living who see the graves of the dead, as for the war dead themselves.

> What shall we say who have knowledge
> Carried to the heart? Shall we take the act
> To the grave? Shall we, more hopeful, set up the grave
> In the house? The ravenous grave?
> The shut gate and the decomposing wall:
> The gentle serpent, green in the mulberry bush,
> Riots with his tongue through the hush—
> Sentinel of the grave who counts us all![15]

It is a poem about the inability of the poet to perform the traditional poet's task of memorializing the war dead. Later poetry, and history, have a way of intruding on poets who are more optimistic. Tate, one of the southern Fugitive Poets and a biographer of both Stonewall Jackson and Jefferson Davis, entertained little optimism for the lost cause of the Confederacy.

Lowell unravels the threads that Tate was weaving and draws nearer to what Homer shows us at the end of the *Iliad*. In contrast to Tate's "Ode," "For the Union Dead" meets the challenge of history by working with it rather than turning away in resignation. Forged out of two earlier poems, "The Old Aquarium" and "One Gallant Rush: The Death of Colonel Shaw," "For the Union Dead" fuses the poet's memory of the old aquarium on Boston Com-

Figure 27. Augustus Saint-Gaudens, memorial to Colonel Shaw, Boston (Photograph by Jeffrey Nintzel.)

mon with his personal memory and researches into the history of Shaw and the Massachusetts Fifty-fourth.[16] Its images evoke the era of the rising battle for civil rights, inspired not just by Saint-Gaudens's memorial, but also by its dismantling while the Commons underground parking garage was being built.

Lowell had already visited Morris Island and seen the sand and dunes of the barrier islands where the battle over Charleston was waged, and he had seen for himself the obliteration of the Massachusetts Fifty-fourth's battlefield. "For the Union Dead" also can be read as an answer to such earlier poems explicitly on Shaw and his men as the one by Lowell's nineteenth-century relation, James Russell Lowell, who also composed lines for the Shaw Memorial.[17]

> He leads for aye the advance,
> Hope's forlorn—hopes that plant the desperate good
> For nobler Earths and days of manlier mood.

The Union dead here are not only the whites who fought the Confederate dead, but also the blacks for whom that war was fought. Unlike the elegiac

Tate, Lowell is not generic and nameless in his treatment of this scene—a stance that is sometimes thought of as unpolitical—but goes after the city that was the heart of the abolitionist movement as well as the recruiting ground for Shaw. He is quite specific in naming the war dead, quoting but changing the lapidary Latin of the monument. As Helen Vendler observes, Saint-Gaudens had incised the motto of the Society of the Cincinnati about one man's valor in war, "He left behind everything to save the Republic" (*Relinquit Omnia Servare Rem Publicam*), but Lowell made the verb plural, *Relinquunt Omnia Servare Rem Publicam* ("They leave behind everything to save the Republic"), so that the memorial now applies to all the men of the Fifty-fourth Regiment, not just Shaw.[18]

> Two months after marching through Boston,
> half the regiment was dead;
> at the dedication,
> William James could almost hear the bronze Negroes breathe.
> Their monument sticks like a fishbone
> in the city's throat.
> Its Colonel is as lean
> as a compass-needle.

Lowell recalls that Shaw's own father wanted him buried in the ditch where the Confederates had thrown him, to be with his "niggers." He then leaps from that moment in 1863 to a present world that has become indistinguishable from the ditch into which the Confederates threw Shaw's body.

> The ditch is nearer.
> There are no statues for the last war here;
> on Boylston Street, a commercial photograph
> shows Hiroshima boiling
> over a Mosler Safe, the "Rock of Ages"
> that survived the blast. Space is nearer.
> When I crouch to my television set,
> the drained faces of Negro school-children rise like balloons.
> Colonel Shaw
> is riding on his bubble,
> he waits
> for the blessed break.
> The Aquarium is gone. Everywhere,
> giant finned cars nose forward like fish;
> a savage servility
> slides by on grease.

It is not only Lowell's sense of history and his outrage at its neglect that save the story of Battery Wagner and its dead. As Helen Vendler puts it, "For the Union Dead" is "a resurrection rite intending to resuscitate both Shaw and his monument."[19] And it does this for a world where Madison Avenue turns the atomic bombing at Hiroshima into a manufacturer's warranty test of the Mosler safe.

Sand and sea and sky are the same for the Greeks' wall and Battery Wagner. Saint-Gaudens's memorial would seem the first line of defense against this fate. It is far removed from the actual battle site, as such memorials often are. But as Lowell suggests, this reliance on the durability of meaning in a monument is a delusion. Not only was Saint-Gaudens's monument itself exposed to a literal, if temporary, dislocation. One hundred years after the battle at Battery Wagner, with the March on Washington in 1963 and Martin Luther King Jr.'s speech, "I have a dream," the cause for which Shaw and his men died was as unrealized as ever. Lowell's poem gives us an eternal meantime, where we can return to the battle for Battery Wagner and bring the memory of Colonel Shaw and his men once again to life, just as we return to the men fighting before the Achaean Walls at Troy, forever alive in Homer's poetry, and to the words of the loud-crashing sea.

Five THE COMPANION SEEN
BUT NOT HEARD

> Insofar as Eros is physical passion and sensual impulsion, war has been from of
> old its true mate and bedfellow, as the ancient myth makes clear. And erotic
> love of the fuller sort can find a dwelling place in the violence of war that for-
> ever astounds us and remains inexplicable. Here Ares and Aphrodite meet as
> opposites who have a powerful attraction for each other. Love as concern can
> achieve at times its greatest satisfaction and triumph in struggling to preserve
> what Ares is intent on destroying. Though deeply opposed to conflict, this
> love is not as exposed or helpless as is friendship. In the exercise of its ancient
> rights, preservative love sanctifies even the battlefield by its presence and
> holds men back from being delivered over wholly to the lustful powers of de-
> struction. But love as friendship, despite its insulation, must subsist haphaz-
> ardly and as best it may in the midst of war. Its true domain is peace, only
> peace.
>
> J. Glenn Gray, *The Warriors*

Achilles' wide-ranging appetites are not fully unleashed in the *Iliad* until he
begins to slaughter Trojans, hacking his way through to the only goal Patroclus's death suddenly leaves him, killing Hector. At that point in his war it is
easy to imagine him capable of anything.[1] Homer and his Muses sing nothing about the chase and murder of the young Trojan prince Troilus, or of the
slaying of the Amazon queen Penthesilea. A famous vase painting by the
Penthesilea painter in the Antikensammlung in Munich depicts the moment
when Achilles and Penthesilea are falling in love, even as he is driving his
sword into her breast (fig. 28). The downward thrust of the sword into the
helpless suppliant is the ultimate penetration for her, but possibly not for
Achilles. By some accounts he is said to have made love to Penthesilea's
corpse after he killed her. Even more arresting is the piteous gaze of the victim, locked with the furious glare of her killer's eyes seen through his hel-
met's visor. Good killing, like good sex, is much enhanced by eye contact.[2]

The Penthesilea painter well understands the marriage of sexual passion
and lust in battle that Gray speaks of. Many of these alternate stories, each
less flattering to Achilles than the last, appear in sources from late antiquity
such as the fictional eyewitness Dictys of Crete and his *Chronicles of the Trojan
War*. They have inspired alternative versions of Achilles, as Homer shows
him, ever since.[3]

Figure 28. Penthesilea painter, Achilles and Penthesilea, red figure cup (Staatliche Antikensammlung, Munich. Copyright Foto Marburg/Art Resource, New York.)

But particular stories are not so important as perception. No one who follows the *Iliad* into the heart of its battles (chapter 6) needs to see this scene to believe that Achilles would be capable of it. The coupling of Achilles and Penthesilea is a mortal image replaying an old theme: Ares the god of war and Aphrodite the goddess of love, intermingled in a marriage of love and death.[4] The moment captured by the Penthesilea painter will surprise no one who knows the *Iliad* or later poetry and art of war. In war, this love may have time to develop over many years; it often is like the overpowering love of the young. It concentrates itself into a maximal experience of gain and loss; everything love brings us can be lost in an instant to war. It is this twin legacy that makes the Trojan wife Andromache and the Greek warrior Patroclus such complementary figures. In the *Iliad*, it is not just that we come to see the love between men in battle through the lens of the love between men and women, though that is the case with Patroclus and Achilles. It is the contrast between love as experienced at home, apart from war, and love that is found on the battlefield that we also come to know.

THE LAMENT OF THE SOLDIER'S WIFE

> She gave an envious thought to the happier lot of men, who are always free to plunge into the healing waters of action.
> Henry James, *The Portrait of a Lady*

Love is never far from the thoughts of a man in battle. Hector has long since left Andromache behind by the time he ponders on the battlefield outside the walls of Troy whether he should fight Achilles to the death, or attempt to parley with him. Facing Achilles, he realizes that whatever he says or does will make no difference. The way he characterizes his fear suggests how close romance and love are to their apparent antitheses, scorn and hate. Hector's conception of surrender and defeat is inseparable from his notion of femininity.[5]

> Why debate, my friend? Why thrash things out?
> I must not go and implore him. He'll show no mercy,
> no respect for me, my rights—he'd cut me down
> straight off—stripped of defenses like a woman
> once I have loosed the armor off my body.
> No way to parley with that man—not now—
> not from behind some oak or rock to whisper,
> like a boy and girl might whisper to each other . . .
> Better to clash in battle, now, at once—
> *see* which fighter Zeus awards the glory!
>   (22.122–30; 22.146–56, Fagles)

Hector can see clearly the warrior's companion love, but he cannot hear of it, any more than Achilles would hear of it. The ceaseless struggle between the desires of battle and the desires of love is played out in the contemporary Vietnamese writer Bao Ninh's *Sorrow of War,* where the students Kien and Phuong meet for what they think will be the last time before Kien leaves to serve in the North Vietnamese army in its war against the Americans. He is suddenly overcome with fear and tears himself away from Phuong's embrace. She sees at once that Kien is as afraid of love as he is of war.

> "You're afraid, aren't you?" Phuong said, suddenly breaking the silence between them. "Me, too. But just realising it makes me more keen."
> "I just think we shouldn't," he blathered. "I'm going off to war. I'm going away," he said unconvincingly. "Better not."
> "Okay," she sighed. "But there'll never be another time like now."

"I'll come back," he said urgently.

"When? A thousand years from now? You'll be changed and so will I. Hanoi will be different. So will this West Lake."

"Our feelings won't change, that's the most important thing," he said.

She remained silent for a moment then said, "I can see what's going to happen. War, ruin, destruction."

"Maybe, but we'll rebuild."

"You're a simpleton; your father was different, he saw it coming," she said.[6]

The young would-be warrior Kien has yet to cross over the threshold that Achilles and Hector have long since crossed. He tries to think only of duty, scared of giving way to the urge to love. Yet the adolescent Kien shares one important thing with even the maturest of heroes. Neither he nor Hector can be turned away from war by love. They sense the present and future course of events but are too afraid, or feel too doomed, to do more than what the present demands. When Andromache mourns for Hector after he is slain by Achilles, she grieves for the realization of everything she had foreseen would happen. The reality of his death stuns her, but it is something she and other women of Troy foresaw more clearly than Hector could as he returned to the war. As Chapman's Homer phrases it, "In his life great Hector's funerals were."

Like the fast-forward of the story of the Achaean walls (books 7 and 12), and with more resonance than that divinely foretold event, the parting of Hector and Andromache is a memory that Hector and Homer's readers carry into all the battles that follow. Hector would like Andromache's role to be as sharply defined and separated from his own as possible. He uses their household to set a limit to a mutual dread that each of them barely controls.

> Go therefore back to our house, and take up your own work,
> the loom and the distaff, and see to it that your handmaidens
> ply their work also; but the men must see to the fighting,
> all men who are the people of Ilion, but I beyond others.
> (6.490–93, Lattimore)

Aristophanes would take this celebrated declaration of a wife's and a husband's roles in the direction of Phuong and other women skeptical of male rules. In *Lysistrata*, a comedy produced toward the end of the Peloponnesian War in 411 when Athens's future course looked no more certain than Troy's, he turns Hector's division of labors between men and women in war into the climax of his heroine Lysistrata's cross-examination of the men who try to run Athens. Hector's precept becomes an archaic example of male stupidity

in the face of women's common sense. Douglass Parker's version remains the
best realization of the scene in performable English.

> *Lysistrata*: When the War began, like the prudent, dutiful wives that we are,
>   we tolerated you men, and endured your actions in silence. (Small
>   wonder—
>   you wouldn't let us say boo.) You were not precisely the answer
>   to a matron's prayer—we knew you too well, and found out more.
>   Too many times, as we sat in the house, we'd hear that you'd done it
>   —again—manhandled another affair of state with your usual
>   staggering incompetence. Then, masking our worry with a nervous
>   laugh,
>   we'd ask you brightly, "How was the Assembly today, dear? Anything
>   in the minutes about Peace?" And my husband would give his stock
>   reply.
>   "What's that to you? Shut up!" And I did.
> *Kleonike*: *I* never shut up!
> *Commissioner*: I trust you were shut up. Soundly.
> *Lysistrata*: Regardless, *I* shut up.
>   And then we'd learn that you'd passed another decree, fouler
>   than the first, and we'd ask again: "Darling, how *did* you manage
>   anything so idiotic?" And my husband, with his customary glare,
>   would tell me to spin my thread, or else get a clout on the head.
>   And of course he'd quote from Homer: *Ye menne must husband ye warre.*
> *Commissioner*: Apt and irrefutably right.
> *Lysistrata*: *Right*, you miserable misfit?
>   to keep us from giving advice while you fumbled the City away
>   in the Senate? Right, indeed![7]

Whereas Lysistrata enacts a woman's critical detachment, Andromache and
Phuong play the more traditional role of the witness of war who often sees
what may come in war more clearly than the man who goes into it. Phuong
finds Kien's craving for war and death a ridiculous excuse to avoid making
love, and in her hands the scene of seeing a hero off to war turns into a trite
ritual, one she trumps by joining up herself. Since Kien is offering his life for
a cause, she decides to waste her life as well. Phuong is in part an Andromache, the submissive wife, but she has more than a little of Lysistrata in her.
Her sophistication is a significant departure from the role of women in traditional Vietnamese culture, such as *The Tale of Kieu* portrays.

In this most famous of Vietnamese poems, the tribulations of the young
woman Kieu have often been read as a veiled story of the Vietnamese nation

and its fate to be ruled by one foreign empire after another.[8] Kieu's lover
Kim cannot understand why Kieu should sing as she does. Soon she will be
compelled to become a courtesan to save her family. Even then, Kieu, like
Phuong and Andromache, is well ahead of her lover in her song.

> The lamp now flared, now dimmed—and there he sat
> hovering between sheer rapture and deep gloom.
> He'd dug his knees or he'd hang down his head—
> he'd feel his entrails wrenching, knit his brows.
> "Indeed, a master's touch," he said at last,
> "but it betrays such bitterness within!
> Why do you choose to play those plaintive strains
> which grieve your heart and sorrow other souls?"
> "I'm settled in my nature," she replied,
> "Who knows why Heaven makes one sad or gay?
> But I shall mark your golden words, their truth,
> and by degrees my temper may yet mend."[9]

Bao Ninh's Phuong is not about to replay Kieu.[10] But neither is she really a
Lysistrata. When she goes off to war herself, she is beaten and gang-raped
by her own country's soldiers. She and Kien survive the war, physically, but
their love dies. Their parting scene in *The Sorrow of War* is a love story cut
short before its lovers even realize it, an adolescent version of the parting of
Hector and Andromache.

For his part, Hector is the reactive hero, the patriot whose identity is so
strong that he cannot break away from it. He is aware of the probable consequences of his death in battle and hopes to be dead rather than face what
will happen.

> Now, since by my own recklessness I have ruined my people,
> I feel shame before the Trojans and the Trojan women with
>   trailing
> robes, that someone who is less of a man than I will say of me:
> "Hektor believed in his own strength and ruined his people."
> Thus they will speak; and as for me, it would be much better
> at that time, to go against Achilleus, and slay him, and come
>   back,
> or else be killed by him in glory in front of the city.
>   (22.104–10, Lattimore)

He sees much of what Andromache sees, but he cannot act on what she
says. Nor does he foresee all the consequences. Although he can imagine the

humiliation and anguish of Andromache, his death will be anything but one accomplished in glory. It is left to Andromache herself, after Hector is slain, to imagine the fate of their son, Astyanax. First she imagines his sorrows as an orphan with no father to protect him.

> The day of bereavement leaves a child with no agemates to
>   befriend him.
> He bows his head before every man, his cheeks are bewept, he
> goes, needy, a boy among his father's companions,
> and tugs at this man by the mantle, that man by the tunic,
> and they pity him, and one gives him a tiny drink from a goblet,
> enough to moisten his lips, not enough to moisten his palate.
> But one whose parents are living beats him out of the banquet
> hitting his with his fists and in words also abuses him:
> "Get out, you! Your father is not dining among us."
> And the boy goes away in tears to his widowed mother.
>   (22.490–99; 22.489–99, Lattimore)

By the end of the poem, as Hector's corpse is brought back to Troy, she arrives at a more accurate prediction of their son's future, saying to him,

>   or else some Achaean
> will take you by hand and hurl you from the tower into
>   horrible
> death, in anger because Hector once killed his brother,
> or his father, or his son; there were so many Achaeans
> whose teeth bit the vast earth, beaten down by the hands of
>   Hector.
> Your father was no merciful man in the horror of battle.
>   (24.734–39, Lattimore)

We know what Homer expects his audiences to know: at the urging of Odysseus, the Greeks will hurl Astyanax off the walls of Troy to prevent his growing up and avenging his father.[11]

Men admire Hector in his roles as husband, father, and son defending his city. The anthropologist James Redfield turned into a classicist, temporarily, because of his admiration of Hector's civic virtues. Redfield shifted the focus of the poem away from the best of the Achaeans, to the family man and citizen he came to regard as Achilles' chief victim. The last line of the poem (the burial of Hector) became for him more important than the first (the rage of Achilles).

> As I thought about Hector, my affection for him grew. I found in him a martyr to loyalties, a witness to the things of this world, a hero ready to die for

the precious imperfections of ordinary life. I became Hector's partisan; I felt he had been neglected by the critics, unjustly shaded by the glamour of Achilles. I saw his story as that of an admirable man who falls into error without ceasing to be admirable and who dies a death which is tragic because we find it inevitable and in some sense his own fault, but undeserved. For the first time I thought that I understood Aristotle's praise of the story of such a hero as the best kind of tragic plot. I determined to write something about, and in praise of, Hector and Homer.[12]

Hector's humanity is undoubted, but this does not mean that he isn't as much a hero—in practical terms, a killer of men—as anyone else. Andromache says to his son Astyanax that his father was "no man of mercy" (24.739; 24.870, Fagles). More literally, Hector was not *meilichos*—a man who was not "mild," even luxuriously "pleasant." The word has erotic overtones, associated with the allures of Paris, Helen, and the gifts of Aphrodite.[13] On the battlefield Hector aims to be everything that the soft, self-indulgent Paris is not.

There are no such healing waters of action for the soldier's wife. In "The Song of a Soldier's Wife," by Dang Tran Con and Phan Huy Ich, traditionally known to the Vietnamese by its opening line, "When all through earth and heaven rise dust storms," it falls to that wife as well to imagine what her husband's fate will be in war.

> A man will fight a thousand miles from home
> to earn his winding sheet: a horse's skin.
> His very life, as weighty as Mount T'ai,
> he'll drop in battle like so much goose down.
> . . . .
>
> You left and journeyed toward the far Southwest—
> who knows where you are battling at this hour?
> Those who have gone to war for a long time
> have learned to treat their lives like blades of grass.
> Heaven's grace, all fiercely fight.
> Confronting perils, few will reach old age
> . . . .
>
> Inside this door, I live my fated life—
> but were you born to roam at heaven's edge?
> We hoped to join like fish and water once:
> instead, we've split apart—a stream, a cloud.
> I never thought I'd be a soldier's wife,
> condemned to wait and long for him at home.[14]

If women are not born into playing the soldier's wife, the men they see off to war sometimes earn much less sentimental responses.

Hector is constantly worried about what the Trojans might think of him, and this awareness makes his parting with Andromache all the more unbearable. He much prefers to charge back into the thick of battle. It is not only that, as Hector, he has no other choice; it is easier to go out into the fearful future than to abide in Andromache's clairvoyant present. Not so sympathetic to this dilemma, Gertrude Stein gets Hector's number in *Wars I Have Seen*, the delusional sentiments as well as the bravado. Like Robert E. Lee, Hector was a civil servant, a man who went to war because he was supposed to go to war.

> The thing that is most interesting about government servants is that they believe what they are supposed to believe, they really do believe what they are supposed to believe, which has a great deal to do with wars and wars being what they are. It really has. . . .
>
> I once asked some one who should know why public servants in the army in every branch of government did not seem to have the kind of judgment that the man in the street any man or any woman has about what is happening. Oh he answered the reason is simple, they are specialists, and to a specialist his specialty is the whole of everything and if his specialty is in good order and it generally is then everything must be succeeding. In the German army they call these specialists the bees, because in their cells they are supposed to make honey, not money honey. And so this is what makes war, and then makes the failure of war. I have said so often between 1938 and 1943, I cannot understand why men have so little common sense why they cannot understand when there is no possibility of their winning that they will win, why they cannot remember that two and two makes four and no more. And now everybody knows except the public servants they are still believing what they are supposed to believe, nobody else believes it, not even all their families believe it but believe it or not, they do still believe it, believe what they are supposed to believe. And so naturally they believing what they are supposed to believe make it possible for the country to think that they can win a war that they cannot possibly win, and so they go to war, and all because the public servants really believe what they are supposed to believe what they are supposed to believe they really do.[15]

The feminist imagination makes short work of both warriors and the poets who sing about them. As Alice Childress memorably put it, "A hero ain't nothin' but a sandwich."

In an essay accompanying her short novel *Cassandra*, the German writer Christa Wolf asks, "To whom can I say that the *Iliad* bores me?"[16] Wolf revises Homer just as Euripides had done in *The Trojan Women,* by focusing on the women and children who were victims of the Trojan War, and by following alternate versions of the story. The murder of Astyanax, foreseen but not actually realized in the *Iliad,* predictably comes to the center of action in Euripides' play. *Cassandra* begins with the transformation of the voice of Christa Wolf, the East German writer to whom no one will listen, into the voice of the princess of Troy, Cassandra, whose prophecies are fated to be believed by no one. Wolf wants us to see the sanctioned violence of war not head-on, as in Homer's battle scenes, but at an angle, from the sidelines, where the heroic exploits in the Trojan War consist of nothing but sheer, simple butchery.

> Then Achilles the brute came. The murderer came into the temple, which darkened as he stood at the entrance. What did this man want? What was he after, wearing weapons here in the temple? Hideous moment: already I knew. Then he laughed. Every hair on my head stood on end and sheer terror came into my brother's eyes. I threw myself over him and was shoved aside as if I were not there. In what role was his enemy approaching my brother? As a murderer? As a seducer? Could such a thing be—the voluptuousness of the murderer and the lover in one? Was that allowed to exist among human beings? The fixed gaze of the victim. The capering approach of the pursuer, whom I now saw from behind, a lewd beast. Who took Troilus by the shoulders, stroked him, handled him—the defenseless boy from whom I, wretched woman, had removed the armor! Laughing, laughing all over. Gripped his neck. Moved to the throat. His plump, stuffy-fingered, hairy hand on my brother's throat. Pressing, pressing. I hung on the murderer's arm, on which the veins stood out like cords. My brother's eyes were starting out of their sockets. And the gratification in Achilles' face. The naked hideous male gratification. If that exists, everything is possible. It was deathly still. I was shaken off, felt nothing. Now the enemy, the monster, raised his sword in full view of Apollo's statue and severed my brother's head from his torso. Human blood spurted onto the altar as before it had spurted from the carcasses of our sacrificial animals. Troilus, the sacrificial victim. The butcher fled with a horrid and gratified howl. Achilles the brute. I felt nothing for a long time.[17]

By changing Achilles' battlefield exploits into murder, Wolf rewrites the Trojan War myth, making the women who are on the periphery in Homer and such traditional poetry as "The Song of a Soldier's Wife" take center stage. Achilles emerges as a psychopathic killer, gleefully strangling and decapitating the stripling Troilus.

Cassandra offers a portrait of ancient sisterhood that makes hash of ancient myth and tradition, and yet it is not quite so radical as it sounds. In Aeschylus's *Agamemnon* Cassandra and Clytemnestra meet briefly before Cassandra enters the house of Atreus. She is fully aware that she and Agamemnon will be murdered there by Clytemnestra and her lover Aegisthus. *Cassandra* follows faithfully the broad outline of the story of the *Iliad* and the *Agamemnon*—Agamemnon and Cassandra must die—but the musing of Wolf's Cassandra is given a voice altogether different from anything we hear in Homer or Greek tragedy.

> When the queen walked out the gate a little while ago, I let myself feel a last tiny hope that I could get her to spare the children's lives. All I had to do was to look into her eyes. She was doing what she had to do. She did not make things as they are, she is adapting to things as they are. Either she gets rid of her husband, this empty-headed ninny, and makes a good job of it, or she gives up herself: her life, her sovereignty, her lover—who, if I interpret the figure in the background correctly, also looks to be a self-centered ninny, but young, handsome, smooth-fleshed. She indicated to me with a shrug of her shoulders that what was happening had nothing to do with me personally. In different times nothing would have prevented us from calling each other sister.[18]

Wolf's Cassandra is conceived with open disdain for traditional versions of male poets like Homer and Aeschylus, and this Cassandra has no sense of irony. Her musings on Clytemnestra and sisterhood transform the brotherhood of male warriors into a sisterhood of their victims, with the result that the sisterhood of Clytemnestra and Cassandra—an Aristophanic concept if there ever was one—begins to sound like the alliance of Cecily Cardew and Gwendolyn Fairfax in *The Importance of Being Earnest*.

> *Jack*: Cecily and Gwendolyn are perfectly certain to be extremely great
> friends. I'll bet you anything that half an hour after they have met, they
> will be calling each other sister.
> *Algernon*: Women only do that when they have called each other a lot of
> other things first.

In her strong reaction against what she sees as a pernicious heritage, in her resolve to become a contemporary equivalent of Cassandra herself, the betrayed prophet whose visions of the future no one will believe, Wolf has followed her chosen mythical icon all too successfully.

Yet the choice of myth was a shrewd one. It is always the fate of Cassandra not to be heeded. Andromache and Hector come back to life again and again, each with their men and women partisans, the tragedy of loss of husband and wife in war repeated as another variation on a theme, just as Cassandra warns again and again in vain. In all these tales of the soldier's wife we are forever crossing back and forth, between the absurdity of the loss and the sorrow of it. For those locked in necessity and incapable of escape, war stories like *Lysistrata, Cassandra,* and *Wars I Have Seen* are all so much irrelevant fantasy. In her memoir of her life with her husband, the poet Edward Thomas, Helen Thomas records their parting at Christmas in 1916. Edward soon departed for the front and was killed the following April. Helen's recollection is purest Andromache:

> But now my love was overwhelmed by dim forebodings which my natural happiness, hopefulness and vitality were powerless to subdue, and which robbed me of the courage to stay there and make believe to continue a life from which without Edward all significance had gone: forebodings which though vague and unformulated urged me to wrench myself from these associations before they became unbearable to me. . . . The jerry-built cottage is made sacred to me because of those last evenings with Edward there. Only on a few more occasions were we to sit together by our own fireside, and as if I knew it, my heart hurt with unsheddable tears, and, when he had gone, with a bitterness new and dreadful to it.[19]

Edward Thomas was able to write a poem about this parting ("Out in the Dark over the Snow"); he even had much of it in his mind as the events Helen recalls took place. But his is not the only poetry that was made from this archetypal moment in war. Helen's memory is guided by the voice of their young daughter Myfanwy that Edward had earlier turned into poetry. They go upstairs, undress, and Edward reads to her from *Antony and Cleopatra.*

> So we lay, all night, sometimes talking of our love and all that had been, and of the children, and what had been amiss and what right. We knew the best was that there had never been untruth between us. We knew all of each other, and it was right. So talking and crying and loving in each other's arms we fell asleep as the cold reflected light of the snow crept through the frost-covered windows.
>
> We were alone in the room. He took me in his arms, holding me tightly to him, his face white, his eyes full of a fear I had never seen before. My arms were around his neck. "Beloved, I love you," was all I could say. "Helen, Helen, Helen," he said, "remember that, whatever happens, all is well between us for ever and ever." And hand in hand we went downstairs and out to the children, who were playing in the snow.[20]

The love of Edward and Helen suffuses this moment, and Edward is at one with her in sensing what is coming, but he can do nothing but return to the war. This wife's soldier has no other option, nor does she.

GENTLE PATROCLUS

> The essential difference between comradeship and friendship consists in a
> heightened awareness of the self in friendship and in the suppression of self-
> awareness in comradeship. Friends do not seek to lose their identity, as
> comrades and erotic lovers do. On the contrary, friends find themselves in
> each other and thereby gain greater self-knowledge and self-possession.
> J. Glenn Gray, *The Warriors*

Ancient scholarly tradition assigned the title *Patrokleia* or *The Story of Patroclus*
to book 16 alone: the story of Patroclus's donning Achilles' armor, his entry
into battle, his killing of Zeus's son Sarpedon, and his own death at the
hands of Hector. But *Iliad* 16 is part of a larger sequence of events, the focus
of the second and longest day of fighting in the *Iliad*. Patroclus's story is in
the middle of a poem that opens with the anger of Achilles and ends with the
funeral rites of Hector, the ultimate victim of Achilles' wrath. Within the *Iliad*, the death of Patroclus is the cardinal event, determining the progress
from Achilles' anger to the funeral of Hector. In Glenn Gray's terms, the
story of Achilles could be summarized as one in which a hero begins with
Patroclus as his dearest comrade in war, and then discovers through the loss
of Patroclus what that love actually means.

Patroclus is a constant presence with Achilles. But until Patroclus joins in
the action of the war, in book 11, he does not utter a word. This is an eloquent silence.[21] When he does speak for the first time, in a gentle, even innocent tone, the poet lets us know that the emergence of Patroclus's voice is
also his first step toward death.

> At once he spoke to his own companion in arms, Patroclus,
> calling from the ship, and he heard it from inside the shelter,
>   and came out
> like the war god, and this was the beginning of his evil.
> The strong son of Menoitios spoke first, and addressed him:
> "What do you wish with me Achilles? Why do you call me?"
> (11.602–6; 11.601–5, Lattimore)

Before this moment, we learn the nature of the love between the two not
through a speech or a conversation, but through a scene of domestic happiness.

> With this he was pleasuring his heart, and singing of men's
>   fame,
> as Patroclus was sitting over against him, alone, in silence,
> watching Aiakides [Achilles] and the time he would leave off
>   singing.
> (9.189–91, Lattimore)

He is then commanded by Achilles once again to prepare a meal for them, and does so.

> So he spoke, and Patroclus obeyed his beloved companion,
> and tossed down a great chopping-block into the firelight,
> and laid upon it the back of a sheep, and one of a fat goat,
> with the chine of a fatted pig edged thick with lard, and for
>   him
> Automedon held the meats, and brilliant Achilles carved
>   them,
> and cut it well into pieces and spitted them, as meanwhile
> Menoitios' son, a man like a god, made the fire blaze greatly.
>   (9.205–11, Lattimore)

When Patroclus returns from his reconnaissance of the battle, Achilles taunts him for his tears, in the way that warriors in all-male armies are given to doing.[22]

> Why then are you crying like some poor little girl, Patroclus,
> who runs after her mother and begs to be picked up and
>   carried,
> and clings to her dress, and holds her back when she tries to
>   hurry,
> and gazes tearfully into her face, until she is picked up?
> You are like such a one, Patroclus, dropping these soft tears.
>   (16.7–11, Lattimore)

Achilles' gift for figurative thinking carries beyond his insult, to wider implications for Homer's more suspicious audiences. If Patroclus is acting the little girl, who else could Achilles be but the mother?

From his first, silent appearance in book 1, doing Achilles' bidding, accompanying Achilles in his withdrawal from the war, Patroclus plays the role of a silent, faithful wife, not speaking until spoken to.[23] Achilles' old friend and tutor Phoenix is the closest thing to a father Achilles has at Troy, and Phoenix does not hesitate to exploit the wifelike devotion of Patroclus to persuade him to return to the war. For this rhetorical purpose he turns to a cautionary tale of the hero Meleager and his withdrawal from war to the company of his wife, Cleopatra.

> Over and over the old horseman Oeneus begged him, he
> took a stand at the vaulted chamber's threshold,
> shaking the bolted doors, begging his own son!
> Over and over his brothers and noble mother

> implored him—he refused them all the more—
> and troops of comrades, devoted, dearest friends.
> Not even they could bring his fighting spirit round
> until, at last, rocks were raining down on the chamber,
> Curetes about to mount the towers and torch the great city!
> And then, finally, Meleager's bride, beautiful Cleopatra
> begged him, streaming tears, recounting all the griefs
> that fall to people whose city's seized and plundered—
> the men slaughtered, citadel burned to rubble, enemies
> dragging the children, raping the sashed and lovely women.
> How his spirit leapt when he heard those horrors—
> and buckling his gleaming armor round his body,
> out he rushed to war.
>   (9.581–96; 9.709–25, Fagles)

Phoenix's story is as prophetic as it is provocative: Achilles will at last reenter battle, and even at Patroclus's urging. But he will do so at a point when the original reasons for doing so have evaporated, replaced by an even harsher reality than the one that Meleager confronts after he has returned to his war. Unlike Cleopatra, Patroclus will have to die to accomplish as much.

> And so Meleager saved them all
> from the fatal day, he gave way to his own feelings,
> but too late. No longer would they make good the gifts,
> those troves of gifts to warm his heart, and even so
> he beat off that disaster . . . empty-handed.
>   (9.597–99; 9.725–29, Fagles)

Meleager is no subtle model for Achilles. As Homer's audiences can hear, Cleopatra is by Meleager's side at every stage in Phoenix's story, accompanying him as he withdraws from the besieged city to his own house—just as Achilles has withdrawn from Agamemnon's war, to his tent and the company of Patroclus. The similar role Patroclus and Cleopatra play is reflected in the Phoenix's serious wordplay on their names, *Patro-klos* and *Kleo-patra*: *kleos*, "glory," and *pateres*, "ancestors."[24] If Cleopatra is a mirror image of these word roots in Patroclus's name, Patroclus performs roles that are a reflection of Cleopatra's role, as wife to Meleager. He serves Achilles as a companion in withdrawal; he will be the one who pleads, just as Cleopatra pled with Meleager.

A warrior like Patroclus is often the pivotal figure of a war story. The mourning of the warrior for such a lost comrade surfaces in Philip Caputo's Vietnam memoir, *A Rumor of War*. Under the pressure of trying to preserve the memory of his friend Walter Levy, Caputo slips in midsentence into a direct address to the dead.

> I still could not remember what he had said to me that night in Georgetown. It could not have been important, yet I wanted to remember. I want to remember now, to remember what you said, you, Walter Neville Levy, whose ghost haunts me still. No, it could not have been anything important or profound, but that doesn't mater. What matters is that you were alive then, alive and speaking. And if I could remember what you said, I could make you speak again on this page and perhaps make you seem as alive to others as you still seem to me.[25]

Caputo speaks across the barrier between the living and the dead, in much the same way that the shade of Patroclus appears to Achilles in a dream.

> The ghost came and stood over his head and spoke a word to
>   him:
> "You sleep, Achilleus; you have forgotten me; but you were
>   not
> careless of me when I lived, but only in death. Bury me
> as quickly as may be, let me pass through the gates of Hades."
>   (23.69–71, Lattimore)

The love between Patroclus and Achilles continues to make male commentators uncomfortable. The suspicion that something funny is going on in, of all places, the *Iliad*, surfaces in Homer's two most popular American translators.[26] Thus Lattimore's version of Patroclus's exasperated words to Nestor.

> Now I go back as messenger to Achilles, to tell him.
> You know yourself, aged sir beloved of Zeus, how *he* is;
> a dangerous man; he might even be angry with one who is
>   guiltless.
>   (11.652–54; 11.651–53, Lattimore)

This is no more than a faint raising of a professorial eyebrow, a gesture that Robert Fagles repeats in his more recent version.

> Well you know, old soldier loved by the gods,
> what sort of man *he* is—that great and terrible man.
>   (11.653–54; 11.773–74, Fagles)

The italics lend an arch touch to what is simply a formulaic end-of-line phrase, "what sort of man he is."[27] The epic-sized rage of Achilles shrinks to the self-indulgence of a spouse whose ways are all too familiar. *Honestly* . . .

Lattimore and Fagles are nonetheless aiming in the right direction. The story of Achilles and Patroclus is like the story of Hector and Andromache, and as Homer sings it, this story also has to do with love, not lust. Progress in the professional study of sexuality has, curiously, made it harder, not easier, for some of Homer's readers to see the difference. Now we can move easily from discreet italics that merely hint at love between men, to what might be termed the real thing. By the time memoirs and fiction and poetry from the American Vietnam War came to be written, in 1980s America, wartime male anxieties could be as much a target for parody as they had been in antiquity, in *Lysistrata*. Charles Nelson's *Boy Who Picked the Bullets Up* is an epistolary novel of letters written by "Kurt Strom," a nom de guerre more suited to a porn star than a soldier. Strom is a gay medic serving in the Marine Corps, whose sexual exploits are like those of soldiers in all wars: relentless and energetic—only with other men. Nelson's novel is a gay reductio ad absurdum of Joseph Heller's *Catch-22*, itself already the most celebrated reductio of its war (World War II) as *The Good Soldier Schweik* was of its predecessor. Nelson has an ear attuned to American stand-up comedy, in which we can hear war run through the wringer of punch lines. He also turns the straight male's fear of women into the gay man's fear of macho aggression.

Marines are trained to hate queers. Marines take great offense when they are called queers. Should a recruit be unable to hack basic training, he is known as queer. Whenever a marine fucks up, he is assumed queer. It's rock bottom to these guys. The pits. A queer has no reason to live, so he's best done away with. Kill a queer for Uncle Sam.

Lieutenant Sanford led a seminar in Homosexuality to celebrate Paranoia Week. He had the ultimate solution to the problem. "I believe the government should stand all faggots before a firing squad. If I ever thought that one of my men was a faggot, I'd shoot him in the back and call it self-defense." He looked at me.

Oh, Lieutenant Sanford, I thought, you needn't worry about defending your spindly body, your purple lips, your receding chin, and your two-inch pecker. I thought the aforementioned; I never said it aloud. What I said aloud was, "Oh, Lieutenant Sanford, you can do better than that. Fit the punishment to the crime. Pull the pin of a grenade and shove it up the queer's ass."

"Have him suck on a punji stick and ram it down his throat," yelled a grunt.

"Stick leeches up the queer's dick and they'll suck him to death," cried another.

"Tie him to stakes in the latrine and drown him with piss," a third grunt advised.

"Or we could shit on him until he smothers," added a fourth.

Whatever have I started?[28]

What makes Nelson's fantasy work is that it reads like a faithful transcript of war and how American men are trained for it. Stanley Kubrick has a similar scene in *Full Metal Jacket*, where marines are drilled to see their dicks and their rifles as their basic tools for war.

The far-from-routine memoirs of Kurt Strom are a refreshing contrast to the indirection of earlier war memoirs and fiction; for example, *Seven Pillars of Wisdom*, where the altogether different T. E. Lawrence can describe this bond between warriors as an aberration, something caused by the absence of women.

> The Arab was by nature continent; and the use of universal marriage had nearly abolished irregular courses in his tribes. The public women of the rare settlements we encountered in our months of wandering would have been nothing to our number, even had their raddled meat been palatable to a man of healthy parts. In horror of such sordid commerce our youths began indifferently to slake one another's few needs in their own clean bodies—a cold convenience that, by comparison, seemed sexless and even pure. Later, some began to justify this sterile process, and swore that friends quivering together in the yielding sand with intimate hot limbs in supreme embrace, found there hidden in the darkness a sensual co-efficient of the mental passion which was welding our souls and spirits in one flaming effort. Several, thirsting to punish appetites they could not wholly prevent, took a savage pride in degrading the body, and offered themselves fiercely in any habit which promised physical pain or filth.[29]

Lawrence's sermon borders on the pornographic, as sermons on vice tend to. In his book on British love in the interwar period, Philip Hoare notes that love and sex on the remote battlefield such as Lawrence reports could be written off as an un-British perversion.[30] He limns actions without explaining them, counting on his reader's imagination to fill in the one correct perversion each veiled reference implies.

It is not explicitness about love in war that is the hardest thing to grasp, but simply love itself. In *Love and War in the Apennines*, a memoir of the British campaign in Italy, Eric Newby reports that masturbation was difficult in an enemy prison camp's dormitory, and that any kind of sex with other men was even more challenging. "Whatever loves there were between prisoners could only be expressed by looks and words or perhaps a surreptitious pressure of the hand, otherwise they had to remain locked away within the hearts and minds of the lovers until they could be free or were moved to some more private place."[31] The frustration of a love that Newby could only observe in discreet silence is recorded in great detail in *The Cage*, a little-known prisoner-of-war memoir from World War II by Dan Billany and David Dowie that Newby cites in passing. The manuscript was delivered to their families after the war. It is presumed both men were killed at some point either while escaping or while in captivity in Italy. In the course of this fragmentary roman à clef, the fictive Alan records his growing love for a fellow soldier in a prisoner-of-war camp. It is love poetry in a rudimentary form, a good example of what the historian of sexuality Jonathan Ned Katz has recently shown to be the tongue-tied dilemma of men in love with men.[32] David, the object of love, finds Alan's feelings for him comprehensible, and for that reason frightening.

> His own demands betrayed him. I was willing to give a lot, but always he seemed to be asking for just a little more. His eyes were always on the margin of my generosity, craving for whatever was just beyond. It was so bewildering and exasperating, because surely he could see that affection is all a matter of trust, and if he wholeheartedly enjoyed as much love as I could freely give, then in time I would gain reassurance and give him more. . . . What did he want? To be taken in my arms, to be kissed, to be trusted with the warmth of my own life? To sleep in my arms, as he sometimes said? Well, he could not have those things, not primarily because they might be unnatural, but just because he wanted them and could not be happy with the genuine affection I gave him short of those things. It seems obvious enough to me that there's no harm in affection and in intimate contacts, but they must arise out of real tenderness, must come to their true place, when the emotions they represent have developed to the point where they demand expression. Alan couldn't wait for that. He was afraid it would not happen.[33]

The chief problem proves to be not the existence of such love, but David's inability to respond to it. Finally, he learns to embrace Alan's friendship: "He cared for me, in myself, not for what I meant to him. He genuinely liked all that I was; he did feel the good in me. The barrier between us was gone completely, not a trace of it remained."[34] Here is a triumphant ending, not unlike the final moments of movie romance, which was perhaps the only model Billany and Dowie could have had for the expression of their love. Their disappearance and presumed death give the end of the manuscript an added poignancy.

> Emotions followed each other, but all were coloured by sadness and this new-found tenderness. I felt sad, and yet utterly satisfied, utterly relieved.

The world was richer. Whatever happened now—for things must some-times go astray, there would be failures, shadows—but through all that, whatever happened now, something had changed profoundly; it would be all right now. The days that were coming would be better than those that had gone. I *would* take his hand. I would lead him back to the world of life. I never would desert him now till I had set him back on the road he had strayed from. We should not be fighting each other any more. For us the war was over. [35]

As Glenn Gray observes of soldiers in that same war, what matters most to those facing death is not how their bonds match anyone's categories of sex-uality, but how they will face the pain of loss. [36] In the *Iliad* love seems to be articulated only as it is about to be lost. In Achilles' case, it is lost even before it is understood. What Hector means to Andromache is clear to us from the moment we see them together. What Patroclus means to Achilles might never have been fully realized without his death.

Loss tinges the poetry of war, and Aphrodite is as much to be reckoned with as Ares. When Paris is miraculously lifted from certain death on the battlefield and returned to a reluctant Helen by Aphrodite's powers, we see how intertwined war and love can be.

> "Come, then, rather let us go to bed and turn to love-making.
> Never before as now has passion enmeshed my senses,
> not when I took you the first time from Lakedaimon the lovely
> and caught you up and carried you away in seafaring vessels,
> and lay with you in the bed of love on the island Kranae,
> not even then, as now, did I love you and sweet desire seize
>   me."
> Speaking, he led the way to the bed; and his wife went with
>   him.
>   (3.441–47, Lattimore)

There are many ways to discover love's importance to us. Few are as efficient as war.

Six THE POETRY IS IN THE KILLING

> I think it is sentimental to discuss the subject of war, or peace, without ac-
> knowledging that a great many people enjoy war—not only the idea of it, but
> the fighting itself. In my time I have sat through many, many hours listening
> to people talking about war, the prevention of war, the awfulness of war, with
> it never once being mentioned that for large numbers of people the idea of
> war is exciting, and that when a war is over they may say it was the best time
> in their lives. This may be true even of people whose experiences in war were
> terrible, and which ruined their lives.
>
> Doris Lessing, *Prisons We Choose to Live Inside*

To the dismay of peaceful readers, Homer's descriptions of wounding and
killing are copious and exquisitely detailed. Although modern critical descriptions of the *Iliad* never fail to acknowledge the major role battles play in
the poem, these scenes are rarely at the center of commentary. We linger
over the deaths of Patroclus and Hector because we get to know them so
well. Few other heroes gain such loving readerships. Today, a reader of the
Iliad is likely to skip over the fray, from the quarrel of Agamemnon and
Achilles, and go to such famous moments as the parting of Hector and Andromache and the meeting of Priam and Achilles in book 24. These are cardinal moments in the poem, and each of these inspiring, tragic moments
arises from scenes like this:

> The spear smashed in the bone and he fell to the ground
>   headlong
> on his face. Meanwhile warlike Menelaos stabbed Thoas
> in the chest where it was left bare by the shield, and unstrung
>   his limbs' strength.
> Meges, Phyleus' son, watched Amphiklos as he came on
> and was too quick with a stab at the base of the leg, where the
>   muscle
> of a man grows thickest, so that on the spearhead the sinew
> was torn apart, and a mist of darkness closed over both eyes.
>   (16.310–16, Lattimore)

Relentless as they are, these scenes lead us to larger considerations, reflections
beyond sheer blood and guts. But blood and guts, in fact, mean everything.

Our squeamishness at recognizing their connection to the rest of the poem and to us is due to our imagined distance from war.

Only the greatest heroes of the Greeks and an occasional Trojan champion such as Aeneas survive their wounds to fight another day. As we might expect in a Greek poem about a Greek war, the Trojan enemies and their allies suffer more. Yet death in battle has a way of leveling differences. As Elaine Scarry has observed in *The Body in Pain*, our wounds and deaths in wars denationalize us, reducing us to a fundamental, stateless human identity.

> The "unmaking" of the human being, the emptying of the nation from his body, is equally characteristic of dying or being wounded, for the in part naturally "given" and in part "made" body is deconstructed. When the Irishman's chest is shattered, when the Armenian boy is shot through the legs and groin, when a Russian woman dies in a burning village, when an American medic is blown apart on the field, their wounds are not Irish, Armenian, Russian, or American precisely because it is the unmaking of an Irishman, the unmaking of an Armenian boy, the unmaking of a Russian woman, the unmaking of an American soldier that has just occurred, as well as in each case the unmaking of the civilization as it resides in each of those bodies.[1]

Thus, while the patriotic disposition to dwell on the killing of the enemy is alive and well-served in Homer, in the end the funeral rites of Achilles' hated enemy Hector become the poem's culmination, a moment of pathos surpassing even the funeral games for Patroclus.

Half of the *Iliad*'s war music is devoted to battle, told in precise details that become as characteristic of the poem as its similes.[2] In a war poem filled with the compression of opposites, Patroclus's metamorphosis is the most extreme. The gentlest of warriors becomes the most ferocious, and in the shortest time. Once he enters the battle in Achilles' armor, no one is more merciless with his enemies.

> He fell thunderously, and Patroclus in his next outrush
> at Thestor, Enops' son, who huddled inside his chariot,
> shrunk back, he had lost all his nerve, and from his hands the reins
> slipped—Patroclus coming close up to him stabbed with a
>   spear-thrust
> at the right side of the jaw and drove it on through the teeth, then
> hooked and dragged him with the spear over the rail, as a
>   fisherman
> who sits out on the jut of a rock with line and glittering

> bronze hook drags a fish, who is thus doomed, out of the
> water.
> . . . .
>
> Next he struck Euryalos, as he swept in, with a great stone
> in the middle of the head, and all the head broke into two
> pieces
> inside the heavy helmet, and he in the dust face downward
> dropped while death breaking the spirit drifted about him.
>   (16.401–8, 411–14, Lattimore)

These gruesome deaths come without comment from Patroclus himself. But the techniques of fisherman and spearman are closely related not only in the poet's mind. Not too long before his own death, Patroclus's frenzy carries him so far from where he began that he articulates what we would think only a poet and a muse could conceive. After Sarpedon, the son of Zeus, his other great trophy is Hector's charioteer, Kebriones:

> The sharp stone hit him in the forehead
> and smashed both brows in on each other, nor could the bone
> hold
> the rock, but his eyes fell out into the dust before him
> there at his feet, so that he vaulted to earth like a diver
> from the carefully wrought chariot, and the life left his bones.
>   (16.740–43; 16.739–43, Lattimore)

As if he too were hearing the poet, Patroclus picks up on the image of the graceful death-leap of Kebriones and turns it into battle poetry, on the spot.

>   Now
> you spoke in bitter mockery over him, rider Patroclus:
> "See now, what a light man this is, how agile an acrobat.
> If only he were somewhere on the sea, where the fish swarm,
> he could fill the hunger of many men, by diving for oysters;
> he could go overboard from a boat even in rough weather
> the way he somersaults so easily to the ground from his
> chariot
> now. So, to be sure, in Troy also they have their acrobats."
>   (16.744–50; 16.743–50, Lattimore)

Patroclus hears the poetry we hear: the simile of the fisherman Thestor, hundreds of lines before (16.406–8).[3] When he says the Trojans "also have their acrobats," he seems somehow to have overheard his enemy Aeneas praising his victim Meriones for dancing out of the way of his spear.[4]

> Meriones, though you are a dancer my spear might have
> > stopped you
> now and for all time, if only I could have hit you.
> > (16.617–18, Lattimore)

Poet's song and warrior's song blend into a single melody as Patroclus turns killing itself into poetry. With apologies to Wilfred Owen, who found po-etry in the pity of war, war's poetry is also to be found in the killing.

FACING BATTLE

> A battle must obey the dramatic unities of time, place and action.
> John Keegan, *The Face of Battle*

Few of Homer's commentators have wished the *Iliad* a battle longer than it is. With fully half the poem devoted to violence and mayhem, there are as many battle scenes as a romance would devote to the obsessions of lovers and their intrigues.[5] Pope knew battle scenes were likely to be as unpopular with Homer's newest readers as with those reading them for the hundredth time.[6] He explains not only their proportions in the poem, but their variety. Killing one's enemies can be carried out with as much craft and studied vari-ation as any other art. Consider this sequence from Achilles' slaughter of Trojans in book 20:

> > > Now Tros with his hands was reaching
> > for the knees, bent on supplication, but he stabbed with his
> > > sword at the liver
> > so that the liver was torn from its place, and from it the black
> > > blood
> > drenched the fold of his tunic and his eyes were shrouded in
> > > darkness
> > as the life went. Next from close in he thrust at Moulios
> > with the pike at the ear, so the bronze spearhead pushed
> > > through and came out
> > at the other ear. Now he hit Echeklos the son of Agenor
> > with the hilted sword, hewing against his head in the middle
> > so all the sword was smoking with blood, and over both eyes
> > closed the red death and the strong destiny. Now Deukalion
> > was struck in the arm, at a place in the elbow where the
> > > tendons
> > come together. There through the arm Achilles transfixed him
> > with the bronze spearhead, and he, arm hanging heavy,
> > > waited

and looked his death in the face. Achilles struck with the
   sword's edge
at his neck, and swept the helmed head far away, and the
   marrow
gushed from the neckbone, and he went down to the ground
   at full length.
(20.468–83, Lattimore)

Apart from the sheer volume of deaths in this brief scene of slaughter, what
impresses us most is Achilles' ingenuity—and the poet's. Neither of them
wades into a killing the same way twice: a sword to the liver, a pike in the ear,
a sword into the head, and finally, the climax of a double mortal blow for
Deucalion, who is transfixed at the elbow with a spear, and then decapitated
with a sword.

The battles of the *Iliad* have the "inquisitorial approach" that John Keegan
desires: get at the truth of what happens in battle, do not aim simply for a
verdict about what led to victory or defeat.[7] Keegan excludes traditional
military history, of the kind that Basil Liddell-Hart writes, with its deliberate
focus on generalship and strategy rather than the accidents of human misery.
What Keegan does convey in *The Face of Battle* is the aesthetics of the battle,
much the same kind of scenes that the *Iliad* gives us in such abundance:

> Wounds and their treatment, the mechanics of being taken prisoner, the na-
> ture of leadership at the most junior level, the role of compulsion in getting
> men to stand their ground, the incidence of accidents as a cause of death in
> war, and above all, the dimensions of the danger which different varieties
> of weapons offer to the soldier on the battlefield . . . hand weapon, single-
> missile weapon, and multi-missile weapon . . . to demonstrate, as exactly as
> possible, what the warfare, respectively, of hand, single-missile and multiple-
> missile weapons was—and is—like, and to suggest how and why the men
> who have had (and do have) to face these weapons control their fears,
> staunch their wounds, go to their deaths.[8]

Keegan's inquisitorial approach is in full force in a war writer like Paul
Fussell, who combines the roles of critic and soldier into one angry profes-
sion. His treatment of Ernie Pyle, the most popular American war correspondent in World War II, exposes the gap between the soldier's and the
civilian's imaginations of war. It points to the realities that the soldier would
know, and the poet.

> One of Pyle's best-known pieces is his description of the return to his com-
> pany in Italy of the body of Captain Henry T. Waskow, "of Belton, Texas."
> Such ostentatious geographical precision only calls attention to the genteel

vagueness with which Pyle is content to depict the captain's wound and body. Brought down from a mountain by muleback, Captain Waskow's body is laid out on the ground at night and respectfully visited by officers and men of the company. The closest Pyle comes to accurate registration is reporting that one man, who sat by the body for some time, holding the captain's hand and looking into his face, finally "reached over and gently straightened the points of the captain's shirt collar, and then he sort of arranged the tattered edges of the uniform around the wound."9

In his impatience Fussell misses the memorializing purpose of identifying Captain Waskow for the folks at home; this is the purpose of "of Belton, Texas," in particular. Is not this detail like Homer's precision in genealogy and geography? We think of Patroclus's victim Thestor, Enops's son, or young Simoeisios and his mother who bore him beside the banks of Simois. Genealogy is only gratuitous when we make it so. Fussell is also not sensitive to the feelings of Captain Waskow's family, who might, after all, be expected to have read Ernie Pyle, and would take no pleasure in such an autopsy. But he is trying to make us see what his real war was like.

> While delivering an account satisfying in its own terms, this leaves un-touched what normally would be thought journalistically indispensable questions, and certainly questions bound to occur to readers hoping to de-rive from the Infantry's Friend an accurate image of the infantry's experi-ence. Questions like these:
>   1. What killed Captain Waskow? Bullet, shell fragments, a mine, or what?
>   2. Where was his wound? How large was it? you imply that it was in the traditionally noble place, the chest. Was it? Was it a little hole, or was it a great red missing place? Was it perhaps in the crotch, or in the testicles, or in the belly? Were his entrails extruded, or in any way visible?
>   3. How much blood was there? Was the captain's uniform bloody? Did the faithful soldier wash his hands after toying with those "tattered edges"? Were the captain's eyes open? Did his face look happy? Surprised? Satisfied? Angry?[10]

This has an incisiveness Achilles would envy. Fussell is driven by a rage from his war that is as strong fifty years after the event as ever. There is a level of precision in those angry questions that the war photographer and camera-man strive to capture, but what Fussell wants Pyle to have recorded would have gone far beyond the limits that journalists had to observe in reporting to the home front on American casualties in World War II.[11] It is important to realize that what Fussell is after, authenticity, does not require actual experience. What he wants Pyle to have reported is something that society sends soldiers off to find out, somewhere else, anywhere else but at home.

With characteristic savagery, Virginia Woolf makes the same point in *Mrs. Dalloway*. Set in a fine June afternoon in postwar London, *Mrs. Dalloway* captures with great precision the ability of those confronted with violence not to see it, and the power of those who are not witnesses to it to recapture that violence, completely, in their imagination. The veteran Septimus Smith kills himself at the moment a Dr. Holmes is barging his way past Smith's wife, Rezia.

> There remained only the window, the large Bloomsbury lodging house window, the tiresome, the troublesome, and rather melodramatic business of opening the window and throwing himself out. It was their idea of tragedy, not his or Rezia's (for she was with him). Holmes and Bradshaw like that sort of thing. (He sat on the sill.) But he would wait till the very last moment. He did not want to die. Life was good. The sun hot. Only human beings—what did *they* want? Coming down the staircase opposite an old man stopped and stared at him. Holmes was at the door. "I'll give it you!" he cried, and flung himself vigorously, violently down on to Mrs. Filmer's area railings.[12]

Everyone at the actual scene of Septimus's death takes care to avoid looking at or even thinking about the suicide: how it was done, what happened, why it happened—above all, what it might mean. Dr. Holmes exclaims, "The coward!" But Septimus's wife Rezia "ran to the window, she saw; she understood." Holmes protects her by drugging her to sleep: "she must not see him, must be spared as much as possible." As Rezia dozes off, she sees her landlady, Mrs. Filmer. "'He is dead,' she said, smiling at the poor old woman who guarded her with her honest light-blue eyes fixed on the door. (They wouldn't bring him in here, would they?) But Mrs. Filmer pooh-poohed. Oh no, oh no! They were carrying him away now. Ought she not to be told? Married people ought to be together, Mrs. Filmer thought. But they must do as the doctor said."[13] The discretion of the doctor is an attempt to turn everyone present away from the reality of death, and on the actual scene of Septimus's suicide, it may succeed. But not in Clarissa Dalloway's imagination.

> He had killed himself—but how? Always her body went through it first, when she was told, suddenly, of an accident; her dress flamed, her body burnt. He had thrown himself from a window. Up had flashed the ground: through him, blundering, bruising, went the rusty spikes. There he lay with

a thud, thud, thud in his brain, and then a suffocation of blackness. So she saw it. But why had he done it? And the Bradshaws talked of it at her party?

She had once thrown a shilling into the Serpentine, never anything more. But he had flung it away.[14]

Clarissa's party is suffused with her sense of being alive, a sense heightened by the news of a young man's suicide. Thus a war veteran's death becomes a sacrifice, where the lifeblood of the ritual victim furnishes the surrounding community with a new vitality.

What Fussell and Woolf are both after is what the *Iliad* provides in abundance. Here is a terse summary of one sequence that begins toward the end of book 4, a relatively brief passage marking a quick crescendo of battle, leading into book 5 and an even greater struggle when the hero Diomedes gets to shine because of the absence of Achilles. That book will be a proper *aristeia* or show of prowess (*aretē*) in battle for Diomedes, something for which every hero strives. With a glance back to Fussell's list, we might reduce the information in Homer to basic questions: Who is killing or wounding? Who is wounded or killed? What is the weapon used? How and where wounded? What is the outcome of the action?

In the space of eighty-two lines (4.457–538), roughly two and a half pages in the translations of Lattimore or Fagles, and, say, less than ten minutes of spoken or sung verse:

1. Antilochus kills Thalysias's son Echepolus with a spear through his forehead.

2. Agenor kills Elephenor, Chalkodon's son, with a spear in the side.

3. Ajax kills Simoeisios, the son of Anthemion Simoeisios, with a spear beside the right nipple.

4. In outrage at this, Priam's son Antiphos aims at Ajax, but instead his spear cast kills Leukos with a wound in the groin.

5. Odysseus in reaction to that death kills Demokoon, a bastard son of Priam, with a spear to his head that runs through one temple and comes out the other.

6. Peiros kills Amaryngkeus's son Diores, first wounding him with a boulder, smashing the tendons in his right ankle, then spearing him next to the navel in such a way that the spear disembowels him and his guts spill out on the ground.

7. Finally, tit for tat, Thoas the Aetolian spears Pieros in the chest above the nipple, and Pieros, dying, drags the spear from his chest and strikes Thoas in the middle of the belly. They both fall dead, sprawled beside one another in the dust.

This is only the beginning of a series of battles that will rise to unimaginably more-savage levels once Achilles returns to the war, but perhaps it is enough to suggest that Homer is quite aware of the soldier's angry questions. What killed him? Where was his wound? Was there much blood?

Even in this numbing summary the studied variation is unmistakable. The particular battle sequence from which this comes does not win the greatest prize of all for the Greeks in the first day's fighting, the capture or killing of Paris, but Diomedes will go on to wound both Aphrodite and Ares. Perhaps his greatest achievement—for those partial to the Greeks, certainly among the most satisfying in the whole poem—is not just his killing of Pandarus, whose arrow had wounded Menelaus and broken the truce, but the way Diomedes kills him.[15] It is a fine example of retributive justice, where the punishment seems to fit the crime. As a warrior fighting against Diomedes, Pandarus is out of his league, not using the weapon he uses best, the bow and arrow. He throws a spear that grazes Diomedes and boasts about it. Diomedes' answer is a spear cast guided by Athena. As he often does, Fagles turns up the volume of what is already a gruesome passage in Lattimore.

> With that he hurled and Athena drove the shaft
> and it split the archer's nose between his eyes—
> it cracked his glistening teeth, the tough bronze
> cut off his tongue at the roots, smashed his jaw
> and the point came ripping out beneath his chin.
> (5.290–93; 5.321–25, Fagles)

The trajectory of the spear is so high in the air that it comes down at an acute angle to produce the grotesque wound that pays back Pandarus, symmetrically, for wounding Menelaus with an arrow, breaking the truce, and resuming the war.[16] And yet, even as he is paid back, the entire life story of Pandarus first unfolds before us, immediately before he goes to his death at the hands of Diomedes. Aeneas calls him to go into battle and shoot more Greeks with his arrows, but Pandarus is already disenchanted with his lovely weapon. His father, Lycaon, had urged him to go to Troy with his horses and chariot, but he had refused—unwisely, he now sees.

> So I left them and made my way on foot to Ilion
> trusting my bow, a thing that was to profit me nothing.
> For now I have drawn it against two of their best men, Tydeus'
> son, and the son of Atreus, and both of these I hit
> and drew visible blood, yet only wakened their anger.
> So it was in bad luck that I took from its peg the curved bow

on that day when I carried it to lovely Ilion
at the head of my Trojans, bringing delight to brilliant Hector.
Now if ever I win home again and lay eyes once more
on my country, and my wife, and the great house with the
        high roof,
let some stranger straightway cut my head from my shoulders
if I do not break this bow in my hands and throw it in the
        shining
fire, since as a wind and nothing I have taken it with me.
        (5.204–16, Lattimore)

So goes an early version of the sniper's lament. Pandarus's speech marks not only a turn back to the more prestigious mode of combat for warriors in Homer, fighting with weapons face-to-face; it is also more than a little apotropaic. (The bullet with our name on it won't get us if we say there is a bullet with our name on it.) If Pandarus can swear off the weapon he has used up to now, with such skill—it's not his fault if the greatest Greek heroes lead charmed lives—perhaps he will escape the battlefield retribution that any man in battle might fear is headed his way. The murderous little boy lurking in every Greek man is urged to say, Take that, Pandarus. The simple pleasures of seeing an enemy on the other side get his just deserts is no longer so simple. Pandarus is brought alive, unforgettably, like Simoeisios and countless others in Homer, at the very moment he is about to die.

Many of Homer's later civilian readers have found such overkill overdone. For them Ovid's parody of Homeric battle scenes in the *Metamorphoses* is richly deserved. Like any effective parody, Ovid's springs from an intimate understanding of what drives the original poetry. Here, in his incongruous world, Nestor is a Polonian elder giving an interminable account of the fabled battle of the Lapiths and Centaurs—a myth about civilization versus the barbarians, recalled on the metopes or frieze sculptures of the Parthenon, no less. Homeric battle turns into a tavern brawl or gladiatorial combat in a Roman amphitheater. There have been many versions published since that get more words of the original across, but Rolfe Humphries' translation has the right mix of brio and absurdity:

Amycus robbed the inner shrine and from it
Bore off a chandelier with glittering lamps,
Lifted it high, the way an axe is lifted
To strike a white bull for sacrifice,
And dashed it at the head of Celadon,
Smashing his face so that no man would know it.
His eyes bulged from their sockets, and his cheek-bones

Splintered, and what had been his nose was driven
Into his palate. Pelates of Pella
Wrenched off a maple table-leg and used it
To knock Amycus down with, with his chin
Driven into his breast. That made things even,
As he spat out black blood and teeth together.
A second blow finished him off. Then Gryneus,
Staring, wild-eyed, at the smoking altar near him,
Cried out, "Why not use this?" and caught it up
With all its fires and hurled it at the throng
And crushed two men, Broteas and Orios,
Whose mother, so folks said, was named Mycale
And she, or so they said, had incantations
To bring the horns of the moon to earth, no matter
How much she struggled. "You shall not escape me
If I can find a weapon" one Exadius
Cried out, and found a weapon, a stag's antlers
Hung on a pine-tree as a votive offering.
And Gryneus' eyes were pierced by those twin prongs,
Eyeballs gouged out; one of them stuck to the horn,
The other rolled down his beard till a blood-clot caught it.[17]

Ovid's parody works because it plays on the artifice that underlies literary accounts of battle. It is just such precision that makes us believe some war stories—even when many of the wounds described are fantastic inventions—and disbelieve others. But it isn't "reality" at all that we are being mesmerized by. Homer's anatomical exactitude is no more than an illusion of what a battle wound might really be like.[18] Those who hate war and want nothing to do with such grisly stories would have little to hate or to flee from if they did not face such battle scenes. Those who look forward to war and seek it out, whatever the cost, have a powerful stimulus to see if battle will be as terrible as the poets make it seem, or as funny.

HOW THEY DIE

> Whatever is not war, whatever war destroys or threatens, the *Iliad* wraps in poetry; the realities of war, never.
> Weil, *The "Iliad"; or, The Poem of Force*

In his study of the psychological costs of learning to kill in modern society, Dave Grossman maintains that there are fewer psychiatric problems in sailors and pilots because no one is trying to kill them, specifically, personally, nor do they have to see anyone they are killing. "Instead of killing people up close and personal, modern navies kill ships and airplanes. Of course there are people in these ships and airplanes, but psychological and mechanical distances protect the modern sailor."[19] The American veteran Alvin Kernan tells what it was like to see pilots in an aircraft carrier plane crash in the sea and vanish almost immediately, without a trace left behind, being and nothingness summed up in a sentence.

> The quickness with which active life, so much energy and skill in the banking plane, disappeared as if it had never been, stunned me.
>
> It was the instantaneous contrast of something and nothing that caught my attention.[20]

This kind of instantaneous transformation is characteristic of modern air warfare. Pilots and their planes can simply disappear, and as Samuel Hynes points out in his war memoir *Flights of Passage,* this can create a problem for traditional modes of commemoration.

> On the whole, memoirs of those at sea have a little less of the horrors of land warfare, if only because the resolution, as final of course as any, comes so rapidly. A striking theme about sea warfare and especially air war is the speed, the finality, the god-awful neatness of it. So often there is little trace left of what or who is lost. . . . The reality of death comes to you in stages. First it is an ideal—all men are mortal, as in the syllogism. Then it is something that happens to strangers, then to persons you know, but somewhere else, and at last it enters your presence, and you see death, on a runway or in a field, in a cloud of dust and a column of smoke. Though even that doesn't make your own death conceivable.[21]

But quickly as it comes, the essential transition from being to nonbeing is nonetheless there.

> Our friend Bergie—the church-in-the-wildwood tenor, the gentle husband, the "father" of our Santa Barbara family—had simply vanished from our lives. There was no body, no grave, and no funeral, no one, it seemed, to mourn for. T and Joe and I put his possessions together—there was almost nothing worth saving—and gave them to the Adjutant to send home, and took his cot apart and moved it out of the tent. For a while there was a patch of dead wheat where the cot had been; but gradually it was worn away, until it was like the rest of the tent floor.[22]

A patch of dead wheat gradually worn away: Hynes experienced in microcosm what those who know Battery Wagner could see in larger scale.

Compared to Okinawa or the Somme, air and naval wars seem cleaner wars in most respects. In other ways they may have been worse. The essential horror of death in battle was more accelerated than ever, often with everything over before either victim or onlooker could realize what had happened. Elmer Bendiner's *Fall of Fortresses*, a memoir of the American bombing command in World War II, has just such moments, linking as it does the serene, almost Olympian detachment and beauty of the air with the sudden sharp realities of mortal death in air combat. He describes the situation of his plane's ball turret gunner, the kind of airman Randall Jarrell turned into the subject of a short poem, "Death of the Ball Turret Gunner":

> I do not know how he withstood the torture wrapped within himself, powerless amid bullets and explosions, oppressed by the realization that at any instant he might be spattered to a mass of ugly tissue, like a cat run over on the highway. This might happen to any man in the crew, but the rest of us had the illusion of motion, of elbow room to give us security. There was nothing that Leary could do about his fate. He was as powerless as a rivet in his ball turret. He had been reduced to a neuter.[23]

Bendiner makes us live through what the poet Jarrell never experienced, but what Jarrell's poetry causes us to see. He also records a kaleidoscopic inventory of poetic images in his comments on the war as it exists in his memory. "Our war did not allow for sustained emotions. It spattered the brain with images of headless corpses, then washed it clean with the sight of a girl laughing at the piano player, then shattered it again with a dying plane sending its sacrificial smoke into the sky. It froze the brain at twenty below, boiled it with the smell of gunpowder, and let it fall asleep in a pub."[24]

Bendiner writes of an evening in the Brevet, a pub for airmen in London: not a place for Grand Guignol or for solemn politics, but a place for lullabies, for seductions—what the alluring Hedy Lamar playing Tondelayo in the movies was all about. "In the morning I had been over Germany watching *Tondelayo*'s sister plane"—a B-25D bomber had been named after Hedy Lamar's character—"through my port window. Along the fuselage to the tail ran a scarlet streak. It had taken me a moment to understand that there was no top turret and that the fuselage was painted with the blood of a gunner who had manned it before it was blown away. And here I was in the evening, charmed by total irrelevancies at the Brevet. I talked and smiled as if I had not seen what I had seen only some ten hours earlier."[25] The soldier often has too little time to think about what is happening to him. Or if there is time, too little to think larger thoughts.

Part of the power of Christopher Logue's *War Music* comes from its compression of heroic experience, so that the death of a hero in an ancient poem from a vanished civilization becomes for us a death in the present, for the present. In Logue's version, one of Patroclus's mortal killers, Euphorbus, is turned into the onomatopoetic "Thackta," and his spear cast is changed from behind the shoulders ("a Dardanian man hit him between the shoulders with a sharp javelin") to the thighs. Logue's poetry narrows and deepens the focus on mortality, capturing the awful sense of the growing separation between the dying man and the unconcerned Trojan warriors who are onlookers. There is full awareness of the shock of a wound, as much clinical precision as Fussell could desire, compressed to the point where we feel along with Patroclus the thrust of Thackta's javelin.

> All of them lay and stared;
> And one, a boy called Thackta, cast.
> His javelin went through your calves,
> Stitching your knees together, and you fell,
> Not noticing the pain, and tried to crawl
> Towards the Fleet, and—even now—feeling
> For Thackta's ankle—ah!—and got it? No . . .
> Not a boy's ankle that you got,
> But Hector's.
>
> Standing above you,
> His bronze mask smiling down into your face,
> Putting his spear through . . . ach, and saying:
> "Why tears, Patroclus?
> Did you hope to melt Troy down
> And make our women fetch the ingots home?
> I can imagine it!
> You and your marvellous Achilles;
> Him with an upright finger, saying:
> *Don't show your face again, Patroclus,*
> *Unless it's red with Hector's blood.*"
> And Patroclus,
> Shaking the voice out of his body, says:
> "Big mouth.
> Remember it took three of you to kill me.
> A god, a boy, and, last and least, a hero.
> I can hear Death pronounce my name, and yet
> Somehow it sounds like *Hector.*
> And as I close my eyes I see Achilles' face
> With Death's voice coming out of it."

> Saying these things Patroclus died.
> And as his soul went through the sand
> Hector withdrew his spear and said:
>   "Perhaps."[26]

The language here contorts and writhes around Hector's spear: ". . . ach."
Compare Lattimore's literal version of the same lines:

> He spoke, and as he spoke the end of death closed in upon
>   him,
> and the soul fluttering free of his limbs went down into
>   Death's house
> mourning her destiny, leaving youth and manhood behind
>   her.
>   (16.855–57, 22.361–63, Lattimore)

The soul of the young warrior mourning its destiny loses mythical detail in
Logue, but not poetry: "And his soul went through the sand."

The final pages of *The Ghost Road*, Pat Barker's concluding novel of a tril-
ogy about Wilfred Owen, Siegfried Sassoon, and other soldiers in the Great
War who were patients of the psychologist William Rivers, builds to a similar crossover moment.

> Prior was about to start across the water with ammunition when he was
> himself hit, though it didn't feel like a bullet, more like a blow from some-
> thing big and hard, a truncheon or a cricket bat, only it knocked him off his
> feet and he fell, one arm trailing over the edge of the canal.
>
> He tried to turn to crawl back beyond the drainage ditches, knowing it
> was only a matter of time before he was hit again, but the gas was thick here
> and he couldn't reach his mask. Banal, simple, repetitive thoughts ran round
> and round his mind. *Balls up. Bloody mad. Oh Christ.* There was no pain, more a
> spreading numbness that left his brain clear. He saw Kirk die. He saw Owen
> die, his body lifted off the ground by bullets, describing a slow arc in the air
> as it fell. It seemed to take forever to fall, and Prior's consciousness fluttered
> down with it. He gazed at his reflection in the water, which broke and re-
> formed and broke again as bullets hit the surface and then, gradually, as the
> numbness spread, he ceased to see it.[27]

Prior crosses the divide between the living and the dead as elusively as Patroclus. Both deaths leave us in awe.

To witness the death of others in war is to realize that the same thing can
happen to you. One does not require a set piece on the battlefield to reach

that point. It can happen simply by accident. Alvin Kernan tells of two pilots lost over the side of an aircraft carrier in the Pacific:

> In an instant the plane was in the water off the starboard side, broken in half between the radioman and the pilot, neither of whom, knocked out by the crash, heads hanging limply forward, moved. Then in an instant both pieces were gone, the water was unruffled, and the ship sailed on. The quickness with which active life, so much energy and skill in the banking plane, disappeared as if it had never been, stunned me.
>
> It was the instantaneous contrast of something and nothing that caught my attention, and like some eighteen-year-old ancient mariner, I went around for days trying to tell people what had *really* happened, how astounding it was.[28]

Our curiosity about war's mystery is pervasive. When there is no possible way of recovering a direct account of death in war, we will use every kind of ingenuity to reconstruct what the killing may have been like. Forensic pathology can even make up for a direct report of war. One earlier example of such an event is the Russian secret police's massacre of thousands of Polish officers in the Katyn forest in 1940, a notorious war crime ordered by Stalin that was for some years attributed to the Germans. The executions were orchestrated so that each victim was compelled to go to his death completely alone. As the historian Allen Paul reconstructs the event in his book *Katyn*:

> For the victims, these last seconds were marked, almost certainly, by disorientation and helplessness. It seems likely that their thoughts—geared so recently at hopes of reparation—suddenly swirled in fear and dismay as the first shots were fired outside the bus. . . . Only the bullets were merciful at this scene of slaughter. They pierced like estoques to the occipital bone, coursing upward from this small protrusion at the base of the skull, then passing through the brain to a point of egress between the nose and hair line. This angle suggests that each victim's head was bent forward and that the executioner stood close behind him, firing slightly downward. A shot thus aimed offered two practical advantages: it caused instant death and minimal loss of blood.[29]

Even the execution teams may have been murdered to remove any possibility of later testimony from eyewitnesses. Paul relies on a forensic pathologist's report from the exhumed bones of the victims at Katyn to create a sense of what it might have been like to be one of the Polish officers about to be executed. Precise anatomical descriptions are a major reason the scene moves us, speculative and unprovable as it is. The combination of imagined personal terror and detached, clinical description is not easily forgotten.

Until barriers of technology are breached, so that we at last can smell and feel as well as hear and see what happens to human bodies in war, we cannot imagine what people have to endure. The memoirs of E. B. Sledge about his service in the marines in the Pacific during World War II come as close as possible to the physical realities of war—the equivalent in prose to Goya's graphic designs in *The Disasters of War*, or the battles of the *Iliad*.[30] One thing that Sledge wants to convey is what war is like to a culture based on indoor plumbing. "In combat, cleanliness for the infantryman was all but impossible. Our filth added to our general misery. Fear and filth went hand in hand. It has always puzzled me that this important fact is omitted from otherwise excellent personal memoirs by infantrymen. It is, of course, a vile subject, but it was as important to us then as being wet or dry, hot or cold, in the shade or exposed to the blistering sun, hungry, tired, or sick."[31] This theme is laid out early at Peleliu, then reaches something like an apotheosis in the mud and maggots of Okinawa six months later. Although one's own dead (marines in this case) would naturally be removed, the enemy dead were often left to rot where they fell. It is not so widely appreciated as it might be that for all their geographical and temporal remove from the trench warfare of the western front of World War I, the Americans and Japanese went through essentially the same experience, and in far worse conditions because of tropical climate.[32]

> The bodies were badly decomposed and nearly blackened by exposure. This was to be expected of the dead in the tropics, but these Marines had been mutilated hideously by the enemy. One man had been decapitated. His head lay on his chest; his hands had been severed from his wrists and also lay on his chest near his chin. In disbelief I stared at the face as I realized that the Japanese had cut off the dead Marine's penis and stuffed it into his mouth. The corpse next to him had been treated similarly. The third had been butchered, chopped up like a carcass torn by some predatory animal.
>
> My emotions solidified into rage and a hatred for the Japanese beyond anything I ever had experienced. From that moment on I never felt the least pity or compassion for them no matter what the circumstances. My comrades would field-strip their packs and pockets for souvenirs and take gold teeth, but I never saw a Marine commit the kind of barbaric mutilation the Japanese committed if they had access to our dead.[33]

Sledge is no detached artist, and even thirty years later could not control his rage at what he remembered. He was coming onto ground that possibly only poets and artists can stand to occupy for long. In two of the worst (and

Figure 29. Goya, *Disasters of War*, no. 37, "This is worse" (Courtesy of Hood Museum of Art, Dartmouth College, Hanover, New Hampshire; gift of Adolph Weil Jr., Class of 1935.)

artistically, the best) scenes from Goya's *Disasters of War*, we see how an artist can patiently convey war's inhumanity, by an exquisite design and attention to details (figs. 29 and 30). Goya captures the artistry of such mutilation with a delicacy and precision in his composition that, like Homer's studied variation of battle deaths, actually intensifies the horror of what we see.[34]

Sledge's resolve that American marines would never be guilty of such barbaric acts doesn't last even for the length of his own memoir. A friend named Mac comes in with a severed, dried Japanese hand, which he thinks would be more interesting than a tooth to have as a souvenir. Mac was

> a decent, clean-cut man but one of those who apparently felt no restraints under the brutalizing influence of war—although he had hardly been in combat at that time. He had one ghoulish, obscene tendency that revolted even the most hardened and callous men I knew. When most men felt the urge to urinate, they simply went over to a bush or stopped wherever they

Grande hazaña. con muertos.

Figure 30. Goya, *Disasters of War*, no. 39, "Heroic feat! with dead men!" (Courtesy of Hood Museum of Art, Dartmouth College, Hanover, New Hampshire; gift of Adolph Weil Jr., Class of 1935.)

happened to be and relieved themselves without ritual or fanfare. Not Mac. If he could, that "gentleman by the act of Congress" would locate a Japanese corpse, stand over it, and urinate in its mouth. It was the most repulsive thing I ever saw an American do in the war. I was ashamed that he was a Marine officer.[35]

This is the same officer whom Sledge once sees on a patrol, "taking great pains and effort to position himself and his carbine near a Japanese corpse. After getting just the right angle, Mac took careful aim and squeezed off a couple of rounds. The dead Japanese lay on his back with his trousers pulled down to his knees. Mac was trying very carefully to blast off the head of the corpse's penis. He succeeded. As he exulted over his aim, I turned away in disgust."[36]

Sledge was outraged by the mutilation and dishonor meted out to his fellow soldiers, and to begin with he was capable of as much disgust at his fellow marines' similar treatment of the enemy. But by the time his memoir nears its end, in the trench warfare of Okinawa, it is only his own comrades' deaths that move him; dead Japanese did not bother him "in the least."[37] Then he too was finally caught in the Yes and No of war, the contradictions that are as impossible for us to untangle as the feelings we have about Achilles strumming away on the lyre from Eëtion's city. And everywhere there is the abiding fascination with how they die—more truthfully, how we die.[38]

Seven THE FIRE FROM HEPHAESTUS

> Even invasion spectacles suffered dramatic devaluation as the soldier's
> purview narrowed to combat. Were they not extraordinary things? Yes,
> agreed Bill Mauldin: "Invasions are magnificent things to watch . . ." But what
> of the solider who was one of those thousands of fragments constituting the
> spectacle that so delighted distant observers? That more often invited feelings
> of impairment than of exaltation, of acute personal vulnerability rather than
> any reassuring sense of massive combined strength, as if such great numbers
> must inevitably diminish and ultimately overwhelm the individual. Magnifi-
> cent to watch, but, Mauldin added, "awful things to be in."
>
> Gerald Linderman, *The World within War*

The shield of Achilles in book 18 of the *Iliad* is the ultimate war fantasy. Homer's readers have always been dazzled by his translation of the arts of the
divine craftsman of the gods into the sublime poetry of the shield. Here the
most frightening instrument of war becomes poetry whose music must be
heard to be believed; only then can its allure be fully grasped. But the shield
also defies summary and translation. Like the images it creates, its sounds are
inimitable.

The divine origin of Achilles' arms is also significant. Hephaestus is famous as the maker of Pandora, and his shield for Achilles is no less seductive.
It is at once a cosmic vision of an existence that no mortal can experience
and a spectacle no one can resist. This transcendent fantasy of the world on
an instrument of death plays to our fascination with the spectacles of war, all
those awesome sights we love to observe from what we imagine to be a safe
distance.[1]

Progress in the technology of warfare has enabled us to realize the full
power of what Hephaestus creates. The arms of Achilles carry him into
combat with the elements of creation itself, and now we can do the same.
The fabled rivers of Troy found their kin in the tributaries of the Ota River at
Hiroshima, seething with the dying and the dead, on August 6, 1945.

FROM BATTLE ROUT TO THE LOVELIEST OF VERSES

> Sad Tydings, Son of *Peleus*! thou must hear;
> And wretched I, th'unwilling Messenger!

136

Dead is *Patroclus!* for his Corps they fight;
His naked Corps: His Arms are *Hector's* Right.
Antilochus to Achilles, *Iliad* 18.21–24 (Pope)

The poetry of the shield of Achilles arises from the death of Patroclus and the disintegration of the Achaeans as a fighting force. The masses of men who were marshaled so magnificently to the multiple similes of book 2 race to their ships, as the Greeks fall back in the struggle over Patroclus's corpse.[2] Instead of the integrative similes in book 2 that introduce the catalogue of ships, of goatherds separating and pasturing their flocks, or of birds or insects swarming, there comes at the end of book 17 an equally sweeping series of similes of an army disintegrating before our eyes. One such image follows another: weary pack animals straining to carry away a corpse, a riverbank resisting the powerful floodwaters of Trojans, daws and starlings screaming at the hawks Hector and Aeneas, who have come to murder their little birds.[3]

Nothing that was orderly remains the same. As the Greeks had assembled, the gleam of their weapons looked as lovely and distant as a fire in a forest along the top of a distant mountain.

> As obliterating fire lights up a vast forest
> along the crests of a mountain, and the flare shows far off,
> so as they marched, from the magnificent bronze the gleam
>   went
> dazzling all about through the upper air to the heaven.
> (2.455–58, Lattimore)

Now those same Greeks are locked in a struggle that is like the fire that rises when men storm a city; it is as if the Greeks had turned into the very citadel of Troy that they are seeking to take, and were themselves the victims of storming and devastation.

> So these, straining, carried the dead man out of the battle
> and back to the hollow ships, and the fight that was drawn fast
>   between them
> was wild as fire which, risen suddenly, storming a city
> of men sets it ablaze, and houses diminish before it
> in the high glare, and the force of the wind on it roars it to
>   thunder;
> so, as the Danaans made their way back, the weariless roaring
> of horses, chariots, and spearmen was ever upon them.
> (17.735–41, Lattimore)

The host of men that pressed forward into the array of battle in book 2 was so eager that

> now battle became sweeter to them than to go back
> in their hollow ships to the beloved land of their fathers.
> (2.453–54, Lattimore)

That same army has become a nonarmy, completely undone:

> the young Achaian warriors
> went, screaming terror, all the delight of battle forgotten.
> Many fine pieces of armour littered the ground on both sides
> of the ditch, as the Danaans fled. There was no check in the
> fighting.
> (17.758–61, Lattimore)

We arrive at a moment in war where spectacles arise that would never have been imagined before, ones so marvelous that they even seem, somehow, to justify the destruction and deaths that bring them into being. The spectacles of war free us to engage in what Klaus Theweleit terms "fantasies of transcendence": "a tradition of freeing the thinking brain from the depths of the most pressing situations and sending it off to some fictive summit for a panoramic overview."[4] The shield of Achilles is one such panoramic overview of war and the cosmos, arising from just such depths.

No object in the *Iliad* is of more significance for understanding the appeal of war than the shield of Achilles.[5] Like any shield, this one has an ambiguous, double purpose built into it. Shields are instruments of war, movable walls, and like walls may not in themselves seem to be death-dealing weapons. Unlike the sword, the spear, or the arrow, they do not wound. But they enable the warrior to survive his enemy's attack until he can deliver his own. They are an indispensable companion to the weapons of war.[6] In an advance in war, a shield marks an incorporation of the enemy into one's own territory, just as in retreat it marks a contraction. The poet helps us see this in the way he characterizes the shield of the hero Ajax.

> Now Aias came near him, carrying like a wall his shield
> of bronze and sevenfold ox-hide which Tychios wrought him
> with much toil;
> Tychios, at home in Hyle, far the best of all workers in leather
> who made him the great gleaming shield of sevenfold ox-hide
> from strong bulls, and hammered an eight-fold of bronze
> upon it.
> (7.219–23, Lattimore)

Ajax's shield is itself no ordinary thing, nor is Agamemnon's, with its Gorgon's head, and Fear (*Deimos*) and Terror (*Phobos*, book 11.36–37). The shield that Hephaestus makes for Achilles is all of these things, and more.

Hephaestus is well aware that what he is creating only confirms Achilles' mortality; the shield of Achilles is also the tomb of Achilles.[7] As he turns to the making of Achilles' armor, Hephaestus says to Thetis,

> If only I could hide him away from pain and death,
> that day his grim destiny comes to take Achilles,
> as surely as glorious armor shall be his, armor
> that any man in the world of men will marvel at
> through all the years to come—whoever sees its splendor.
> (18.464–68; 18.542–47, Fagles)

The shield of Achilles brings the fire of Hephaestus everywhere it goes. In the later reception of the *Iliad,* the story of its making marks the beginning of a long Western tradition of ekphrasis.[8] Unlike its illustrious progeny, Achilles' shield stays still only long enough to be made, its design described in its making. Its scenes seem to be as alive and moving as the human being for whom it is made. It is the most movable of artistic creations, continuing to play out a drama of action, distance, and time.[9] Like any other weapon of war, it realizes its true purpose as soon as the warrior for whom it was made moves into battle.

The poetry of the shield enables us to see war's spectacles in inverse proportion to the way they are actually experienced in war. As Bill Mauldin observed, the Normandy invasion was magnificent to watch at a distance, but it was living hell to be on Omaha Beach. Through the art of Homer and his Muses, we are taken into the center of the forge of war itself—as if to the moment of nuclear fission, to the explosion of bombs and the center of the firestorm, where we can see into the destructive energy of war being unleashed at an inhumanly close range. From the moment Thetis delivers the shining arms from Hephaestus to her son, all mortals but Achilles begin to pull back, and the further they get from them, paradoxically, the more terrifying those arms become, the more indistinguishable they are from the fire of the god who created it. The gleam (*selas*) from the shield is reflected in the hero from whose eyes emanate a gleam of identical power. And then the gifts from Hephaestus are put to the use for which they were made: Achilles killing men; Achilles fighting with nature itself in battle with the rivers Xanthus and Scamander.

THE RING OF THE SHIELD

> Poetry is not felt: it is said. Or rather: the proper way to feel poetry is to say it.
> Octavio Paz, *The Bow and the Lyre*

The story of what Hephaestus creates is part of the plot of the *Iliad,* but the scenes on the shield itself have no beginning or end. Each one has the rudiments of what could be a plot for the mortal beings portrayed there, but no scene ever follows through to a conclusion. What we hear of is suggestive of the world of the *Iliad,* but that world is seen with all its particularities erased, reduced to generic scenes. Here are the facts as a recent commentator presents them.

> The description begins with Hephaestus setting to work, gathering and using his tools and metals. The describer then turns to the scenes depicted on this shield. The first is the heavens: the sun, moon, and four constellations (the Pleiades, the Hyades, Orion, and the Bear). There follows a city at peace, divided into two scenes showing social rituals: a wedding procession and the lawful settlement of a blood feud. After the city at peace comes a city at war; this picture of a walled city besieged by invading armies is the longest of the scenes, and includes plans, battles, and ambush, and the participation of gods in the fray. The next five scenes are of agriculture and husbandry: the ploughing of a field, a harvest, a vineyard with children dancing (accompanied by a boy singing and playing a lyre), a scene depicting the herding of cattle with a vividly described attack of lions, and a brief description of a sheepfold. The final scene is that of a dance floor with young dancers performing an elaborate dance upon it. The entire Shield (as the entire earth) is encircled by the river Ocean. The eighteenth book of the *Iliad* then ends with a brief nine lines describing the rest of the weapons and Thetis's departure with the new arms for Achilles.[10]

Such summaries help organize our thinking, but these are preliminary moves, warm-up exercises like scales and arpeggios, not music. As Hephaestus says, we are meant to be overwhelmed and dazzled by the making of the shield. An inventory has no place in aesthetic experience. Homer's poetry is itself an account of the making of the shield, a translation by Homer of an artist's work into poetry. It is not only that the shield of Achilles never existed as an actual object. It lives in the sound of Homer's poetry, not the silence of letters in a written or printed text. Each of us will imagine what we can from the song of the shield's making, and to do this, as Octavio Paz advises, we must face the music.

A good example is *Iliad* 18.576, a line S. E. Bassett regarded as the most beautiful in all of Homer.[11] It comes from the middle of a pastoral scene describing a river and a field of reeds that cattle are being driven to, cattle that themselves are miraculously wrought of gold and of tin, yet thronging forward like living beings, lowing as they move out of the dung of their farmyard toward the river's banks. And as they go, they move toward Bassett's most beautiful line. Transliterated from Greek to English, it is *par potamon keladonta, para hrodanon donakēna,*

literally, "to a river murmuring, to waving reed-thickets."[12]

None of Homer's good translators merely decodes him into English; most re-create the melodious effect of Homer's Greek line in their own. While no single one of them captures everything, all of them together show first one facet and then another, with a cumulative expertise not unlike the tradition of Homer's commentators.

Martin Hammond's English prose, for example, is scrupulously exact in getting every word in Homer across to his readers. The phrasing in the second part of the sentence is also well on the way to capturing the aural effects in the original.

> The cows were fashioned in gold and tin, and were mooing as they hurried from the farmyard to their pasture by a purling river, beside the beds of swaying reeds.[13]

"By a purling river, beside the beds of swaying reeds" is as elegant a single line as in any of the verse translations, though "purling" will be more familiar to English than American ears. At the other end of the scale from Hammond, his Elizabethan predecessor John Chapman's fourteeners create rougher sounds than the melodious heifer lowing to the skies in Keats's "Ode on a Grecian Urn."

> A herd of Oxen then he carv'd with high-raisd heads, forg'd all
> Of Gold and Tin (for colour mixt), and bellowing from their
>   stall
> Rusht to their pastures at a flood, that eccho'd all their throtes,
> Exceeding swift and full of reeds.
> (18.523–26, Chapman)

Chapman's cows are as rapid and lively as Homer's herd, so lively that the sinister flood and reeds to which they race now sound more like an environmental hazard than a garden spot.

Four verse translators, Lattimore, Fitzgerald, Fagles, and Lombardo, are each as responsive to the original as their sense of fidelity to the text and their six- or five-stress lines allow. Taking their translations in chronological order, dating respectively from 1951, 1974, 1990, and 1997, we find Fitzgerald's five-stress line consciously departing from Lattimore's six beats, and then Fagles, in turn, knowingly departing from both of them. Lombardo goes his own way with an actor's preference for a five-stress line that leaves out anything that gets in the way of a version suitable for stage performance.[14] The first three are well aware of the challenge of Bassett's verse and attempt to capture it as much as possible. Lombardo is less concerned to do this, preferring to moo with Hammond rather than low with Lattimore.

> He made upon it a herd of horn-straight oxen. The cattle
> were wrought of gold and of tin, and thronged in speed and
>   with lowing
> out of the dung of the farmyard to a pasturing place by a
>   sounding
> river, and beside the moving field of a reed bed.
>   (18.573–76, Lattimore)

> The artisan made next a herd of longhorns,
> fashioned in gold and tin: away they shambled,
> lowing, from byre to pasture by a stream
> that sang in ripples, and by reeds a-sway.
>   (18.670–73, Fitzgerald)[15]

> And he forged on the shield a herd of longhorn cattle,
> working the bulls in beaten gold and tin, lowing loud
> and rumbling out of the farmyard dung to pasture
> along a rippling stream, along the swaying reeds.
>   (18.670–73, Fagles)

> On it he made a herd of straight-horn cattle.
> The cows were wrought of gold and tin
> And rushed out mooing from the farmyard dung
> To a pasture by the banks of a roaring river,
> Making their way through swaying reeds.
>   (18.716–20, Lombardo)

As usual Lattimore is precise about getting the meaning of the words across, morpheme for morpheme, but not even his loose six-stress line can capture all of Homer's line in one line, possibly because his ear called for the addition of *and* to make the whole sentence run well. In his five-stress lines, Fitzgerald doesn't hesitate to throw out words if they get in the way; he turns the barnyard dung into a cow barn (byre) and changes parts of speech midstream, with the liveliest diction of any of the four in his "sang in ripples" and "reeds a-sway." Fagles builds on Fitzgerald's way of treating the line and gets the anaphora of *par . . . para,* in an exact rendering of Homer's conjunctionless two half-lines and their parallel structures. Lombardo interrupts the river and the reeds, making no attempt to get the music of one line into one line of his.

With these contemporary translations in mind it is not hard to see how much elegance and vitality Pope's version of 1725 retains.[16] Already sure of how to make his own music, he re-creates a seemingly effortless version of Homer's.

> Here, Herds of Oxen march, erect and bold,
> Rear high their horns, and seem to lowe in Gold,
> And speed to Meadows on whose sounding shores
> A rapid Torent thro' the Rushes roars.
> (18.665–68, Pope)

The synaesthesia of "seem to lowe in Gold" seems a particularly felicitous idea, even though "to lowe in Gold" is only in general what is happening in this scene of the shield. Pope also omits one of Hephaestus's precious metals that Lattimore renders precisely ("the cattle were wrought of gold and of tin," *hai de boes chrusoio teteuxato kassiterou te*). Gone, too, is the dung of the farm-yard (*mukēthmōi d'apo koprou*). Like some of his successors, Pope creates poetry by knowing what to leave out. The cattle's move from dung to gold in lines 574 and 575 is a tiny but telling characteristic of Hephaestus's magical art at work, fusing the divine and the mundane at a level that Pope couldn't reach without lapsing into diction unsuitable for the sublime of his day.[17] But he captures, at one and the same time, and in one phrase, both Hephaestus's fusion of the living image with its representation in flowing, inanimate metal, and Homer's transformative art that renders Hephaestus's craft into poetry of equal splendor.

The shield of Achilles is a fusion of poetry and crafts, the visual and verbal spheres of artistic creation.[18] What the god and the poet have created is now put to a most unlovely use.

AN OLYMPIAN VIEW OF WAR

> Sooner or later in life everyone discovers that perfect happiness is unrealizable, but there are few that pause to consider the antithesis: that perfect unhappiness is equally unattainable. The obstacles preventing the realization of both these extreme states are of the same nature: they derive from our human condition, which is opposed to everything infinite.
> Primo Levi, *If This Is a Man*

Achilles' anger grows greater as he looks at the weapons Hephaestus has created, and as he handles them he takes delight and happiness in seeing them and holding them. Pope suffuses the whole scene with fire.

> Unmov'd, the Hero kindles at the Show,
> And feels with Rage divine his Bosom glow:

From his fierce Eye-balls living Flames expire,
And flash incessant like a Stream of Fire.
        (19.19–22)

Achilles' eyes blaze forth as the arms themselves will when he moves into battle.[19]

As when from across water a light shines to mariners
from a blazing fire, when the fire is burning high in the
        mountains,
in a desolate steading, as the mariners are carried unwilling
by storm winds over the fish-swarming sea, far away from
        their loved ones,
so the light from the fair elaborate shield of Achilleus
shot into the high air.
        (19.375–80, Lattimore)

The faraway gleam recedes from the mariners unwillingly swept from their loved ones. The blazing fire is far away, high aloft, a sign whose meaning they would know, but one impossible to read in the grip of the storm at sea. The more distant we are from the shield, the less readable it becomes. Draw closer, and the sinister meaning of its distant gleam is no riddle at all.[20] Hephaestus is another way to say "fire."

As when the north wind of autumn suddenly makes dry
a garden freshly watered and makes glad the man who is
        tending it,
so the entire flat land was dried up with Hephaistos burning
the dead bodies.
        (21.346–49, Lattimore)

Perhaps because he is so near the immortal gods, Achilles understands the limits of such divine artistry better than ordinary mortals could.[21] He has an equally clear idea of what Patroclus now is: a dead flesh that will soon be rotting. The conjunction of imperishable object and mortal body in Achilles' imagination is telling. It contradicts our immortal longing to enjoy the fantasy world that Hephaestus's art and Homer's song have opened up to us. Achilles knows better; he knows the difference between immortal and mortal, and between artifacts and human bodies, and he thinks of Patroclus—more precisely, the remains of Patroclus. Nothing better underscores the mortal condition than Achilles' admiration of Hephaestus's creation, followed by his practical concern for Patroclus's corpse.

Of recent translators and poets Christopher Logue best brings out the

crucial difference between immortal artist and mortal recipient. He will
have nothing to do with this divinely sanctioned weapon. Was he immune
to its music? Unwilling to take up a double challenge from an Olympian and
a poet inspired by the Muses? For whatever reason, Logue eliminates the
gorgeous story of the shield's making altogether, reducing all of Olympus
and the cosmos of the shield to a divine union label. The entire absence of
the shield is more stunning than any attempt to re-create it could ever have
been.

> And as she laid the moonlit armour on the sand
> It chimed;
> And the sound that came from it
> Followed the light that came from it,
> Like sighing,
> Saying,
> *Made in Heaven.*

> And those who had the neck to watch Achilles weep
> Could not look now.
> Nobody looked. They were afraid.

> Except Achilles: looked,
> Lifted a piece of it between his hands;
> Turned it; tested the weight of it; and then
> Spun the holy tungsten, like a star between his knees,
> Slitting his eyes against the flare, some said,
> But others thought the hatred shuttered by his lids
> Made him protect the metal.

> His eyes like furnace doors ajar.

> When he had got its weight
> And let its industry console his grief a bit:
> "I'll fight,"
> He said. Simple as that. "I'll fight."
> . . . .
> "But while I fight, what will become of this"—
> Patroclus—"Mother?
> Inside an hour a thousand slimy things will burrow.
> And if the fight drags on his flesh will swarm
> Like water boiling."[22]

No slimy things for Patroclus. It is understandable that we have always pre-ferred to concentrate on the shield of Achilles rather than the rotting corpse of Patroclus. But Achilles is a better interpreter of the gifts of the gods. We lose sight of the reality of our mortality, most especially when confronted with the seductive, immortal images that Hephaestus devised.

In our zeal to live up to Hephaestus's prediction, we have tried so hard to see what is in the shield for us that we risk seeing what is not for us at all. The world that appears in the shield is not the world of the *Iliad,* or our world. As Walter Marg has observed, even the men in battle on the shield do not really seem like human beings; they are a mob, nameless, like ants chewing away on a piece of wood.[23] Yet we are drawn to it in no small part because of the pastoral visions of the world that it contains, scenes of peace juxtaposed with scenes of war.

Such pastoral green thoughts in a green shade arise in counterpoint to the horrors of war.[24] In *Under Storm's Wing,* Helen Thomas looks back through the war and her husband's death, to their life together in the English country-side before the war. It is a vanished world, as dead and receding in time as Edward himself. It has coherence, it moves in and with the seasons of the year, it is a pastoral memory created as part of a memorial of loss.

> It is this full life of homely doings that I remember chiefly at the farm—the early morning expeditions with Edward to a large pond about three miles away to fish for perch and roach and even pike; the walks to Penshurst and Leigh and Ightham Moat; the picking and storing of apples; the making of quince jam; the finding of an owl's or a nightingale's nest; the woodpecker which cut the air in scallops as it flew from oak to oak; the white owl which brought its young to the roof ridge to be fed; the beautiful ploughhorses with their shining brass ornaments; the cows going into their stalls like people going into their pews in church; the building and thatching of the ricks; the hedging and ditching; the wood-cutting and faggot-binding by men whose fathers had done the same work and whose fathers' fathers too; the work of the farm, leisured as the coming and going of the seasons; the lovely cycle of ploughing, sowing and reaping; the slow experienced labourers, whose knowledge had come to them as the acorns come to the oaks, whose skill had come as the swallows' skill, who are satisfied in their hard life as are the oaks and the swallows in theirs. How I loved it all, and with what joy and strength it filled my being, so that when I needed joy and strength they did not fail me.[25]

This is the stuff from which similes are made, all images of a pastoral world like the one that Hephaestus creates.

And he forged a king's estate where harvesters labored,
reaping the ripe grain, swinging their whetted scythes.
Some stalks fell in line with the reapers, row on row,
and others the sheaf-binders girded round with ropes,
three binders standing over the sheaves, behind them
boys gathering up the cut swaths, filling their arms,
supplying grain to the binders, endless bundles.
                    (18.550–56; 18.639–45, Fagles)

And he forged a thriving vineyard loaded with clusters,
bunches of lustrous grapes in gold, ripening deep purple
and climbing vines shot up on silver vine-poles.
And round it he cut a ditch in dark blue enamel
and round the ditch he staked a fence in tin.
And one lone footpath led toward the vineyard
and down it the pickers ran
whenever they went to strip the grapes at vintage—
girls and boys, their hearts leaping in innocence,
bearing away the sweet ripe fruit in wicker baskets.
                    (18.561–68; 18.654–63, Fagles)

In contrast to the images of the shield, Helen Thomas's scenes are animated by life as it was actually lived, with seasons of growth and ripening and decay. The divine animation of the shield is nothing like the unique life that Thomas records.

Nor like any life as it is lived. W. H. Auden's "Shield of Achilles" offers a bleak landscape of rapes, executions, and reprisals that reads like a sardonic send-up of the beautiful images of Homer's shield, a narrower vision of the world, far more particular and monochromatic.[26] Unlike Thetis in the *Iliad*, who comes for the arms for her son and takes them to him, this Thetis has seen the shield of Achilles before, and expects to see it again.

She looked over his shoulder
For vines and olive trees,
Marble well-governed cities
And ships upon untamed seas.
But there on the shining metal
His hands had put instead
An artificial wilderness
And a sky like lead.[27]

Whoever she is, she seems to know Keats's sonnet "On First Looking into Chapman's Homer" and the still, unravished bride of quietness in the "Ode on a Grecian Urn." The search for vines and olive trees and cities and ships upon untamed seas comes to a full stop with "instead" and scenes of the total devastation of landscape that modern bombardment can accomplish—that, or the scrupulously cleared terrain of the concentration camp. Compare Primo Levi's account in *The Reawakening*, his sequel to *If This Is a Man*. In a passage that might be termed "On First Looking into the Mother Camp at Auschwitz," he sees for the first time the infamous crowning legend over the entrance gate, *Arbeit Macht Frei*, "Work Gives Freedom."

> When Yankel's cart crossed the famous threshold, we were amazed. Buna-Monowitz, with its twelve thousand inhabitants, was a village in compari-son: what we were entering was a boundless metropolis. There were no one-story "Blocks," but innumerable gloomy, square, grey stone edifices, three floors high, all identical; between them ran paved roads, straight and at right angles, as far as the eye could see. Everything was deserted, silent, flattened by the heavy sky, full of mud and rain and abandonment.[28]

Levi's images in *The Reawakening* and others like them are familiar from war-time newsreels and later documentaries, and it is these images that Auden's poem evokes, not a world that readers of Keats would recognize.

> She looked over his shoulder
> For ritual pieties,
> White flower-garlanded heifers,
> Libation and sacrifice,
> But there on the shining metal
> Where the altar should have been,
> She saw by his flickering forge-light
> Quite another scene.

Auden is juxtaposing the world whose memory Levi has preserved with the world that Keats imagined. His target is not the images of Homer's shield, still less the poetry of Keats, but the deluded expectations of readers of such transcendent poetry. The gap between the world we want to see and the world we know we actually live in grows greater and greater.

> Barbed wire enclosed an arbitrary spot
> Where bored officials lounged (one cracked a joke)
> And sentries sweated for the day was hot;
> A crowd of ordinary decent folk
> Watched from without and neither moved nor spoke
> As three pale figures were led forth and bound
> To three posts driven upright in the ground.

Although Auden seems to offer a more restricted view of the world than Homer's unfolding of Hephaestus's grand designs, "The Shield of Achilles" is a most perceptive translation of Homer's and Hephaestus's arts for our present world. Auden sees that a crucial issue in the shield of Achilles is not just what it contains, but how we contemplate it.

> The thin-lipped armourer,
>   Hephaestos, hobbled away,
> Thetis of the shining breasts
>   Cried out in dismay
> At what the god had wrought
>   To please her son, the strong
> Iron-hearted man-slaying Achilles
>   Who would not live long.

The horrible dissonance of Auden's poetry suggests that the more we idealize the shield, the more we accept the values of the world of Zeus it affirms, the more we guarantee that we shall remain in the Olympians' fixed schemes of a mortality whose search for transcendence is, for the gods at least, synonymous with meaninglessness. Auden's poem may explain why Logue refused to give an account of the lovely images of the shield altogether. Logue's union label *Made in Heaven* is a brilliant joke summing up the whole tradition of shields and the poetry of them.

There has always been something mythologically correct about our mortal fascination with the shield of Achilles. Along with having a propensity to make things as fearsome as they are beautiful, Hephaestus is shrewdly attentive to the psychology and status of the men who receive his works.[29] Like any wise artist in a well-run court, he works to support the supremacy of the one who runs it: in the Olympian world, that ruler is father Zeus. Hephaestus fashions the scepter of Agamemnon that is described in the assembly scene in book 2, a symbol of kingly power made originally for Zeus, who gave it to Hermes, who gave it to Pelops, who gave it to Atreus, who in turn gave it to Thyestes, who gave it to Agamemnon (*Iliad* 2.100–108).

Hephaestus is an artisan with a mission, an enforcer of the way Zeus wants things to be. He is sensitive to his clients—and victims. When Thetis first comes to him, he remembers that he would have suffered greatly if the sea goddesses Eurynome and Thetis had not hidden him from his mother, Hera, for nine years. Under their tutelage he labored at ring composition, literally, making *daidala polla*, "many intricate things": pins bending back, curved clasps, cups, necklaces. The shield of Achilles is at once a warrior's weapon and a made-to-order pattern growing out of the arts he practiced with Thetis and Eurynome.

Like those necklaces and clasps, the shield has not so much a beginning and an end as a circle of existence, and a world where no preference or value is assigned at any point. The song of the *Iliad* itself is a different kind of circle. It is renewable because it is a poem of infinite artistic experience; its power lies in its subjects being nonrenewable things: unique, individual lives and destinies, irrevocable decisions and their consequences, the wrath of Achilles and the devastation it caused. Recall how this difference between the unending cycle of the world and individual mortality gives meaning to the life of a hero.

> High-hearted son of Tydeus, why ask about my birth?
> Like the generation of leaves, the lives of mortal men.
> Now the wind scatters the old leaves across the earth,
> now the living timber bursts with the new buds
> and spring comes round again. And so with men:
> as one generation comes to life, another dies away.
> (6.145–49; 6.169–74, Fagles)

To those endless generations of leaves Glaucus can counterpose his genealogy. His own achievements become a way of transcending mortality and achieving an enduring fame. In the Olympian view, this notion of transcending the limits of mortal life is contemptible. Apollo backs away from a quarrel with Poseidon, because they should not fight

>   for the sake of insignificant
> mortals, who are as leaves are, and now flourish and grow
>   warm
> with life, and feed on what the ground gives, but then again
> fade away and are dead.
> (21.463–66, Lattimore)

Whereas Glaucus can use the evanescent quality of mortal life and the season of leaves to frame his life and give meaning to it, Apollo can only see humanity and its successive generations as vegetative creatures without significance—certainly nothing that should lead to a quarrel between fellow gods.

But the vision of the shield abides and persuades us of its wonders, doing precisely what Hephaestus predicts it will. In its way, the shield of Achilles is even more scandalous a seduction than Pandora, a more sophisticated snare than the moralizing stories about her in Hesiod. We get not simply a description of Hephaestus's arts, but an enactment of them, working their magic on whoever wants to embrace the transcendent and the immortal.

Many World War II memoirs about the air war in Europe capture the beauty and exaltation of war at this Olympian distance. In *The Fall of Fortresses*, Elmer Bendiner tells about hearing of the effects of the Hamburg raid of 1943 in which firestorms were created, and has positively Hephaestean thoughts about the experience. "Many of the men who thus manipulated the primal elements of fire, earth, air and water were mild and tender fellows. I knew them well; I was one of them. We were not unconcerned with the hell we left behind us. The hells were perceived, however, only as pillars of smoke, not as human anguish, and, happily for us, soldiers inhibit their imaginations. Most of the flyers who cracked up in combat did so out of fear for their own lives, not out of remorse, which is a civilian luxury to be enjoyed in peacetime."[30] Bendiner becomes most poetic when recalling the beauty of seeing combat in the air:

> Gleaming in silver with white contrails spinning behind them, the Fortresses pulsed and throbbed. The sound of engines beat a rhythm for which my mind devised melodies. We strung out for perhaps ten miles or more across the sky as we left Orfordness.
>
> I exulted in that parade. I confess this as an act of treason against the intellect, because I have seen dead men washed out of their turrets with a hose. But if one wants an intellectual view of war one must ask someone who has not seen it.[31]

Bendiner is amazingly calm and collected in recording his work as he flies along. "The afternoon was brilliant, but, as I remember it, the earth was somber, smudged, dark green and purple. In the gloom those orange-yellow fires curling black smoke upward were grotesque. I was as incredulous as I had been when first I saw a fuselage red with the blood of a gunner's head blasted along with his turret. As we followed that trail of torches it seemed unreal. I see it now as a funeral cortege with black-plumed horses and torches in the night."[32] Much the same spirit characterizes their own losses. "Of course, we had followed the terrible trail of burning Fortresses, but the death of hundreds far away is not nearly so horrible as the death of one man next to you. Were it otherwise, no man could live out a single day of war, perhaps not even of peace."[33] Anyone who follows accounts of battle by witnesses rather than of men in the thick of the killing and dying, tends to turn up the same reports of ecstatic, visionary experiences.

In *The World within War* Gerald Linderman assembles a remarkable sequence of war correspondents' reports that read like so many glosses on the dazzling arts of the shield of Achilles. Here are eyewitnesses to war who, in spite of themselves, experience it as a fine spectator sport, even though they know intellectually that what they are watching is not just entertainment. Ernie Pyle was entirely candid about the thrill of witnessing war's spectacles in his reports from London during the Blitz.

> [On] that night this old, old city was—even though I must bite my tongue in shame for saying it—the most beautiful sight I have ever seen.
>
> It was a night when London was ringed and stabbed with fire . . .
>
> I gathered a couple of friends and went to a high, darkened balcony that gave us a view of a third of the entire circle of London. As we stepped out onto the balcony a vast inner excitement came over all of us—an excitement that had neither fear nor horror in it, because it was too full of awe.
>
> You have all seen big fires, but I doubt if you have ever seen the whole horizon of a city lined with great fires—scores of them, perhaps hundreds.
>
> There was something inspiring just in the awful savagery of it. . . . Immediately above the fires the sky was red and angry, and overhead, making a ceiling in the vast heavens, there was a cloud of smoke all in pink. Up in that pink shrouding there were tiny, brilliant specks of flashing light—antiaircraft shells bursting. . . .
>
> The thing I shall always remember above all other things in my life is the monstrous loveliness of that one single view of London on a holiday night—the Thames sparkling with the pinpoints of white-hot bombs. All of it roofed over with a ceiling of pink that held bursting shells, balloons, flares and the grind of vicious engines. And in yourself the excitement and anticipation and wonder in your soul that this could be happening at all.
>
> These things all went together to make the most hateful, most beautiful single scene I have ever known.[34]

"The most hateful, most beautiful single scene I have ever known": that oxymoron describes everything about the shield of Achilles, in its most concentrated form. The British war correspondent Malcolm Muggeridge was no different from an American when it came to the excitement of living through the Blitz, even though it was the City and Fleet Street in his own capital that were being bombed.

> There was something rather wonderful about London in the Blitz, with no street lights, no traffic and no pedestrians to speak of; just an empty, dark city, torn with great explosions, racked with ack-ack fire, lit with lurid flames, acrid smoke, its air full of the dust of fallen buildings. I remember particularly Regent's Park on a moonlit night, full of the fragrance of the rose gardens; the Nash Terraces, perfectly blacked-out, not a sign of a light anywhere, white stately shapes waiting to be toppled over—as they duly were, crumbling into rubble like melting snow. Andreas and I watched the

great fires in the City and Fleet Street from St. James's Park. It was a great il-
lumination, a mighty holocaust; the end of everything, surely. . . . I felt a
terrible joy and exaltation at the sight and sound and taste and smell of all
this destruction; at the lurid sky, the pall of smoke, the faces of bystanders
wildly lit in the flames.[35]

Of all the reports of transcendent experiences in war that Linderman has
gathered, the one that takes the cake is a comment made by Colonel Charles
Codman of General George S. Patton's staff. In a letter to his wife, during
the campaign in Sicily, he wrote: "And speaking of wonderful things, we had
quite a show from the palace window last night. [The air raid] was very noisy
but colorful in the extreme. The high-water mark—and perhaps the most
beautiful as well as [most] satisfactory sight I have ever beheld—was a flam-
ing enemy bomber spattering itself and its occupants against the side of a
mountain. God, it was gorgeous—completely cured [my] sulfa hang-over."[36]
Faced with a choice between war's realities and what Primo Levi might term
the perfect happiness of its spectacles, we'll choose entertainment every
time.

THE RIVERS OF HIROSHIMA

> Now we are all sons of bitches.
> Kenneth Bainbridge, director of the Trinity atomic bomb test, July 16, 1945

Achilles is not done with Hephaestus once he has his shield and armor. Nor
are we. Hephaestus returns in another guise, as a divine force of pure fire, in
book 21, when Achilles battles with the river Scamander. The river threatens to engulf Achilles in its waves, and Hera calls in Hephaestus to save him.
This is a fantastic, wholly supernatural encounter of elemental forces, a
battle between fire and water, provoked by Achilles' slaughter of Trojans.
The number of dead and dying grows so great that the very rivers themselves become choked with corpses and blood. Scamander rebels at this
violation of his waters.[37]

> Stop, Achilles! Greater than any man on earth,
> greater in outrage too—
> For the gods themselves are always at your side!
> But if Zeus allows you to kill off all the Trojans,
> drive them out of my depths at least, I ask you,
> out on the plain and do your butchery there.
> All my lovely rapids are crammed with corpses now,
> no channel in sight to sweep my currents out to sacred sea—
> I'm choked with corpses and still you slaughter more,

you blot out more! Leave me alone, have done—
captain of armies, I am filled with horror!
(21.214–21; 21.240–50, Fagles)

The battle grows more ferocious, drawing in the river Xanthus as well, with
Scamander hurling masses of water and corpses at Achilles, Achilles first
fighting, then fleeing the flood, until finally it appears that even Achilles will
be overwhelmed. Then Hera calls to her son, the god of fire, and Hephaestus unleashes his flames. In Fagles's deliberately breathless version:

> First he shot into flames and burned the plain,
> ignited hordes of corpses, squads Achilles slaughtered—
> he scorched the whole plain and the shining river shrank.
> Hard as the autumn North Wind hits a leveled field
> just drenched in a downpour, quickly dries it off
> and the farmer is glad and starts to till his soil—
> so the whole plain was parched and the god of fire devoured
> all the dead, then blazing in all his glory veered for the river—
> an inferno—the elms burned, the willows and tamarisks
>   burned
> and the lotus burned and the galingale and reeds and rushes,
> all that flourished along the running river's lush banks
> and the eels writhed and fish in the whirlpools leapt high,
> breaking the surface left and right in a sheen of fire,
> gasping under the Master Smith Hephaestus' blast.
>   (21.343–55; 21.390–403, Fagles)

Then the river Xanthus himself is in danger of being destroyed. Xanthus
pleads with Hephaestus, but to no avail. To savor the simile, we might switch
to Lattimore's slower lines:

> He spoke, blazing with fire, and his lovely waters were
>   seething.
> And as a cauldron that is propped over a great fire boils up
> dancing on its whole circle with dry sticks burning beneath it
> as it melts down the fat of swine made tender, so Xanthos'
> lovely streams were burned with the fire, and the water was
>   boiling
> and would not flow along but was stopped under stress of the
>   hot blast
> strongly blown by resourceful Hephaistos.
>   (21.361–67)

The culinary metaphor accords well with what happens to any animal body when being rendered of its fat. Hera answers this prayer and calls off Hephaestus.

Achilles' battle with Scamander and Xanthus has long seemed more appropriate to Hesiod's accounts of divine, elemental wars in the *Theogony*. There Earth (Gaia) and Sky (Ouranos) and Ocean (Oceanus) and other primal beings create the world by their conflicts. But the most fantastic part of the *Iliad* recounts something now a matter of course for us, among the most familiar of all images of war. Richard Rhodes's *Making of the Atomic Bomb* tells of a similar conflict of fire and water in the rivers of Hiroshima.

In the hours after the detonation, so many people ran to one of the banks of the Ota River that the testimony of those survivors who witnessed this first nuclear holocaust created "river stories," a whole genre of Hiroshima survivors' accounts.[38] Like Linderman's sequence on the spectacle of bombing in Europe in World War II, Rhodes's series of vignettes gains its power from its accumulation of detail. The great difference is that we are now hearing what it was like to be at the center of war's spectacle, rather than a distant witness to it. For example, this report from a third-grade boy:

> Men whose whole bodies were covered with blood, and women, whose skin hung from them like a kimono, plunged shrieking into the river. All these become corpses and their bodies are carried by the current toward the sea.[39]

Or a young ship designer whose response to the bombing was to rush home immediately to Nagasaki:

> I had to cross the river to reach the station. As I came to the river and went down the bank to the water, I found that the stream was filled with dead bodies. I started to cross by crawling over the corpses, on my hands and knees. As I got about a third of the way across, a dead body began to sink under my weight and I went into the water, wetting my burned skin. It pained severely. I could go no further, as there was a break in the bridge of corpses, so I turned back to the shore.[40]

Or a fifth-grade boy:

> The river became not a stream of flowing water but rather a stream of drifting dead bodies. No matter how much I might exaggerate the stories of the burned people who died shrieking and of how the city of Hiroshima was burned to the ground, the facts would still be clearly more terrible.[41]

Eyewitness reports like these suggest that we are in a better position than ever to appreciate the fiery arts of Hephaestus, thanks to the past century's signal scientific achievement. The atomic bomb blasts at Hiroshima and

Nagasaki remain to date the greatest spectacles of war, and by far the dead-liest. From the moment of its first detonation at the Trinity test site in New Mexico, this most destructive of war's inventions has been described in count-less ways: through eyewitness narratives, forensic pathology, and reports of the effects of the bomb. But Rhodes's reconstruction of the detonation in millionths of a second is perhaps the most chilling of all, simply for the way it explains how the bomb played with the elements of creation itself.

> Time: 05.29.45. The firing circuit closed; the X-unit discharged; the detona-tors at thirty-two detonation points simultaneously fired; they ignited the outer lens shells of Composition B; the detonation waves separately bulged, encountered inclusions of Baratol, slowed, curved, turned inside out, merged to a common-inward-driving sphere; the spherical detonation wave crossed into the second shell of solid fast Composition B and accelerated; hit the wall of dense uranium tamper and became a shock wave and squeezed, liquefying, moving through; hit the nickel plating of the pluto-nium core and squeezed, the small sphere shrinking, collapsing into itself, becoming an eyeball; the shock wave reaching the tiny initiator at the cen-ter and swirling through its designed irregularities to mix its beryllium and polonium; polonium alphas kicking neutrons free from scant atoms of beryl-lium: one, two, seven, nine, hardly more neutrons drilling into the sur-rounding plutonium to start the chain reaction. Then fission multiplying its prodigious energy release through eighty generations in millionths of a sec-ond, tens of millions of degrees, millions of pounds of pressure. Before the radiation leaked away, conditions within the eyeball briefly resembled the state of the universe moments after its first primordial explosion.[42]

Compared to this scientific reconstruction of a split second, Hephaestus's crafts seem slower, but, oddly, not so very distant.

> And the bellows, all twenty, blew on the crucibles,
> breathing with all degrees of shooting, fiery heat
> as the god hurried on—a blast for the heavy work,
> a quick breath for the light, all precisely gauged
> to the god of fire's wish and the pace of the work in hand.
> Bronze he flung in the blaze, tough, durable bronze
> and tin and priceless gold and silver, and then,
> planting the huge anvil upon its block, he gripped
> his mighty hammer in one hand, the other gripped his tongs.
> (18.470–77; 18.549–57, Fagles)

The effect of the fireball at Hiroshima is more familiar to us now than any-thing the Olympian Hephaestus made. Yet there is a correspondence in these arts. As in the *Iliad*, nearness to the fire turns out to be a crucial factor. Rhodes summarizes an account of the effects of this blast on human beings, from an official report of the Committee for the Compilation of Materials on Damage Caused by the Atomic Bombs in Hiroshima and Nagasaki:[43]

> The temperature at the site of the explosion . . . reached 5,400 degrees F . . . and primary atomic bomb thermal injury was found in those exposed within [two miles] of the hypocenter. . . . Primary burns are injuries of a special nature and not ordinarily experienced in everyday life. . . . Extremely intense thermal energy leads not only to carbonization but also to evaporation of the viscerae. People exposed within half a mile of the Little Boy fireball, that is, were seared to bundles of smoking black char in a fraction of a second as their internal organs boiled away. "Doctor," a patient commented to Michihiko Hachiya a few days later, "a human being who has been roasted becomes quite small, doesn't he?" The small black bundles now stuck to the streets and bridges and sidewalks of Hiroshima numbered in the thousands.[44]

Rhodes goes on to create a simple graph to measure the correlation between distance from the hypocenter above ground zero, where the bomb exploded (eighteen hundred feet), and the percentage of people killed. The percentage rises strictly, impersonally, depending on how close one was to the hypocenter.[45] It is part of our mental equipment now to know that the nearer we are to ground zero, the higher the kill rate rises. In the first use of atomic weapons at Hiroshima, the kill rate reached 100 percent within a half mile of the hypocenter. This familiar piece of modern science may help us look at the fear of Achilles' men and even the anguish of Hector and the Trojans in a more understanding way.

None had the courage
to look straight at it. They were afraid of it.

Eight TOWARD THE AUTUMN NIGHT
OF OGUMA HIDEO

> The familiar destructiveness of war represents not, as is commonly supposed,
> finality, but uncertainty, a hovering on the edge of what, like death, can never
> be fully known.
>
> Jacqueline Rose, "Why War?"

When Troy finally fell to the trick of the Trojan horse, the Trojan War did
come to an end, but this terminal event so celebrated in art and literature did
not close the war. It was the end for Troy and the Trojans, but not for the
Greeks. They had years of wandering ahead of them, the *nostoi* or returns
that would give rise to the original tale of nostalgia, the soldier's homesick-
ness that finds its first Western expression in the *Odyssey*. There was no such
homecoming for many. Not one of Odysseus's companions makes it home
alive. The death of Achilles and the fall of Troy are a constant presence in
the *Iliad*, and the fate of Troy's women and children becomes increasingly
clear. These tales about war's end are not so much stories told, as ones threat-
ening to be told. Their omission is often taken as a sign of Homer's excellence as a poet. He knew when to stop his story as well as how he should
start it. But there is more than a great poet's sense for formal excellence at
work here. The end of the *Iliad* is as wise about how wars stop as it is about
how they start.[1]

"Start" and "stop," advisedly: not *ended* or *begun*, nor *won* nor *lost*. Such terms
as *triumph, defeat, victory, fall, armistice, surrender,* and that all-purpose word *peace*
are what we use to mark a moment in war that is as arbitrary and elusive as its
beginnings. War stories mirror the confusion in war. If there is a winner, so
goes common parlance, there must be a loser; if there is joy and exultation,
there must be mourning and fear. War stories' authors are often content to
stop in midstream and revel in their survival, or mourn their loss; whether
numb or happy, no one seems bothered with the incompleteness of the tale.[2]

The *Iliad* captures this uncertain leap from war to peace.[3] Even with properly solemn funeral rites, as in books 23 and 24, the story turns inconclusive,
plunging us into the middle of yet other war stories: the rape of Cassandra,
the murder of Astyanax and Priam. These are events we are fated not so
much to hear, as to dread. Homer takes special care to show us how these ex-

158

tremes of uncertainty are brought together. Ending with the deaths and funeral rites of Patroclus and Hector, with the death of Achilles and the fall of Troy imminent and unavoidable, the poem stops, poised forever on the knife edge of the future. Homer brings us through the mourning songs of Troy to an awareness of the equally chaotic stories about war's endings that modern artists particularly want to capture. We can see the *Iliad*'s ending reborn, in the "Long, Long Autumn Nights" that the Japanese poet Oguma Hideo captures in his 1935 elegy for the old women of Korea, who were among the earliest victims of Japanese imperialism before the official beginning of World War II. Like the women at Troy, these old women become Hecubas and Andromaches whose suffering and humiliation at the hands of their Japanese conquerors come to life in Oguma's poetry.

THRENODY

> Time's wrong-way telescope will show
> a minute man ten years hence
> and by distance simplified.
>
> Through that lens see if I seem
> substance or nothing: of the world
> deserving mention or charitable oblivion
>
> not by momentary spleen
> or love into decision hurled,
> leisurely arrive at an opinion.
>
> Remember me when I am dead
> and simplify me when I'm dead.
> Keith Douglas, "Simplify Me When I'm Dead"

As the young British soldier and poet Keith Douglas (1920–44) knew so well, to remember the dead is to simplify the dead. Every monument and memorial is bound to obey Douglas's sardonic command. Monuments fix a moment of mourning in dirt and stone. Homer captures this static quality of the tomb when he likens the grief of the immortal horses of Achilles over the death of Patroclus to a grave stele.

> But standing clear of the fray Achilles' horses wept
> from the time they first had sensed their driver's death,
> brought down in the dust by man-killing Hector.
> Diores' rugged son Automedon did his best,
> lashed them gently now, now shouting oath on oath.
> But both balked at returning now to the ships
> moored at the Hellespont's far-reaching shore

or galloping back to fight beside the Argives.
Staunch as a pillar planted tall above a barrow,
standing sentry over some lord or lady's gravesite,
so they stood, holding the blazoned chariot stock-still,
their heads trailing along the ground, warm tears flowing
down from their eyes to wet the earth . . . the horses mourned,
longing now for their driver, their luxurious manes soiled,
streaming down from the yoke-pads, down along the yoke.
And Zeus pitied them, watching their tears flow.
He shook his head and addressed his own deep heart:
"Poor creatures, why did we give you to King Peleus,
a mortal doomed to death . . .
you immortal beasts who never age or die?
So you could suffer the pains of wretched men?
There is nothing alive more agonized than man
of all that breathe and crawl across the earth."
                    (17.426–47; 17.493–515, Fagles)

The immobility of the immortal horses has a stillness that no living thing
can match. For if we were to emulate them, in unceasing mourning, we
would destroy ourselves. Niobe wept for her children and stayed unmoving;
her grief turned her into stone. As Achilles urges Priam to overcome his grief
and rejoin the living by having something to eat, he tells of Niobe's transformation.

> But she remembered to eat when she was worn out with
>   weeping.
> And now somewhere among the rocks, in the lonely
>   mountains,
> in Sipylos, where they say is the resting place of the goddesses
> who are nymphs, and dance beside the waters of Acheloios,
> there, stone still, she broods on the sorrows that the gods gave
>   her.
> Come then, we also, aged magnificent sir, must remember
> to eat, and afterwards you may take your beloved son back
> to Ilion, and mourn for him; and he will be much lamented.
>   (24.613–20, Lattimore)

The tomb is the necessary marker for honoring and preserving the memory
of the dead, but it is as alien and unchanging to us as the immortal horses of
Achilles. They are living, breathing, but immortal witnesses, as different
from what they weep for as the grave stele is from the lord or lady buried be-

neath it. Zeus pities them because they have come to know what it is to be mortal, and yet their grief makes them seem totally alien from human beings: stonelike, markers of a vanished life. In Homer's poetry, as now, mortals move in a world where there are monuments to the dead of war, and funeral rites that lead to the making of tombs. The last two actions we hear of in his song turn on mourning, monuments, and feasting. Hector's corpse is burned on a funeral pyre, and the next morning the men of Troy extinguish the flames. Hector's burial is the last line from Homer, a concise example of what Walter Benjamin has said about the way the plots of life and of storytelling are interwoven.

> It is . . . characteristic that not only a man's knowledge or wisdom, but above all his real life—and this is the stuff that stories are made of—first assumes transmissible form at the moment of his death. Just as a sequence of images is set in motion inside a man as his life comes to an end—unfolding the views of himself under which he has encountered himself without being aware of it—suddenly in his expressions and looks the unforgettable emerges and imparts to everything that concerned him that authority which even the poorest wretch in dying possesses for the living around him. This authority is at the very source of the story. . . . Death is the sanction of everything that the storyteller can tell. He has borrowed his authority from death. In other words, it is natural history to which his stories refer back.[4]

So far as the commanders of war are concerned, these endings that are not endings can be the happiest of times. They are what the first poets of war have always aimed at. The funeral games for Patroclus are the last respite in the *Iliad*'s war. The bright, shining happiness of the Greek army in book 23 is a momentary thing, but real, and it is Achilles who creates it. His brisk management of the funeral games of Patroclus stands in egregious contrast to the doom that hovers over both Troy and him.

This reconstitution of the Greeks at Troy is far less celebrated than the quarrel and division and strife that mark the opening of the poem, but it is as impressive as any strategic move Agamemnon, Odysseus, or Nestor manages to make. This harmonious moment is due entirely to the strategic thinking of Achilles. The greatest of all destroyers of cities and killers of men turns into an impressive rebuilder of military society. His constructive intelligence and strategic common sense are as overwhelming in their own way as his earlier rage. For a moment, he reveals himself as the best of the commanders, with a gift for reconciliation that makes even Nestor's eloquence fade.

The hero who has enjoyed his play in war as man slaughtering, *homo necans*, now appears as *homo ludens*, the human being at play.[5] His example is infectious. When Antilochus, Nestor's son, cheats Menelaus in the chariot race, he answers Menelaus's bitter complaints with a fulsome apology and restitution, which Menelaus promptly accepts. Whenever someone doesn't get a prize, Achilles sees that he does. Agamemnon is silent throughout the ceremonies. At the end of the games, he rises to enter the contest for the best spear-thrower, but Achilles stops him.

> "Son of Atreus, for we know how much you surpass all others,
> by how much you are greatest for strength among the spear-
>   throwers,
> therefore take this prize and keep it and go back to your
>   hollow
> ships; but let us give the spear to the hero Meriones;
> if your own heart would have it this way, for so I invite you."
> He spoke, nor did Agamemnon lord of men disobey him.
> The hero gave the bronze spear to Meriones, and thereafter
> handed his prize, surpassingly lovely, to the herald Talthybius.
>   (23.890–97, Lattimore)

Here is a swift-footed goody-two-shoes we never expected to see. Not only does Achilles honor a man he once called a "staggering drunk" and "a king who devours his people,"[6] he seems to have forgotten his own precept to Odysseus: he hates like the gates of Death itself the man who says one thing and hides another in his heart.

Achilles' elegant flattery of Agamemnon is political cunning of a high or-der—higher, possibly, than any yet seen in the poem, as there is no gap whatever between the flattery and its desired results. The irony is that the best rhetorician of the *Iliad* speaks when it no longer matters to him. In his orchestration and administration of the funeral rites and games for Patro-clus, Achilles helps recreate a society, reaffirming the values of a world he will shortly have no part of. It is not only because he will die that this is so. He is focused on a deeper level than any public, political institution can pos-sibly address.[7]

> And the games broke up, and the people scattered to go away,
>   each man
> to his fast-running ship, and the rest of them took thought of
>   their dinner
> and of sweet sleep and its enjoyment; only Achilles
> wept still as he remembered his beloved companion, nor did
>   sleep

> who subdues all come over him, but he tossed from one side
>   to the other
> in longing for Patroklos, for his manhood and his great
>   strength
> and all the actions he had seen to the end with him, and the
>   hardships
> he had suffered; the wars of men; hard crossing of the big
>   waters.
>   (24.1–8, Lattimore)

He fastens Hector's corpse behind his chariot and drags it around Patroclus's tomb three times, then leaves it sprawled face-down in the dust.[8] Nothing changes. In mourning Patroclus he knows he is also mourning himself.[9]

This dissonance between public show and private woe is profound, and it has its parallels in the mourners at Troy, who go through equally bitter rites.[10] Troy faces what the Greek army and its warrior society do not: the imminent loss of the whole city, death itself. Priam knows this and expects it, as do Andromache and the women of Troy. What both the Greeks and the Trojans show us is the need for such sustaining structures, despite their inadequacy. Everything that human beings put together, above all the political and physical spaces they organize to live within, can be undone by war. Every ritual, every lament, every connection that is made is overshadowed by this awareness.

Hector's wife Andromache has been a mourner engaged in funeral rites from the first moment we see her to the last, and only Achilles rises to her level, and beyond. In their grief men's and women's worlds, elsewhere so rigidly defined, suddenly coalesce into a common sphere.[11] It would be difficult to judge who, between Achilles and Andromache, is the more bereft, the more grief-stricken at the end. For his part, Priam may not be so clever a tactician as Nestor, but at this level of human communication he does not need to be.

> "Honour then the gods, Achilleus, and take pity upon me
> remembering your father, yet I am still more pitiful;
> I have gone through what no other mortal on earth has gone
>   through;
> I put my lips to the hands of the man who has killed my
>   children."
> So he spoke, and stirred in the other a passion of grieving
> for his own father. He took the old man's hand and pushed
>   him

gently away, and the two remembered, as Priam sat huddled
at the feet of Achilleus and wept close for manslaughtering
     Hector
and Achilleus wept now for his father, now again
for Patroclus. The sound of their mourning moved in the
     house.
        (24.503–12, Lattimore)

This recognition of the father in an enemy brings Achilles back to his mortal identity as the son of Peleus, his mortal father, rather than the son of his immortal mother, Thetis.

Fathers and sons started this war, and it is fitting that they supervise its ending. Paternity is an abiding preoccupation not only of heroic warriors, but of their innumerable successors in later wars. War is the father of all, as a famous fragment of Heraclitus puts it.[12] When Odysseus meets the shade of Achilles in the postwar world of the dead in the *Odyssey*, Achilles characteristically brushes aside Odysseus's flattering words and asks first of all about his son Neoptolemus, and then about his father (*Odyssey* 11.466–503). In *Everybody's Autobiography*, her 1937 sequel to *The Autobiography of Alice B. Toklas*, Gertrude Stein suggests why any hero like Achilles would come to his senses and think about his father: better late than never.

> There is too much fathering going on now and there is no doubt about it fathers are depressing. Everybody nowadays is a father, there is father Mussolini and father Hitler and father Roosevelt and father Stalin and father Lewis and father Blum and father Franco is just commencing now and there are ever so many more ready to be one. Fathers are depressing. England is the only country now that has not got one and so they are more cheerful there than anywhere. It is a long time now that they have not had any fathering and so their cheerfulness is increasing.
>
> I have been much interested in watching several families here in Belley that have lost their father and it is interesting to me because I was not grown when we lost our father. As I say fathers are depressing any father who is a father or any one who is a father and there are far too many fathers now existing. The periods of the world's history that have always been most dismal ones are the ones where fathers were looming and filling up everything.[13]

Fathers were indeed looming and filling up Europe and the world when Stein wrote this book, some two years before the beginning of World War II.

While Homer has fathers looming and filling up everything, he is no less analytical than Stein about what the father-and-son bond can and cannot accomplish in a world governed by father Zeus. If these ties signify anything now, it is what Priam and Achilles have lost and are about to lose. The reconciliation is momentary, because Achilles' drive to slaughter Trojans is only temporarily in check. Priam will return to Troy, and, after a truce for eleven days of mourning, the war will resume on the twelfth. Achilles will soon die, and so will Priam, and Troy along with him, and they both know this.

What unites Priam and Achilles is not an abstract pity for an enemy, but a recognition of a suffering each endures. Priam weeps for his son, Hector, not for Patroclus; Achilles weeps for his father, Peleus, and for Patroclus, not for Hector. These are parallel lives in parallel mourning, joined for a moment by each one's recognition of the other's grief—literally, compassion.[14] Both Priam and the Olympian gods had calculated that the sight of a pitiful old man begging to ransom the body of his son would make Achilles think first of all of his father. As Hermes tells Priam,

> But you go in yourself and clasp Achilles' knees,
> implore him by his father, his mother with lovely hair,
> by his own son—so you can stir his heart.
>   (24.465–67; 24.546–48, Fagles)

For all their power, these moments of reconciliation in one war have never deterred others from going off joyfully to their own wars—and their own reconciliations. Nor are such humane interludes in war and postwar life guaranteed a respectful audience even when they occur. No one outside Achilles' tent shares his civilized thoughts: not Agamemnon, who would at least hold Priam himself for ransom, nor the grieving women of Troy. To Hecuba, Achilles is nothing but a fiend to be punished.

> I wish I could set teeth
> in the middle of his liver and eat it. That would be vengeance
> for what he did to my son; for he slew him when he was no
>   coward
> but standing before the men of Troy and the deep-girdled
>   women
> of Troy, with no thought in his mind of flight or withdrawal.
>   (24.212–16, Lattimore)

As he sets off on his journey to Achilles, disgusted at his sons who survive when Hector does not, kindly old Priam does not contradict her.[15] His reconciliation with Achilles is a momentary miracle in the war, and lasts for exactly as long as Achilles will hold back the Achaeans. Priam's last word to him is an attempt, perhaps, to leave the door open: "On the twelfth day we shall fight again, if we must." The last word we hear from Achilles is a promise to hold off for the agreed time, and nothing more.

> All will be done, old Priam, as you command.
> I will hold our attack as long as you require.
> (24.669–70; 24.787–88, Fagles)

The future battle and all it will bring is vividly before us, the immediate sequel to the burial of Hector never in doubt. Inspiring as its discovery may be,
compassion in war does not last.

DISORDERLY CONDUCT

Jean Genet's novel *Funeral Rites* (*Pompes funèbres*, 1953) is a story about the liberation of Paris in August 1944. It was inspired by the death of his lover Jean
Decarnin, who was killed, Genet said, "by the bullet of a charming young
collaborator."[16] Genet makes Riton, the collaborator, his narrator. Riton is a
sexual and political outlaw whose view of the world turns everything about
the liberation of Paris upside down. His inspiration for this, Riton explains,
is the propensity of the age.

> Speech kills, poisons, mutilates, distorts, dirties. I would not complain
> about it if I had decided to accept honesty for myself, but having chosen to
> remain outside a social and moral world whose code of honor seemed to me
> to require rectitude, politeness, in short the precepts taught in school, it was
> by raising to the level of virtue, for my own use, the opposite of the com-
> mon virtues that I thought I could attain a moral solitude where I would
> never be joined. I chose to be a traitor, thief, looter, informer, hater, de-
> stroyer, despiser, coward. With ax and cries I cut the bonds that held me
> to the world of customary morality. At times I undid the knots methodically.
> I monstrously departed from you, your world, your towns, your institutions.
> After being subjected to your legal banishment, your prisons, your inter-
> dicts I discovered more forsaken regions where my pride felt more at ease.[17]

As Leo Bersani observes, *Funeral Rites* is profoundly opposed to everything
that monumental art stands for.[18] Genet's rage against the hypocritical or-
derliness he sees in the world expresses itself through an inversion of conventional history and values. The archvillain of twentieth-century history,
Adolf Hitler, appears as an old queen rimming the young German men he
sends out to die for him. There is plenty of joyful sex. Riton the collaborator
and Erik the German would no more be caught with women than they
would be found marching through the Arc de Triomphe. Instead they enter
into one last fling on the rooftops above Paris, before the certain death that
awaits Nazis and collaborators alike.

> Riton's hand lost its will power and Erik's became more friendly. Gently,
> with the other hand, the German took the machine gun and put it down at

his side. He had not let go of Riton, in fact he made his hug more affection-
ate. He drew the kid's head to him. He kissed him.

"Up . . ."

This single word had the curtness of an order, but Riton was already used
to Erik's ways. He stood up. Leaning back against the brick monument, facing a Paris that was watching and waiting, Eric buggered Riton. Their
trousers were lowered over their heels where the belt buckles clinked at
each movement. The group was strengthened by leaning against the wall,
by being backed up, protected by it. If the two standing males had looked at
each other, the quality of the pleasure would not have been the same.
Mouth to mouth, chest to chest, with their knees tangled, they would have
been entwined in a rapture that would have confined them in a kind of oval
that excluded all light, but the bodies in the figurehead which they formed
looked into the darkness, as one looks into the future, the weak sheltered by
the stronger, the four eyes staring in front of them. They were projecting
the frightful ray of their love to infinity. That sharp relief of darkness against
the brick surface was the griffin of a coat of arms, the sacred image on a
shield behind which two other German soldiers were on the lookout. Erik
and Riton were not loving one in the other, they were escaping from themselves over the world, in full view of the world, in a gesture of victory.[19]

Clearing away the monuments and ceremonies and cant that surround victory in war, Genet seeks to capture the horrors that come with victory, by
forcing us to see through the eyes of the defeated of history, the losers'
song.[20] In the cold light of society's order, the line between killing in war
and simple murder is crossed, effortlessly.

For the last time the thirty-five militiamen lowered their rifles and stood
with arms at rest. They were in groups of five, each group ten feet away
from the next, facing the twenty-three-foot wall. Seven groups commanded
by only a lieutenant. A sergeant fired the coup de grâce. The prison assistant carried off a first batch of seven corpses. On the same spot, on the
blood of the first, the next seven were set up and awaited their turn, astounded by the game at the wall so early in the morning. Astounded by the
white label at heart level. Their faces remained surprised. They were taken
away. Seven others came up, standing, shivering with cold, anxious about
the result. Fire! . . . they died. Finally, the last seven. The thirty-five men of
the firing squad were pale. They tried to march away, and their wobbly legs
could hardly support them. Several were haggard, and none of them would
ever in his life forget the eyes or periwinkle faces of the twenty-eight murdered men. If they were still on their feet, it was because of the block they
formed.[21]

Genet makes us believe that the true obscenity in his war is not betrayals and rooftop couplings into the void, but the murder that any group of men can be made to perform. Erik and Riton acquire a kind of poetic immortality that no one in Paris would believe they deserved.

If the dead could come back to us in fact, as they do so often in memory, the results would be no less challenging to conventional patriotism. Balzac's story *Colonel Chabert* is about an officer who served under Napoleon and was presumed killed and buried at the battle of Eylau in February 1807. He was unconscious and in the hasty aftermath on the battlefield was buried alive. He clawed his way out of the mass grave into which he had been pitched, and the vicissitudes of his getting back to a world that thought he was dead are the subject of the novel, which after many revisions eventually became part of Balzac's *Comédie humaine*. Chabert's experience completely undoes that threshold-crossing movement between life and death. His is not the out-of-body experience so familiar from modern psychic lore, but what might be termed an in-body experience, of the most intense kind:

Apparently my horse had been shot in the flank the moment I was wounded myself. Horse and rider were thus knocked over like a house of cards. Wherever I fell, whether to the left or the right, I must have been covered by my horse's body, which prevented me from being crushed by galloping cavalry or hit by stray bullets. When I woke up, Monsieur, I was in a position and a setting which I couldn't convey to you if I talked till dawn. The little air I was breathing was foul. I wanted to move but had no room. Opening my eyes, I saw nothing. The lack of air was the most dangerous thing, and the most pressing indication of my position. I could get no fresh air, and figured I was going to die. This thought wiped out the unbearable pain that had awakened me. My ears were buzzing horribly. I heard, or thought I heard—though I can't swear to it—groans coming from the pile of corpses I was lying in. Even though the memory of those moments is murky, and despite the fact that I must have endured even greater suffering, there are nights when I still think I hear those muffled moans! But there was something more awful: a silence that I have never experienced anywhere else, the perfect silence of the grave. At last able to lift my hand, I felt dead flesh, and then a gap between my head and the corpses above. I explored this empty space I'd been miraculously left. It seems that thanks to the careless haste of our burial, two dead men above me were propped against each other like the base of a house of cards. Scrabbling around me at once, for there was no time to lose, I felt a huge, detached arm. I owe my rescue to that bone. Without it I would have perished![22]

Chabert's widow remarries, has two children, lives in the fashionable Fau-
bourg Saint-Germain, in the Paris of the Restoration of Louis XVIII; many
years later, by the time of his literal return from the grave, she has become
Countess Ferraud. Reunion with her is impossible. After a brief sampling
of prosperity in Paris, Chabert returns to his former life of destitution. The
miraculous resurrection of a war hero brings him back to a world where he is
an unwelcome embarrassment. Chabert discovers that, so far as the war
dead are concerned, the world would prefer to honor their memory rather
than the actual men themselves. The memory is not the same as the man, and
in spite of desperate attempts to recapture his past, Chabert fails. His fate is a
reductio ad absurdum of the role memory plays in our thinking about war.[23]

Neither *Colonel Chabert* nor *Funeral Rites* is a survivor's story. They are stories about those whom war pursues into the aftermath of war, whether it is
victory or defeat, and there destroys them, as thoroughly as any warrior dis-
patched on any field of battle. What makes for great poetry can also make
for the greatest misery, turning those who live beyond a war, not into poets
or writers, but into madmen.

The horrors of war and the blessings of peace can abide side by side, in
perpetual disequilibrium. Recall *Mrs. Dalloway* and the veteran, Septimus,
who throws himself out the window of his rooms, onto the spikes of his
landlady's fence: he has the memories that a poet or writer would draw on,
and a vivid imagination of the present and the past, but he has been driven
mad by the experience. Woolf's portrayal of this soul in misery is a parody
of the violent images of the Great War poets like Wilfred Owen and Siegfried Sassoon. The opposites they yoke in war and poetry are side by side in
his imagination, their past overwhelming his present. The dead of the war
and the pleasant summer day in London in June refuse to come together for
Septimus in any intelligible way. War and peace coexist in hellish simul-
taneity.

>   "It is time," said Rezia.
>   The word "time" split its husk; poured its riches over him; and from his
> lips fell like shells, like shavings from a plane, and without his making them,
> hard, white, imperishable, words, and flew to attach themselves to their
> places in an ode to Time; an immortal ode to Time. He sang. Evans an-
> swered from behind the tree. The dead were in Thessaly, Evans sang,
> among the orchids. There they waited till the War was over, and now the
> dead, now Evans himself—
>   "For God's sake don't come!" Septimus cried out. For he could not look
> upon the dead.

But the branches parted. A man in grey was actually walking towards them. It was Evans! But no mud was on him; no wounds; he was not changed. I must tell the whole world, Septimus cried, raising his hand (as the dead man in the grey suit came nearer), raising his hand like some colossal figure who has lamented the fate of man for ages in the desert alone with his hands pressed to his forehead, furrows of despair on his cheeks, and now sees light on the desert's edge which broadens and strikes the iron-black figure (and Septimus half rose from his chair), and with legions of men prostrate behind him he, the giant mourner, receives for one moment on his face the whole—

"But I am so unhappy, Septimus," said Rezia, trying to make him sit down.[24]

The war is still working, overwhelming the mind of the soldier who has survived to this point, but will not much longer. The integrative imagination of the poet, the memoirist, is coming apart.

Septimus has been mastered by the very things that a saner artist would draw on to make poetry from war. He is separate from Rezia, as any creative artist must be who is making something, but it is a fatal, disconnected separation. What is created is something that only Septimus can see and hear. He has the song sheet and staves of a musician, would have the voice of the poet, but his only discernible melody is chaos. He has the stuff of war and of poetry in him, and certainly the rage, but he can no more pull them together into order than he can separate the world of the living from the world of the dead. Thus Woolf creates the antithesis of Achilles' hearing and seeing the shade of Patroclus. Unlike Achilles, Septimus can neither grieve nor mourn. Rather than putting an end to his war with mourning and monuments, his life has become one long antirequiem, a melody no one but he can hear.

The perfect opposite of Septimus's fall into madness shapes Nguyen Huy Thiep's story "The General Retires," about the return of a general to a postwar, victorious Vietnam in which he can no longer live. The winners of the America War inhabit an insane world. His son, the narrator, is oblivious to much that his father suffers. Economic realities of the postwar world overwhelm war's survivors. The general's son offers a matter-of-fact memoir.

One night I was reading the Russian magazine, Sputnik, when my father came in quietly. "I want to discuss something with you," he said. I made some coffee which my father didn't drink. "Have you been paying attention to what Thuy's been doing?" he asked. "It gives me the creeps."

The Maternity Hospital where my wife worked carried out abortions. Every day, she put the aborted foetuses into a Thermos flask and brought them home. Mr. Co cooked them for the dogs and pigs. I had in fact known about this, but overlooked it as something of no importance. My father led me out to the kitchen and pointed to a pot full of mash in which there were small lumps of foetus. I kept silent. My father cried. He picked up the Thermos flask and hurled it at the pack of Alsatians. "Vile! I don't need wealth that's made of this!" The dogs barked. My father went off up to the house. My wife came in and spoke to Mr. Co: "Why didn't you put it through the meat grinder? Why did you let Father see it?" Mr. Co stammered: "I forgot, I'm sorry, Aunt."

In December, my wife called someone and sold the whole pack of Alsatians. She said: "Stop smoking those imported Galang cigarettes. This year our income is down by 27,000 Dong and our expenditure is up by 18,000, leaving us 45,000 out of pocket."[25]

We realize what the general's son cannot: that the oblivious narrator and the world around the general are focused so completely on economic survival that even the aborted remains of love and sex have become usable commodities. Shortly thereafter the general dies while away from home on an official visit.

LONG, LONG AUTUMN NIGHTS

> Singer of songs in a world of upheaval,
> Will conditions ever improve?
> Will you ever be allowed to sing songs of joy?
> Oguma Hideo, "O, Precious Despair"

The end of the *Iliad* is god-free, Hermes and Zeus and all the other Olympians eternally remote as the gods eventually always are. A god-free end, but not a godless one: this concentration on nothing but mortals and their rituals is one reason Homer appeals to later readers who may know little of and care less for these gods. All that is left are the mortals, who play out their roles, with no illusions about the reality of their situation. What is striking about this mourning is its range. The *Iliad* inspires us to ask of those who survive wars or who think about them: Who mourns? For whom? Why?

Achilles is left alone in his tent; Andromache, Priam, and all the people of Troy conduct the funeral rites of Hector. And this pause turns into the end of the poem. In this pivotal moment, by the absence of gods, human beings come as near face-to-face as they can with what it means to survive, in mortality. Andromache sees slavery for herself, and the same for Astyanax. Or perhaps there will be a worse fate:

> or else some Achaian
> will take you by hand and hurl you from the tower into
> horrible

> death, in anger because Hektor once killed his brother,
> or his father, or his son; there were so many Achaians
> whose teeth bit the vast earth, beaten down by the hands of
>   Hektor.
> Your father was no merciful man in the horror of battle.
>   (24.734–39, Lattimore)

Andromache's ultimate fear becomes true, as seen in a detail from a vase painting of the fall of Troy by the Brygos painter. Astyanax is the youth being hurled by his foot from the walls of Troy (fig. 31). Hecuba can speak only of the past. Though Achilles dragged Hector again and again around Patroclus's tomb, no trace of that mutilation remains.

> Fresh as the morning dew you lie in the royal halls
> like one whom Apollo, lord of the silver bow,
> has approached and shot to death with gentle shafts.
>   (24.757–59; 24.890–92, Fagles)

Helen's lament, the third and last from the women of Troy, is the final lament of a story that has aimed from its opening line at these mourning and funeral rites.[26] Despite all that Helen had done in abandoning her husband and homeland, despite her responsibility in bringing the war to Troy, she names Hector and praises him, because of his past kindness to her.

> I have never heard a harsh saying from you, nor an insult.
> No, but when another, one of my lord's brothers or sisters, a
>   fair-robed
> wife of some brother, would say a harsh word to me in the
>   palace,
> or my lord's mother—but his father was gentle always, a
>   father
> indeed—then you would speak and put them off and restrain
>   them
> by your own gentleness of heart and your gentle words.
>   Therefore
> I mourn for you in sorrow of heart and mourn myself also
> and my ill luck. There was no other in all the wide Troad
> who was kind to me, and my friend; all others shrank when
>   they saw me.
>   (24.767–75, Lattimore)

Hector's kindness comes shining through Helen's words. Like Patroclus's respectful treatment of Achilles' concubine Briseis, Hector's humanity did not

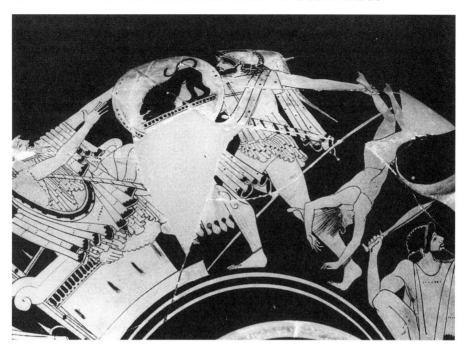

Figure 31. Brygos painter, *The Murder of Astyanax*, red figure vase painting, ca. 490 B.C.E. (Louvre, Paris. Photo by Herve Lewandowski. Copyright Réunion des Musées Nationaux/Art Resource, New York.)

depend on family or patriotic ties. He was kind to Helen in spite of who they were. In her isolation from her husband and people, to say nothing of the despised Paris, she has little else to offer but honor to the memory of a man who was, she says, *ēpios* and *philos*, a kind man and a friend (24.775).

> So she spoke in tears, and the vast populace grieved with her.
> (24.776, Lattimore)

Thus Helen, once a weaver of tapestries, now a mourner whose words can bring tears even to the eyes of her enemies, in person remains the alien, belonging neither to Greek nor Trojan.

Oguma Hideo carries us with Homer and Helen into the center of war's mourning, and he is even more unpatriotic. "Long, Long Autumn Nights" was published in 1935.[27] The occasion was the enforcement of a Japanese edict outlawing traditional Korean dress in Korea, then a province in what promised to be an ever-expanding Japanese empire. As Oguma's translator David Goodman observes, this brutal bureaucratic moment in a long-vanished empire now seems as nothing compared to the enforced prostitution of Korean "comfort women" and other atrocities that were soon to follow.[28] But poets do not measure human suffering by scale. Oguma had already captured in its full horror that same force at work which Simone Weil would describe five years later: *la force* "that does not kill just yet. It will surely kill, it will possibly kill, or perhaps it merely hangs, poised and ready, over the head of the creature it *can* kill, at any moment, which is to say at every moment."[29]

The Japanese of "Long, Long Autumn Nights" has many Korean words throughout its text, such as *nop'a* (the old woman) and *chonyo* (the maiden). The boldest stroke of all is the title, in Korean, not Japanese: *Changjang Ch'uya*.[30] Politically, at the time, nothing could have been more provocative. Today, as poetry, nothing sounds more confident. All the ghostly mourners of war we can imagine seem to come crowding before us in "Long, Long Autumn Nights." It echoes with the anguish that survivors of war know: the victims of Achilles' shield at Troy, the vanished Japanese in the atomic blast at Hiroshima. In the meantime, where poetry always waits for us, who knows how distant we are from these old women of Korea?

As the women walk through the mist,
Suddenly squawk-like screams are heard.
They are struggling with a band of men
And trying to flee the mountain road,
But the men cut them off.

> Damned bitches!
> Wear white will you?
> Then watch how easily it soils!
> You worthless *toktack* shrews!
> Take them off
> Or have your clothes dyed as you wear them!

The careering old women
Are kicked by young feet,
Struck by young fists,
And the young men, whooping it up,
Pursue them as dogs chase aged hens.
They raise brushes
Dripping black ink
And slash across their ancient adversaries' white apparel.

> Who would do such a thing?
> No good can come
> From abusing the aged!

With earsplitting screams the women flee,
But the men give them no quarter
And relentlessly sully their pristine robes.
The pathetic, high-pitched voices trail away,
A moment's clamor interrupting
The quiet Korean night.
Soon it grows quiet again.
Their hair disheveled,
Their miserable white robes
Blackened in the ink attack of
The men from the headman's office,
The old women, their faces twisted,
Struggle to their feet and leave.
When dawn breaks, the old women of the village
Act as if nothing has happened.
Calling their neighbors,
They head for the banks of the Naktong.
They plunge their besmirched raiments in the water,
And for a moment the stream turns black.
But the pollution flows downstream, the water clears,
And the old women's enraged expressions soften, too,
as *tok-tack, tok-tack, tok-tack,*
They begin to beat the laundry.
Striving to affirm all that has happened,
Their expressions change to painful smiles.
They raise frail hands
And strike the rocks.
They sing songs of Korea.
They beat the defiled robes with their mallets.
The mallets that beat weep.
The clothing that is beaten weeps.
The old women who beat weep.
The stones that are struck weep.
All Korea is weeping.

NOTES

INTRODUCTION

1. Cf. Calasso, *Marriage of Cadmus and Harmony*, 103: "Every notion of progress is refuted by the existence of the *Iliad*. The perfection of the first step makes any idea of progressive ascension ridiculous. But at the same time the *Iliad* is an act of provocation as far as forms and shapes are concerned: it defies them and draws them into a fan that has yet to be fully opened. And this state is thanks precisely to the commanding sharpness with which the poem excludes, even expels from within itself, what for centuries to come would be articulated in language. That perfect beginning, through its very appearance, evokes absent counterweights: Mallarmé."

2. Shay, *Achilles in Vietnam*. For a study of Achilles and the ideology of manhood in the American Western, which the authors read as the modern American epic, see Blundell and Ormand, "Western Values."

3. For the connection between the plot of books and the plot of their readers' lives, see Brooks, *Reading for the Plot*, 90–112 ("Freud's Masterplot: A Model for Narrative").

4. Linderman, *The World within War*, 13.

5. Dixon, *Psychology of Military Incompetence*.

6. Gray, *The Warriors*, 59–96.

7. Weil, *The Poem of Force*.

8. Tatum, "The *Iliad* and Memories of War."

9. Weil, *The Poem of Force*, 3.

A NOTE ON READING HOMER

1. Steiner, *Homer in English*.

2. Pope, *The Iliad of Homer*.

3. Ibid., 7:clxxxvii.

4. Arnold, *On Translating Homer*, 30–31. To see Arnold and other critics and theorists in the larger context of the history of translation theory, see Schulte and Biguenet, *Theories of Translation*.

CHAPTER ONE

1. Brooks, *Reading for the Plot*, 90–112; cf. xiv: "Psychoanalysis, after all, is a primarily narrative art, concerned with the recovery of the past through the dynamics of memory and desire."

2. Cf. Proust, *Remembrance of Things Past*, vol. 2, *Within a Budding Grove*, 622: "Our memory does not as a rule present things to us in their chronological sequence but as it were by a reflection in which the order of the parts is reversed."

3. Ninh, *The Sorrow of War*, 214–15.

4. For the continuity between ancient and modern fiction implied here, see Doody, *True Story of the Novel*.

5. For marketing reasons his book is known in English as *Survival in Auschwitz*, though anyone who reads it learns quickly enough that this book by a survivor is not about survival in any ordinary, literal sense of the word; it is a survival of memory through Levi's writing, certainly.

6. Levi, *Survival in Auschwitz* [*If This Is a Man*], author's preface, 9–10.

7. It is essential that an account of such sites be based on personal visits. Just as one needs to say and hear Homer's poetry, not merely contemplate it in silence (see "The Ring of the Shield" in chapter 7, below), so one needs to enter each of these memorial spaces in order to capture something of the feeling the memorial or monument is designed to engender; cf. Young, *The Texture of Memory*, 2.

8. See Griswold, "Vietnam Veterans Memorial," one of the first analyses of the memorial in its political and geographical setting, on which most subsequent comment depends. A close second is Marita Sturken's original essay, "The Wall, the Screen, and the Image," reprinted in an abbreviated and updated version as "The Wall and the Screen Memory." Much of what these and others have observed is already succinctly stated in Maya Lin's original proposal.

9. Lin, *Boundaries*, 4.9–10.

10. While Lattimore's line numbers often correspond to the lines of the original Greek, Fagles and other translators are much freer. To assist anyone interested in comparing translations, or checking the Greek, I will cite the line numbers of the original wherever they differ from a translator's lines.

11. Sturken, "The Wall and the Screen Memory," 58–63.

12. Lin, *Boundaries*, 4.11.

13. Scully, "Terrible Art."

14. For the importance of literature in our conception of what war memorials can be (mainly war memoirs rather than poetry and fiction), see Hynes, "Personal Narratives and Commemoration," an exceptional literary voice in what is mainly a historical collection of essays; cf. also Winter, "Setting the Framework."

15. Scully, "Terrible Art," 28.

16. As Jay Winter observes, Scully's reading of Lutyens's design is a late-twentieth-century critic's view, uncovering things that we can see but ones that Lutyens himself could not have imagined: "He was a conventional patriot, whose wartime swings of mood followed closely the trajectory of the fortunes of the British army. Pacifism was simply not in his bones" (*Sites of Memory*, 106).

17. Scully, "Terrible Art."

18. Dyer, *Missing of the Somme*, 126n: "A monument to 'the untellable,' it is also, strangely and appropriately, unphotographable. No photograph can convey its scale, its balance, its overwhelming effect on the senses."

19. Ibid., 126–27.

20. These messages are from a sample transcribed at Thiepval on 6 September 1996.

21. Dyer, *Missing of the Somme*, 128.

22. Canetti, "The Arch of Triumph," 153.

23. Ibid., 154.

24. For a good reproduction of the sketch, see al-Khalil, *The Monument*, 39 and fig. 20.

25. Ibid., 38–40.

26. Ibid., 2.

27. Ibid., 8.

28. Young, *The Texture of Memory*, 180–82.

29. This and other quotations come from *The Vietnam Wall Experience at Norwich University: "A Time to Remember,"* a guidebook distributed at Disney Field of Norwich University, Northfield, Vermont, during the Moving Wall's exhibition, October 2–6, 1996.

30. It is a "way" (and a major industry) largely unaffected by Mitford's 1963 book; see her revised edition, *The American Way of Death Revisited.*

31. See Zbarsky and Hutchinson, *Lenin's Embalmers.*

32. The line between a site for genuine mourning (which this experience purports to be) and its commercial exploitation is difficult to assess, but the ensemble does suggest something like the sanitizing sentimentality that George Mosse has described in the toys and postcards of France and Germany about the world wars ("The Process of Trivialization").

33. Storr, *Dislocations,* 42. Because it is designed for interaction with visitors, and because it towers over them, Burden's work is even harder to photograph adequately than Lutyens's memorial. For an overview, besides the illustrations in the exhibition catalogue, see Tatum, "Memorials of the America War," 652 and fig. 2.

34. Storr, *Dislocations,* 43.

35. Ibid., 28.

36. Cf. the inscription on a monument at the Ari Burnu Cemetery in ANZAC Cove, dedicated in 1985: "Those heroes that shed their blood and lost their lives . . . You are now lying in the soil of a friendly country. Therefore rest in peace. There is no difference between the Johnnies and the Meamets to us where they lie side by side here in this country of ours . . . You, the mothers who sent their sons from far away countries, wipe away your tears; your sons are now lying in our bosom and are in peace. After having lost their lives on this land they have become our sons as well." When Atatürk wrote his words in 1934, it was very much to Turkey's advantage to consign the war with the British Empire to the past.

37. With Vietnam's long history of struggle against the colonialist French and the Chinese, its memorials require some effort if you want to focus on just those monuments dating from the American Vietnam War; e.g., an imposing monument along the highway in the Mekong Delta, commemorating a successful attack on a French convoy in April 1947 (Tatum, "Memorials of the America War," 640 and fig. 3).

38. Sheehan, *After the War Was Over,* 131.

39. Proust, *Remembrance of Things Past,* vol. 2, *The Guermantes Way,* 89–90.

CHAPTER TWO

1. Godless moderns can never pay too much attention to Homer's gods; see, e.g., Griffin, *Homer on Life and Death,* 144–78 ("Gods and Goddesses") and 179–204 ("The Divine Audience and the Religion of the *Iliad*"). For traditions of gods, Muses, and other aspects of the divine that became part of the machinery of the later epic tradition, see Feeney, *The Gods in Epic.*

2. In a review of the poems of Wilfred Owen, Philip Larkin argued that poetry that comes so directly from experience cannot be so compelling as poetry that is created apart from it: "A 'war poet' is not one who chooses to commemorate or celebrate a war, but one who reacts against having a war thrust upon him: he is chained, that is, to an historical event, and an abnormal one at that. However well he does it, however much we agree that the war happened and ought to be written about, there is still a tendency for us to withhold our highest praise on the grounds that a poet's choice of subject should seem an action, not a reaction. 'The Wreck

of the Deutschland,' we feel, would have been markedly inferior if Hopkins had been a survivor from the passenger list" (561).

3. Proust, *Remembrance of Things Past*, vol. 2, *Cities of the Plain*, 783.

4. Davis, *Badge of Courage*, 83.

5. Ibid., 68–69.

6. Pease, "Fear, Rage, and Mistrials," esp. 156–57: "By stripping the names from the battles
he describes, Crane releases the sheer force of the battle incidents unrelieved by their assimi-
lation into a historical narrative frame. Indeed the war Henry suffers through seems, in its tendency seemingly to start from the beginning with each encounter, to lack any historical
attributes whatever."

7. Crane, *Red Badge of Courage*, 3.

8. A good example is the outrageous conversation he perpetrates with the evidently mind-
less youth Euthyphro, in Plato's *Euthyphro*. See Nehamas, *The Art of Living*.

9. Pease, "Fear, Rage, and Mistrials," 174–75.

10. Norris, "Green Stone of Unrest," 189.

11. *Iliad* 6.146–48. For the etymology linking *hero* (*hērōs*) and *season* (*horos*), see Schein,
Mortal Hero, 69–70, and Nagy, *Best of the Achaeans*, 303.

12. Davis, *Badge of Courage*, 86.

13. Ibid., 154.

14. Alone of Homer's modern English translators, Robert Graves builds the theme into his
title, *The Anger of Achilles*.

15. *The Poetics of Aristotle*, 57. The more vivid the metaphor, the more compelling is Aristotle's point; cf. Fogelin, *Figuratively Speaking*, 107.

16. Cf. "The metaphorical space of a poem may support a variety of different, and sometimes incompatible, readings. This may only show a lack of control, but it can reveal a con-
frontation with unresolved tensions that is the mark of genius" (Fogelin, *Figuratively Speaking*,
112 and n. 11).

17. Kirk allows that it is "one of the most striking and unusual of the Iliadic similes" (*Commentary*, 1:345, on 4.141–47), but he never explains why; for commentators who try, see Moulton, *Similes in the Homeric Poems*, 93 and n. 14, and Hermann Fränkel, *Die homerischen Gleichnisse*, 54,
to both of whose interpretations the present reading owes much.

18. Gray, *The Warriors*, 12.

19. See Lakoff and Johnson, *Metaphors We Live By*, 36. This is a theory of metaphor and simile that, as Fogelin observes, has little to say about metaphor in poetry itself ("A Theory of Figurative Comparisons," in *Figuratively Speaking*).

20. Terry, *Bloods*, 92.

21. Cf. Paz, *The Labyrinth of Solitude*, 57: "The Mexican . . . is familiar with death, jokes
about it, sleeps with it, celebrates it; it is one of his favorite toys and his most steadfast love."

22. Two prints from Goya's series may be seen in chapter 6, below.

23. Fränkel (*Die homerischen Gleichnisse*, 59) thought the processing of the ox-hide might correspond to a similar "processing" of a corpse in battle, but decided that it must be just the "endless going back and forth" ("endlose Hin und Her") that the comparison pointed to. For a more
clinical comment, cf. Edwards, *Commentary*, 99 (on 17.389–99): "Nothing much is known
about the process described. . . . Usually, however, the word [*aloiphē*] means 'fat,' and (nowa-
days at least) the brains are sometimes used in the process."

24. See, for example, the subsections "Racism as a Form of Social Engineering" and "De-
humanization of Bureaucratic Objects" in Zygmunt Bauman's discussion of the "uniqueness
and the normality" of the Holocaust (*Modernity and the Holocaust*, 66–72 and 102–4).

25. For a reading of Simoeisios as emblematic of "the cost in human terms of heroic achievement," see Schein, *Mortal Hero*, 72–77.

26. Power, *War without Mercy*, 224 n. 43, 330 n. 90.

27. For a discussion of this cardinal principle in Homeric criticism, see the chapter "Symbolic Scenes and Significant Objects" in Griffin, *Homer on Life and Death*.

28. *Iliad* 1.43–52.

29. Lynn-George, *Epos*, 151.

CHAPTER THREE

1. Cf. Johnston, *The Ironies of War*, 11–12: "The *Iliad* is, first and foremost, a war poem, our earliest, strangest, and greatest story of men in battle. The term is appropriate not just because a great deal of fighting takes place in the twenty-four books . . . nor because Homer repeatedly describes aspects of the warrior's life. . . . 'War poem' offers a very useful starting point for a discussion of the epic, because the term introduces the central imaginative thrust of the fiction, the exploration of the conduct of human beings individually and collectively when they direct their energies into deadly combat. For the warfare in the *Iliad* does not serve as a merely incidental part of an exciting epic or dramatic narrative nor as a convenient backdrop for an action whose main focus falls elsewhere; the war in Homer's epic, from the opening lines to the very end, forms the organizing principle in a vision of human experience."

2. E.g., two studies published during the American Vietnam War: Fenik, *Typical Battle Scenes*, and Segal, *Theme of Mutilation*.

3. Van Wees, "Homeric Warfare," 668.

4. Van Wees, *Status Warriors*, 262.

5. See Finley, *The World of Odysseus*. If Homer's poetry is any guide to the composition of his audiences, women were welcome to listen, too. The only references to women in van Wees's *Status Warriors* are to the abduction of Helen and to "women's quarters." Homer's poetry would give women much insight into the roles they could play for men, which, as Helen shows, were not always the roles that men thought they should play.

6. Latacz, *Homer*, 15–22 ("The New Relevance of Homer"). Latacz argues for "Homer's nearness," against "irreversible historical alienation," and for "a substantial proximity of ancient and modern." See also David Denby's *Great Books*, a vivid memoir of his nostalgic return to Homer and other classics in the famous Humanities courses at Columbia University.

7. Havelock, *War as a Way of Life*, 34.

8. Ibid., 36.

9. Lepore, *The Name of War*, x.

10. Cf. Keegan, *The Face of Battle*, 303: "What battles have in common is human: the behaviour of men struggling to reconcile their instinct for self-preservation, their sense of honour and the achievement of some aim over which other men are ready to kill them. The study of battle is therefore always a study of fear and usually of courage; always of leadership, usually of obedience; always of compulsion, sometimes of insubordination; always of anxiety, sometimes of elation or catharsis; always of uncertainty and doubt, misinformation and misapprehension, usually also of faith and sometimes of vision; always of violence, sometimes also of cruelty, self-sacrifice, compassion; above all, it is always a study of solidarity and usually also of disintegration—for it is towards the disintegration of human groups that battle is directed. It is necessarily a social and psychological study."

11. Liddell-Hart, *The Real War*, ix–x.

12. For a discussion of the clinical psychology of Achilles' rage, see Shay, *Achilles in Vietnam*, 3–99.

13. Yeats, *Collected Poems*, 133–34.

14. Bornstein, "Afro-Celtic Connections"; for further comment on the connection, see Mishkin, *Harlem and Irish Renaissances*.

15. Killens, *We Heard the Thunder*, 249–50.

16. Keegan, *The Mask of Command*.

17. See his speech to Calchas in *Iliad* 1.106ff.; cf. Kirk, *Commentary*, 1:65 (on 1.108).

18. See the selected list of soldiers' stories in Hynes, *The Soldiers' Tale*, 301–9.

19. Dixon, *Psychology of Military Incompetence*, 21.

20. Ibid.

21. Herodotus, *Histories*, 2.120; for the many alternate versions of Helen and her role in the Trojan War, see Austin, *Helen of Troy*, esp. 118–36 ("Herodotus and Helen in Egypt").

22. Lee's disastrous decision is the eloquent point of departure for Garry Wills's reading of the Gettysburg Address as an American *epitaphios logos* (funeral oration) (*Lincoln at Gettysburg*, 19).

23. Cf. Slatkin, *The Power of Thetis*, 63–64: Achilles appeals to Thetis because of her protection of Zeus.

24. In spite of its echoes of Saddam Hussein and the Gulf War, the phrase and the concept come from Dixon's discussion of problematic mothers and their sons ("Mothers of Incompetence," in *Psychology of Military Incompetence*, 280–87).

25. Ibid., 380; for the extended portrait of Haig, see 371–92.

26. Another instance of Achilles' adaptability as a hero can be found in *Paradise Lost*. Milton did not miss this strategic aspect of Achilles' challenge to authority when he cast Satan into (among other things) an anticipation in mythological time of the rebellion of Achilles, in the process redefining Achilles' rebellion against Agamemnon into Satan's rebellion against God, which begins with "a sense of injured merit" at being passed over for God's favor by God's son.

27. Blainey, *The Causes of War*, 108–9: "Those who studied war's causes, as distinct from its course, ignored him. And yet one of the most dangerous fallacies in the study of war is the belief that the causes of war and the events of a war belong to separate compartments and reflect completely different principles. This fallacy, translated into medicine, would require the causes and course of an illness to be diagnosed on quite different principles."

28. Clausewitz, *On War*, 606–7.

29. McNamara and Van De Mark, *In Retrospect*.

30. Clausewitz, *On War*, 4.11, p. 260.

31. Stein, *Wars I Have Seen*, 7–8.

32. Grant, *Memoirs and Selected Letters*, 207–11.

33. Howard, *Clausewitz*, 74.

34. Clausewitz, *On War*, 136.

35. Grant, *Memoirs and Selected Letters*, preface, 15.

36. De Gaulle, *War Memoirs*, 1.

37. Grant, *Memoirs and Selected Letters*, 665–66.

38. Keegan, *The Mask of Command*, 202. See further the whole chapter (*Mask of Command*, 164–234) on Grant as an unheroic commander (in contrast to a heroic one, such as Alexander, or an antihero, such as Wellington, or a fake hero, such as Hitler), to which this characterization of Grant owes much.

39. Grant, *Memoirs and Selected Letters*, 774.

40. Ibid., 119.

41. Ibid.

42. Porter, *Campaigning with Grant*, 1–2.

43. Ibid., 179.

44. Grant's often costly tactics were widely deplored at the time. Porter has a Clausewitz-ian defense of them: "Grant could have effectually stopped the carnage at any time by with-holding from battle. He could have avoided all bloodshed by remaining north of the Rapidan, entrenching, and not moving against his enemy: but he was not placed in command of the armies for that purpose. It had been demonstrated by more than three years of campaigning that peace could be secured only by whipping and destroying the enemy. No one was more desirous of peace; no one was possessed of a heart more sensitive to every form of human suf-fering than the commander: but he realized that paper bullets are not effective in warfare; he knew better than to attempt to hew rocks with a razor; and he felt that in campaigning the hardest blows bring the quickest relief" (*Campaigning with Grant*, 180). Porter concludes with a stark assessment of why Grant's strategy was necessary. He recognized what war demanded. "When Lee stopped fighting the cause of secession was lost. If Grant had stopped fighting the cause of the Union would have been lost. He was assigned one of the most appalling tasks ever intrusted to a commander. He did his duty fearlessly to the bitter end, and triumphed. In thir-teen months after Lincoln handed him his commission of lieutenant-general, and intrusted to him the command of the armies, the war was virtually ended" (181).

45. Ibid., 471–72. Grant's greatest lieutenant, Sherman, never hesitates to err on the side of completeness, in contrast to his more modest commander, who was famous for his clarity and brevity. Sherman is voluminous, archival, reprinting whatever good things others have to say about him. He included in his thousand pages of narrative hundreds of pages of statistics, letters, and summaries of all kinds, produced with the aid of the official historians of the war who were putting together *The War of the Rebellion: A Compilation of the Official Records of the Union and Confederate Armies*. That project had its beginnings under General in Chief Henry Halleck in 1863 and was not completed until the final volumes appeared in 1901, and an index in 1902.

46. Herodotus, *The Histories*, 390 (7.45–46).

47. Sherman, *Memoirs*, 762–63. With a modicum of self-consciousness, Sherman notices "'Sherman's March to the Sea,' composed by Adjutant S. H. M. Byers of the Fifth Iowa Infantry, when a prisoner in the asylum at Columbia, which had been beautifully written off by a fellow-prisoner, and handed to me in person. This appeared to me so good that I at once sent for By-ers, attached him to my staff, provided him with horse and equipment, and took him as far as Fayetteville, North Carolina, whence he was sent to Washington as bearer of dispatches. . . . I insert the song here for convenient reference and preservation. Byers said that there was an excellent glee-club among the prisoners in Columbia, who used to sing it well, with an audi-ence often of rebel ladies."

48. Royster, *The Destructive War*, 145.

49. Ibid., 89.

50. Moulton argues that this sequence in book 2 is "controlled by an association tech-nique, intensely coordinated by its own coherent movements" (*Similes in the Homeric Poems*, 27; cf. 27–33).

51. Pope, *The Iliad of Homer*, 2.572–85, p. 155.

52. Ibid., on 2.572.

53. This passage in book 2 is thus linked with the similes at the end of book 17 and then the shield of Achilles in book 18 as among the most virtuosic in performance; this undoing of poetry by poetry is crucial to the approach to the shield argued for in chapter 7, below.

54. Moulton, *Similes in the Homeric Poems*, 27–33; Kirk, *Commentary*, 1:162–66.

55. Kirk, *Commentary*, 1:162; on the five similes of book 17 (725–61), see Edwards, *Commentary*, 132–33. This later set of five similes, as disintegrative as the similes of book 2 are constitutive of the army under Agamemnon's renewed leadership, will be treated more fully in chapter 7, below.

56. Pope, *The Iliad of Homer*, book 2; see Mack's comments in the same volume, 7:175.

57. *Iliad* 9.307–429.

58. Martin, *The Language of Heroes*, 80.

59. This repeats a point (which Nestor may have suggested to Odysseus; we can't know) that Odysseus uses in his speech to Achilles: surely his father wanted Peleus to glory in his strength but keep out of trouble by not giving way to anger, and to avoid strife and conflict (9.205). Either Peleus anticipated the quarrel of book 1 in great detail, or this is one more stratagem that backfires.

60. Cf. Hainsworth, *Commentary*, 307–8 (11.790–91 and 792–93): "Nestor moots two possibilities, either Akhilleus will fight personally or he will dispatch Patroklos to the battle as he does in book 16, without any indication being given at this point which, if either, will come to pass. . . . The action of the poem is foreshadowed but partially and ambiguously."

61. All the same, as Ian Johnston has observed (*Ironies of War*, 4), a caveat about this reading is in order. For some who take the orality of the *Iliad* and the implications of oral verse-making seriously, this strategic reading of the significance of the echoing lines 11.792–93 and 15.403–4 crosses the line of what is credible in the interpretation of such poetry; this kind of thinking they find alien to their conception of the poet. See Kirk, *The Songs of Homer*, 351. For an intertextual study of the *Iliad* and *Odyssey* that argues for just such close examinations, see Pucci, *Odysseus Polutropos*.

62. This characterization of Agamemnon and Patroclus is part of a larger pattern throughout the poem, as Carroll Moulton has shown. See his discussion of similes and characterization in *Similes in the Homeric Poems*, 88–116, esp. 103–4: "Personal concern for his own reputation and a defeatist proposal to leave Troy are the subjects of Agamemnon's speech (9.17–28), whereas Patroklos dwells on the general danger, reproaches Achilles for his heartlessness, and requests permission to lead their followers into battle (16.21–45). . . . The repetition of the dark-running spring simile, as well as involving a telling irony of characterization, enforces a structural turning point crucial to the narrative" (a reading generally accepted by Janko, *Commentary*, 315).

63. Marshall, *Men against Fire*, 42.

CHAPTER FOUR

1. Owen, *Story of the Iliad*, 119.

2. Stanley, *The Shield of Homer*, 96.

3. Paz, "The Poetic Revelation," in *The Bow and the Lyre*, 137.

4. O'Brien, *Alexander the Great*, 21.

5. Morris, "Homer and Iron Age," esp. 536.

6. Linenthal, *Sacred Ground*, 3.

7. In his "archaeology" of early Greece, Thucydides warns of the unreliability of landscape as a witness to history in *The Peloponnesian War*; Agamemnon's Mycenae would seem too small a place from which a Trojan War could be launched, while the grand appearance of Athens and its monuments would lead later observers to think the city's power was twice what it actually was (1.10).

8. See Blatt, Brown, and Yacovone, *Hope and Glory.*

9. Oates, *A Woman of Valor,* 176.

10. Ibid., 186.

11. Moore, *The Low Country Engineers,* 33.

12. Ibid., 31–39, esp. 31.

13. Hughes, *American Visions,* 209–10.

14. Lowell read his poem in June 1960 to an enthusiastic audience of thousands of people gathered in the Boston Public Garden (Mariani, *Lost Puritan,* 283).

15. Tate, *Collected Poems,* 22–23.

16. In the opinion of Philip Hobsbaum, the fusion does not work because of "insufficient energy" (*Reader's Guide to Lowell,* 126–27).

17. Ibid., 127.

18. Vendler, "Art, Heroism, and Poetry," esp. 204.

19. Ibid., 207.

CHAPTER FIVE

1. For the psychology of the berserker, see Shay, *Achilles in Vietnam,* 77–99.

2. A recent example of this familiar point can be seen in the World War II epic *Saving Private Ryan,* where a German soldier locked in a death struggle with a Jewish American soldier gradually seduces him into relaxing his resistance to a knife at his throat with whispered reassurances, maintaining eye contact all the while. The knife slowly sinks in, and with a last twist of the blade the *Liebestod* is abruptly over, the American dead, and the German running back into the battle.

3. See Merkle, "Telling the True Story." For other strands in this tradition, see King, *Achilles.*

4. See Gray, *The Warriors,* 59–94 ("Love: War's Ally and Foe").

5. For "the striking antipathy towards effeminacy which characterizes some military organizations," see Dixon, *Psychology of Military Incompetence,* 208–13 ("Anti-effeminacy").

6. Ninh, *The Sorrow of War,* 123–24.

7. Aristophanes, *Lysistrata,* trans. Parker, 41. The archaic English of "Ye menne must husband ye warre" is Parker's inspired way of conveying the "antiquity" of Homer's "The men must see to the fighting," without a footnote. For a literal version of the same scene, see Aristophanes, *Lysistrata,* trans. Halliwell, 112–14.

8. See "Disorderly Conduct" (in chapter 8, below), for an example of the way Vietnamese ideas about nationhood and victory and defeat are invested in a misogynistic portrait of a faithful but money-obsessed wife, in Nguyen Huy Thiep's story "The General Retires."

9. Du, *The Tale of Kieu,* 27, ll. 485–96.

10. For an equally can-do woman, see Phoung's counterpart, the American Mary Anne who follows her high-school sweetheart to Vietnam, in Tim O'Brien's story "The Sweetheart of the Song Tra Bong" (*The Things They Carried,* 99–126).

11. The murder of Astyanax and Priam is the subject of the Brygos painter's vase, discussed in chapter 8 below.

12. Redfield, *Nature and Culture,* xi.

13. Janko, *Commentary,* 307, on 15.741.

14. "The Song of a Soldier's Wife," in Thong, *Heritage of Vietnamese Poetry,* 157–69, ll. 21–24, 91–96, 116–21. Dang Tran Con (1710–45) wrote in classical Chinese in the 1740s when Vietnam was in the middle of one of its many wars against its Chinese rulers. The verse trans-

lation into Vietnamese of Phan Huy Ich (1750–1822) is the most popular and the basis for this English translation (Thong, *Heritage of Vietnamese Poetry*, 259–60).

15. Stein, *Wars I Have Seen*, 52–53.

16. Wolf, "Conditions of a Narrative," in *Cassandra*, 236.

17. Wolf, *Cassandra*, 74.

18. Ibid., 43.

19. Thomas, *Under Storm's Wing*, 106–7.

20. Ibid., 172–73.

21. Cf. Janko, *Commentary*, 313–14. Until he begins to draw himself into the battle, Patroclus's chief trait is this discreet silence; then the least talkative of the heroes becomes among the most eloquent, both in his words and especially in his actions (Scheliha, *Patroklos*, 282).

22. Typical also is the separation of physical love (Briseis and other concubines) from emotional commitment (their love for one another); cf. Dinnerstein, *Mermaid and Minotaur*, 67:

> Men try to handle this danger with the many kinds of sex-segregating institutions that they seem always and everywhere driven to create. Secret societies, hunting trips, pool parlors, wars—all of these provide men with sanctuary from the impact of women, with refuges in which they can recuperate from the temptation to give way to ferocious, voracious dependence, and recover their feelings of competence, autonomy, dignity.
>
> But they need other safeguards too. Short of avoiding women altogether, the best safeguard is to renounce the opportunity for deep feeling inherent in heterosexual love. One way to do this is to keep heterosexual love superficial, emotionally and physically. Another is to dissociate its physical from its emotional possibilities.

This describes precisely the relationship Achilles and Patroclus have with the slave women who serve them, including Briseis, whose appropriation by Agamemnon so enrages Achilles.

23. Halperin, *One Hundred Years of Homosexuality* ("Heroes and Their Pals").

24. Phoenix's telling of this myth reflects his sensitivity to his audience; he is not simply purveying some mythical variant on behalf of the poet. See Edmunds, "Myth in Homer," esp. 428.

25. Caputo, *A Rumor of War*, 212–13.

26. Something did go on in later poetry. A fragment of Aeschylus's lost tragedy *The Myrmidons* (the men Achilles commands at Troy) has been much clutched at for the earliest evidence of an erotic bond between Patroclus and Achilles: "And you felt no compunction for my pure reverence for your thighs—O, what an ill return you have made for so many kisses!" (quoted in Dover, *Greek Homosexuality*, 197).

27. *Eu de su oistha . . . hoios ekeinos* (11.653), literally, "For you know well . . . what sort of man that one is," a phrase that earns the only italicized word in Lattimore's translation; italics appear quite frequently in Fagles's.

28. Nelson, *Boy Who Picked the Bullets Up*, 188–90.

29. Lawrence, *Seven Pillars of Wisdom*, 30. For a more sympathetic assessment of Lawrence as commander, see Dixon, *Psychology of Military Incompetence*, 337–40, esp. 338: "In personality, Lawrence is probably the least authoritarian senior commander the world has ever known."

30. Cf. Hoare, *Oscar Wilde's Last Stand*, 191–226.

31. Newby, *Love and War*, 38.

32. Katz, *Love Stories* ("Searching for Words").

33. Billany and Dowie, *The Cage*, 184–85.

34. Ibid., 189.

35. Ibid., 189–90.

36. Gray, *The Warriors*, 94.

CHAPTER SIX

1. Scarry, *The Body in Pain*, 122–23.

2. This ratio was not too high for some of Homer's followers in the epic tradition; the Romans Lucan and Statius, for example, who wrote under the emperors Nero and Domitian, each try to outdo Homer in the ingenuity of their battle scenes. Some of the most innovative recent work in classics has been on these once unfashionable epics. Exemplary critics include Henderson, "Lucan"; and Feeney, *The Gods in Epic*, 337–91 (on Statius's *Thebaid*). As yet another, Shadi Bartsch, observes, Jonathan Shay might well have grounded his studies in combat trauma and the undoing of character (*Achilles in Vietnam*) in the world of Lucan's heroes and anti-heroes (*Ideology in Cold Blood*, 44–45).

3. See Martin, *Language of Heroes* ("Heroes as Performers").

4. For this interplay of the poet and his hero, see Janko, *Commentary*, 404 (on 16.745–50).

5. Cf. Linderman, *World within War*, 278: "James Jones was inclined to believe in the virtual hegemony of sexual feelings: 'Could it be that all war was basically sexual? Not just in psych[ological] theory, but in fact, actually and emotionally? [Was war a] sort of sexual perversion? Or a complex of perversions?' If so, was there an 'an almost sexual ecstasy' in comradeship?" (citing Jones, *The Thin Red Line*, 277).

6. "Essay on Homer's Battles," in Pope, *The Iliad of Homer*, 252–62. Murrin's *History and Warfare* shows why battle scenes would come to be so unpopular with readers, even of Homer.

7. Keegan, *The Face of Battle*, 73–74; at the same time, he allows that "the treatment of battle in fiction is a subject almost untouched by literary critics, but one which the military historian, with his specialized ability to check for veracity and probability, might very well think of tackling" (76).

8. Ibid., 77.

9. Fussell, *Wartime*, 287.

10. Ibid., 287–88.

11. See Roeder, *The Censored War*.

12. Woolf, *Mrs. Dalloway*, 132.

13. Ibid., 133–34.

14. Ibid., 163.

15. See the discussion of 4.141–47 in chapter 2, above ("The Compression of Opposites").

16. The entire sequence of Pandarus's final battle is in 4.166–296.

17. *Ovid's Metamorphoses*, 292–93.

18. Cf. Friedrich's study of wounding and death in the *Iliad*, *Verwundung und Tod*, e.g., "Scheinrealismus" (Fake realism), 43–51; "Niederer Realismus" (Lower realism), 52–63; "Phantastik im Kleide der Genauigkeit" (The fantastic in the guise of exactitude), 43; "Der Eindruck anatomischer Sachkunde" (The impression of anatomical expertise), 44; "Der strenger Stil" (The austere style), 64–83.

19. Grossman, *On Killing*, 59.

20. Kernan, *Crossing the Line*, 45.

21. Hynes, *Flights of Passage*, 75.

22. Ibid., 206.

23. Bendiner, *The Fall of Fortresses*, 138.

24. Ibid., 145.

25. Ibid., 143–44.

26. Logue, *War Music*, 32–33. The parallel between Patroclus's death and Hector's in

22.361–63 (quoted below) is another touchstone in modern teaching and thinking about the poem; see Janko, *Commentary*, 16.855–57, pp. 420–21.

27. Barker, *The Ghost Road*, 273.

28. Kernan, *Crossing the Line*, 45–46.

29. Paul, *Katyn*, 110–11.

30. Sledge, *With the Old Breed*.

31. Ibid., 92.

32. Ibid., 142–43.

33. Ibid., 148.

34. E.g., Philip Hofer's comments on nos. 37 and 39 in the series in Goya, *The Disasters of War*. "No. 37: 'This is worse.' In a dramatic crescendo, previous etchings in the series have depicted scenes of ever-increasing violence, but this horrific image beggars description. The etching, which technically and in the concentrated force of its composition, is one of Goya's finest, probably records an actual event." "No. 39: 'A heroic feat! With dead men!' This etching represents the utmost extreme of human barbarity, underscored by the eloquently sardonic tone of the title. The scene is certainly one of the most harrowing of the series. It is also one of the finest with regard to the treatment of the naked bodies: subtle shading effects are achieved by skillful drypoint additions, a technique used elsewhere in the *Desastres*, but applied here to greater advantage." For a recent assessment of the relationship between viewer and victim in such art, see Wolf, "Onlooker, Witness."

35. Sledge, *With the Old Breed*, 198–99.

36. Ibid., 198.

37. Ibid., 250.

38. See the death scenes in Nuland, *How We Die*; particularly evocative of these deaths in battle is the account of the murder of the young girl Katie Mason by a paranoid schizophrenic (124–28).

CHAPTER SEVEN

1. See Linderman, *World within War*, 235–62 ("The Appeals of Battle: Spectacle, Danger, Destruction").

2. Cf. Edwards, *Commentary*, 133: "The unusual agglomeration of similes is clearly intended to build this scene to a continuing climax while the narrative shifts to Akhilleus. This is different from the purpose of the series before the Catalogue."

3. For further comparisons of the simile groups in books 2 and 17, see ibid., 132–38.

4. Theweleit, *Male Fantasies*, 146.

5. In oral narratives such as this, the more time the poet devotes to an account of a scene or an object, the more significant it becomes. For this axiom in Homeric criticism, see, e.g., Griffin, *Homer on Life and Death*, 1–49 ("Significant Scenes and Significant Objects").

6. Cf. Lincoln, *Death, War, and Sacrifice*, 143: "shields function not only as an important implement of defense in warfare, but as a moveable social border that separates one's self, group, or territory from the enemy."

7. Cf. Lynn-George's discussion of Hephaestus's words to Thetis: "Shield and tomb are constructs situated on either side of death. But within the *Iliad* the distance between shield and tomb as monuments to life and signs of death is significantly reduced. In this art of death-in-life and life-in-death the shield shares the articulation of the epic itself, where, throughout, the narrative which averts the power of death at the same time also asserts it. . . . In its very failure to preserve life the shield signals survival, less for the bearer than as an object which beyond death, will, like the tomb, constitute a wonder for some future beholder" (*Epos*, 189–90).

8. Heffernan, *Museum of Words*, 3.

9. Edwards, *Commentary*, 207.

10. See Becker, *Shield of Achilles*, 1; cf. 87–150 for an extended essay/commentary on the shield informed by a theoretical study of ekphrasis in the modern sense (the description of a work of visual art), rather than the one antiquity would have known (a description of any kind). Cf. Simon, "Der Schild des Achilleus." The standard book on archaeological parallels (none of which actually fits) is Fittschen, *Der Schild des Achilleus*.

11. Bassett, *The Poetry of Homer*, 156–57 (cited in Edwards, *Commentary*, 226–27).

12. Some of the music is unrecoverable no matter what way we know Homer. Like later classical Greek, Homer's language has tones (on the order of tones in modern Chinese or Vietnamese) whose pitch was signaled by a system of accents devised by Alexandrian scholars. In the postclassical period these tones or pitches gradually changed to stress accents, and the precise way they sounded for Homer's audiences remains a matter of much debate.

13. Hammond, *Iliad*, 322.

14. See Lombardo's translation of the *Iliad*, ix–xiv.

15. Fitzgerald, *Iliad*, "Book Eighteen: The Immortal Shield," 453.

16. Steiner, *Homer in English*, 78: "Collaboration with Elijah Fenton and William Broome will weaken Pope's *Odyssey*. But taken together, these two 'Homers' constitute the principal 'epic act' after Milton in the language."

17. See Maynard Mack's brief but suggestive discussion of Pope's translation in relation to his life and work in the introduction to Pope's *Iliad*, 7:cxi–cclix, esp. ccxlviii–ccxlix on "epic posture." Only small changes in style and diction would be needed to shift from the grandiose style deemed appropriate for heroic poetry, to the parody of epic style characteristic of satires such as *The Dunciad*.

18. Lynn-George, *Epos*, 132: "The structure of the shield's stores in space, its images in time, resists the dichotomy of arts of space and arts of time." Cf. Bal, *Reading "Rembrandt,"* 94–137.

19. Prier, *Thauma Idesthai*, 48.

20. This account of the intermingling fires of Achilles and Hephaestus in Homer's poetry draws on Cedric Whitman's reading of the fiery imagery of the shield and later moments in *Homer and the Heroic Tradition*, 128–53; cf. esp. 28–29: "these images do not form a schematic set of deliberate correspondences; they change and shift constantly, according to the demands of the larger scene-image in which they stand, and the consistency which they show is the consistency of the whole design. By association with action and character, they grow into symbols, but like all symbols, they reflect in their unity a Gestalt, or organism of mental pictures and processes which do not correspond to any single concept. Their wording may change, but this basic set of associations, developing slowly throughout the narrated action, reveals the main threads of the poet's concern."

21. On Achilles as Hephaestus's "ideal reader," see Stanley, *The Shield of Homer*, 3–6.

22. Logue, *War Music*, 68–69.

23. Marg, *Homer über die Dichtung*, 28 and n. 44; for a more idealistic picture of Homer's gods, see Schadewaldt, *Von Homers Werk und Welt*, 352–74 ("Der Schild des Achilleus"), esp. 353.

24. Cf. Fussell, *Great War and Modern Memory*, 231: "If the opposite of war is peace, the opposite of experiencing moments of war is proposing moments of pastoral. Since war takes place outdoors and always within nature, its symbolic status is that of the ultimate anti-pastoral. In Northrop Frye's terms, it belongs to the demonic world, and no one engages in it or contemplates it without implicitly or explicitly bringing to bear the contrasting 'model world'

by which its demonism is measured. When H. M. Tomlinson asks, 'What has the rathe prim-rose to do with old rags and bones on barbed wire?' we must answer, 'Everything.'"

25. Thomas, *Under Storm's Wing*, 104–6.

26. For an account of Auden's fashioning of the poem, see Mendelson, *Later Auden*, 375–77.

27. Auden, "The Shield of Achilles," 596.

28. Levi, *The Reawakening*, 8. This is another book by Levi about the Holocaust that, like his first memoir, *If This Is a Man*, seems condemned to perpetually cheerful repackaging for American and English readers. More measured, less optimistic than *The Reawakening* is his Italian title: *La tregua* is literally *The Truce*, or possibly *The Respite* or *The Remission*, as in a momentary "truce" when one is suffering from a terminal disease.

29. In a classic article on the Song of Ares and Aphrodite in the *Odyssey* ("Das Lied von Ares und Aphrodite"), Walter Burkert demonstrates how important it is, in assessing any single one of Hephaestus's works as represented in poetry, to take some account of his works that appear elsewhere, for different audiences and different purposes; common themes centering on Olympian politics and mortals' relation to them are never far from anything he creates.

30. Bendiner, *The Fall of Fortresses*, 154.

31. Ibid., 168–69.

32. Ibid., 172.

33. Ibid., 184.

34. Linderman, *World within War*, 241–42.

35. Ibid., 242.

36. Ibid.

37. Now we are accustomed to think that it is possible to wage war against nature itself, and not only through nuclear weapons. See Stevens, *The Trail*, part 3, 125–207 ("The War against Nature"), esp. 125 ("A deliberate war against nature. . . . Once nature dies, man also dies. . . . Soil is more valuable than man. It dies more easily and leaves no successor. Many of the wounds of nature can never be healed. This is, in effect, war waged against the future"); and Sihanouk, *My War against the CIA*, 258–60, and esp. 219 ("America's course was set for Viet Nam when the New World was discovered").

38. Rhodes, *Making of the Atomic Bomb*, 725.

39. Osada, *Children of the A-Bomb*, 178.

40. Trumbull, *Nine Who Survived*, 76.

41. Ibid., 219; all texts quoted here are from Rhodes, *Making of the Atomic Bomb*, 725–26.

42. Ibid., 670.

43. Committee for Compilation of Materials, *Hiroshima and Nagasaki*, 119.

44. Rhodes, *Making of the Atomic Bomb*, 714–15, quoting Hachiya, *Hiroshima Diary*, 92.

45. Rhodes, *Making of the Atomic Bomb*, 746.

CHAPTER EIGHT

1. Cf. Blainey, "A Day That Lives in Infamy," in *The Causes of War*, 159: "The leap from peace to war is usually seen as the most revealing event in the fluctuating relations between nations. The leap from war to peace is equally revealing."

2. See "An Epilogue on Epilogues" in Hynes, *The Soldiers' Tale*, 279–85.

3. Endings in narrative have been a popular theme in literary criticism since Frank Kermode's *Sense of an Ending*. Much that Kermode, Peter Brooks (*Reading for the Plot*), and other critics have written about endings is most illuminating about the design of the *Iliad*, even though none of them mentions it.

4. Benjamin, *Illuminations*, 94. This argument is repeatedly invoked by Peter Brooks in *Reading for the Plot* (22, 28, 95, 103).

5. See Huizinga, *Homo Ludens*, 89–104 ("Play and War").

6. *Iliad* 1.225, 231 (Fagles). Other translators play with this rant, too, ranging from the John Wayne–style invective of Lombardo ("You bloated drunk, / With a dog's eyes and a rabbit's heart," "bleeding your people dry"), to John Chapman's splendid Elizabethan English: "Thou ever steep't in wine, Dog's face, with heart but of a Hart," "Thou subject-eating King."

7. Strachey, *Unconscious Motives of War*, 142: "Mourning doesn't solve a reality problem, but an internal one, of guilt." For a sustained reading of the Achilles case by a classicist and psychoanalytic critic, see MacCary, *Childlike Achilles.*

8. In this way the funeral rites of book 23 intensify rather than dispel what Achilles feels. Killing Hector and sacrificing a dozen Trojan captives is a nice example of the end stages of the psychoanalytic theory that war is a "paranoid elaboration of mourning"; cf. Fornari, *The Psychoanalysis of War*, xviii: "The experience of mourning . . . becomes not sorrow for the death of a loved person, but the killing of the enemy who is falsely thought to be the destroyer of the loved object."

9. Cf. Pietro Pucci's analysis of the laments of Briseis and Achilles in *Iliad* 19.282–339: "Briseis recalls the real death of her husband and brothers and symbolically mimes her own death by disfiguring and staining with blood her face, neck and breast. Achilles, in an ascetic fasting that mimes death, evokes the imagined death of his father and son and mentions his close real death. He is therefore lamenting from the posture more radically marginal and suspended from all human connections, that of this community with death. The readers are better able to perceive in this extreme posture also the signs that point to Achilles' marginal position in the earlier parts of the poem, his relative detachment from the political allegiance, his commitment to *kleos* rather than *timē*, his unique leaning to private attachments (Patroclus, Phoenix, Briseis), and his display of unchecked emotions. It is then not a mere chance that the greatest hero mourns over his comrade in an antiphonal lament with his slave and concubine" ("Antiphonal Lament," 272). Nor, we could add, that he then mourns also with the father of the man who killed his friend.

10. Such public ceremonies were from the beginning highly formalized rituals organized in a community, and these rituals endure in often essentially the same form into the Byzantine Christian era and the present. After that public ritual, what Achilles suffers alone is, strictly speaking, his own business. See Alexiou, *Ritual Lament*, especially the index of motifs and images on pp. 271–74.

11. Monsacré, *Les larmes d'Achilles*, 137–42 ("Les pleurs dans l'espace héroique de l'*Iliade*").

12. Cf. Kirk and Raven, *The Presocratic Philosophers*, 195: "War is the father of all and king of all, and some he shows as gods, others as men; some he makes slaves, others free" (Heraclitus, fr. 53).

13. Stein, *Everybody's Autobiography*, 137; cf. Abraham, *Are Girls Necessary?* 94–95.

14. In contemporary usage, the right term to describe what Achilles feels may be *compassion* rather than *pity*. See Nussbaum, *Upheavals of Thought*, 301–2.

15. As Charles Segal observes, this is a finely balanced moment in the *Iliad* that should not be mistaken for a pacifist turn: "Although the resolution of the corpse scene is now in sight, Hecuba's outburst is a reminder that the savagery released by the war still lingers and can flare up again despite the compassionate and conciliatory purposes of Zeus. Homer remains a realist to the end" (*Theme of Mutilation*, 62).

16. Bersani, "The Gay Outlaw," 155.

17. Genet, *Funeral Rites*, 124.

18. Bersani, "The Gay Outlaw," 177.

19. Genet, *Funeral Rites*, 181–82.

20. Cf. Bersani, "The Gay Outlaw," 180 (quoting a passage that does not appear in Frechtman's translation): "The poet . . . is interested in error since only error teaches truth. . . . Poetry or the art of using remains (*La poésie ou l'art d'utiliser le restes*). These errors may serve, or be, the beauty of the future" (*Pompes funèbres*, 190).

21. Genet, *Funeral Rites*, 162–63.

22. Balzac, *Le Colonel Chabert*, 21–23.

23. Brooks, *Reading for the Plot*, 226.

24. Woolf, *Mrs. Dalloway*, 63–64.

25. Thiep, "The General Retires," 122.

26. As many commentators also note, the brief commands of Priam, ordering the Trojans to prepare for Hector's funeral pyre and burial, return us to the opening of the *Iliad*, and another father and child: the priest of Apollo Chryses, asking Agamemnon to return his daughter Chryseis (1.17–21, 24.778–81).

27. David Goodman terms "Long, Long Autumn Nights" an "epic poem" in his well-documented translation; his introduction is still virtually the only critical essay on Oguma's work that I have found in English. See Oguma, *Long, Long Autumn Nights*, 1–21. Readers of Homer might get their hopes up at the term "epic," but it is a slightly misleading term for a poem of roughly four hundred lines. Dennis Washburn informs me that Oguma's work is a hybrid combining elements of Western modernist practices with an earlier Japanese tradition of war poetry and narration (for example, *The Tale of the Heike*, a long narrative poem from the thirteenth to fourteenth centuries C.E. that evolved out of a long oral and musical tradition that might be broadly compared to the oral tradition of Homeric poetry). Oguma's political beliefs were quite dangerous to hold in the 1930s and 1940s, as Goodman observes. As for his place in Japanese poetry more generally, Washburn writes, "It is not only safe to say that his treatment of Koreans and Chinese was exceptional; he has had little company since the war. Only Korean-Japanese writers ever really deal with these issues in detail, though Oe Kenzaburo has been politically active in issues dealing with human rights and reparations toward China and Korea" (e-mail communication).

28. Goodman, introduction to Oguma, *Long, Long Autumn Nights*, 17.

29. Weil, *The Poem of Force*, 4.

30. "Long, Long Autumn Nights" translates *Changjang Ch'uya*; cf. Goodman, introduction, 17.

BIBLIOGRAPHY

Abraham, Julie. *Are Girls Necessary? Lesbian Writing and Modern Histories.* New York: Routledge, 1996.

Alexiou, Margaret. *The Ritual Lament in Greek Tradition.* Cambridge: Cambridge University Press, 1974.

Annual Report of the Chief of Engineers to the Secretary of War for the Year 1878. Part 1. Washington, D.C.: Government Printing Office, 1878.

Aristophanes. *Birds, Lysistrata, Assembly-Women, Wealth.* Trans. Stephen Halliwell. Oxford: Clarendon Press, 1997.

————. *Lysistrata.* Trans. Douglass Parker. In *Aristophanes: Four Comedies,* ed. William Arrowsmith. Ann Arbor: University of Michigan Press, 1983.

Aristotle. *The Poetics of Aristotle.* Trans. Stephen Halliwell. Chapel Hill: University of North Carolina Press, 1987.

Arnold, Matthew. *On Translating Homer.* London: Longmans, Green, Longman, and Roberts, 1861.

Athanassakis, Apostolos, trans. *Hesiod: Theogony, Works and Days, Shield.* Baltimore: Johns Hopkins University Press, 1983.

Auden, W. H. "The Shield of Achilles." In *Collected Poems,* ed. Edward Mendelson. New York: Vintage, 1991.

Austin, Norman. *Helen of Troy and Her Shameless Phantom.* Ithaca, N.Y.: Cornell University Press, 1994.

Bal, Mieke. *Reading "Rembrandt": Beyond the Word-Image Opposition.* Cambridge: Cambridge University Press, 1991.

Balzac, Honoré de. *Le Colonel Chabert.* Ed. Pierre Citron. Paris: Marcel Dider, 1961.

Barker, Pat. *The Ghost Road.* New York: Penguin, 1995.

Bartsch, Shadi. *Ideology in Cold Blood: A Reading of Lucan's "Civil War."* Cambridge, Mass.: Harvard University Press, 1997.

Bassett, S. E. *The Poetry of Homer.* Berkeley: University of California Press, 1938.

Bauman, Zygmunt. *Modernity and the Holocaust.* Ithaca, N.Y.: Cornell University Press, 1989.

Becker, Andrew Sprague. *The Shield of Achilles and the Poetics of Ekphrasis.* Lanham, Md.: Rowman and Littlefield, 1995.

Bendiner, Elmer. *The Fall of Fortresses: A Personal Account of the Most Daring, and Deadly, American Air Battles of World War II.* New York: Putnam, 1980.

Benjamin, Walter. *Illuminations*. Ed. Hannah Arendt. Trans. Harry Zohn. New York: Schocken, 1968.

Bersani, Leo. "The Gay Outlaw." In *Homos*. Cambridge, Mass.: Harvard University Press, 1995.

Billany, Dan, and David Dowie. *The Cage*. London: Longmans, Green, 1949.

Blainey, Geoffrey. *The Causes of War*. New York: Free Press, 1988.

Blatt, Martin H., Thomas J. Brown, and Donald Yacovone, eds. *Hope and Glory: Essays on the Legacy of the Fifty-fourth Massachusetts Regiment*. Amherst: University of Massachusetts Press, 2001.

Blundell, Mary Whitlock, and Kirk Ormand. "Western Values, or the People's Homer: *Unforgiven* as a Reading of the *Iliad*." *Poetics Today* 18, no. 4 (1997): 533–69.

Bond, Edward. "Notes on Imagination." In *Coffee*. London: Methuen, 1995.

Bornstein, George. "Afro-Celtic Connections: From Frederick Douglass to *The Commitments*." In *Literary Influence and African-American Writers: Collected Essays*, ed. Tracy Mishkin. New York: Garland Press, 1996.

Brooks, Peter. *Reading for the Plot: Design and Intention in Narrative*. Cambridge, Mass.: Harvard University Press, 1984.

Brown, Christopher G. "Ares, Aphrodite, and the Laughter of the Gods." *Phoenix* 43 (1989): 283–93.

Burkert, Walter. "Das Lied von Ares und Aphrodite." *Rheinisches Museum*, n.f. 103 (1960): 130–44.

Calasso, Roberto. *The Marriage of Cadmus and Harmony*. Trans. Tim Parks. New York: Knopf, 1993.

Canetti, Elias. "The Arch of Triumph." In *The Conscience of Words*. New York: Seabury Press, 1979.

Caputo, Philip. *A Rumor of War*. New York: Ballantine, 1977.

Carson, Anne. *Economy of the Unlost (Reading Simonides of Keos with Paul Celan)*. Princeton, N.J.: Princeton University Press, 1999.

Clausewitz, Carl von. *On War*. Trans. and ed. Michael Howard and Peter Paret. Princeton, N.J.: Princeton University Press, 1984.

Committee for the Compilation of Materials on Damage Caused by the Atomic Bombs in Hiroshima and Nagasaki. *Hiroshima and Nagasaki: The Physical, Medical, and Social Effects of the Atomic Bombings*. Trans. Eisei Ishikawa and David L. Swain. New York: Basic Books, 1981.

Crane, Stephen. *The Red Badge of Courage: An Episode of the American Civil War*. Ed. Henry Binder. New York: W. W. Norton, 1982.

Davis, Linda H. *Badge of Courage: The Life of Stephen Crane*. New York: Houghton Mifflin, 1998.

de Gaulle, Charles. *Mémoires de guerre: L'appel 1940–1942*. Paris: Libraire Plon, 1954. Translated as *War Memoirs* by Jonathan Griffin, vol. 1 (London: Collins, 1955).

Denby, David. *Great Books: My Adventures with Homer, Rousseau, Woolf, and Other Indestructible Writers of the Western World*. New York: Simon and Schuster, 1997.

Dinnerstein, Dorothy. *The Mermaid and the Minotaur: Sexual Arrangements and Human Malaise*. New York: Other Press, 1971.

Dixon, Norman. *On the Psychology of Military Incompetence*. London: Random House, 1994.

Doody, Margaret Anne. *The True Story of the Novel*. New Brunswick, N.J.: Rutgers University Press, 1996.

Dover, Kenneth. *Greek Homosexuality*. Cambridge, Mass.: Harvard University Press, 1978.

Du, Nguyen. *The Tale of Kieu*. Trans. Huynh Sanh Thong. New Haven, Conn.: Yale University Press, 1983.

Dyer, Geoff. *The Missing of the Somme*. London: Penguin, 1995.

Edmunds, Lowell. "Myth in Homer." In *A New Companion to Homer,* ed. Ian Morris and Barry Powell. Leiden: Brill, 1997.

Edwards, Mark W. *The Iliad: A Commentary.* Ed. Geoffrey S. Kirk. Vol. 5. Cambridge: Cambridge University Press, 1991.

Ehrhart, W. D. "Making the Children Brave." In *Unaccustomed Mercy: Soldier-Poets of the Vietnam War.* Lubbock: Texas Tech University Press, 1989.

Engelhardt, Tom. *The End of Victory Culture: Cold War America and the Disillusioning of a Generation.* New York: Basic Books, 1995.

Fagles, Robert, trans. *Homer: The Iliad.* Introduction and notes by Bernard Knox. New York: Viking Penguin, 1990.

Feeney, Dennis. *The Gods in Epic: Poets and Critics of the Classical Tradition.* Oxford: Clarendon Press, 1991.

Fenik, Bernard. *Typical Battle Scenes in the "Iliad": Studies in the Narrative Technique of Homeric Battle Description.* Wiesbaden: F. Steiner, 1968.

Finley, M. I. *The World of Odysseus.* Rev. ed. London: Chatto and Windus, 1977.

Fittschen, K. *Der Schild des Achilleus.* Göttingen: Archaeologica Homerica, 1973.

Fitzgerald, Robert, trans. *Homer: The Odyssey.* New York: Farrar, Straus and Giroux, 1998.

———. *The Iliad.* Garden City, N.Y.: Doubleday, 1974.

Fogelin, Robert J. *Figuratively Speaking.* New Haven, Conn.: Yale University Press, 1992.

Fornari, Franco. *The Psychoanalysis of War.* Bloomington: Indiana University Press, 1966.

Fränkel, Hermann. *Die homerischen Gleichnisse.* Göttingen: Van der Hoeck und Ruprecht, 1921.

Friedrich, Wolf-Hartmut. *Verwundung und Tod in der Ilias: Homerische Darstellungsweisen.* Göttingen: Van der Hoeck und Ruprecht, 1956.

Fussell, Paul. *The Great War and Modern Memory.* Oxford: Oxford University Press, 1975.

———. *Wartime: Understanding and Behavior in the Second World War.* Oxford: Oxford University Press, 1989.

Genet, Jean. *Pompes funèbres.* Collection Imaginaire. Paris: Gallimard, 1953. Translated as *Funeral Rites* by Bernard Frechtman (London: Faber and Faber, 1973).

Giap, Vo Nguyen, and Van Tien Dung. *How We Won the War.* Ypsilanti, Mich.: Recon Publications, 1976.

Grant, Ulysses S. *Memoirs and Selected Letters: Personal Memoirs of U. S. Grant.* New York: Library of America, 1990.

Graves, Robert, trans. *The Anger of Achilles: Homer's "Iliad."* Garden City, N.Y.: Doubleday, 1959.

Gray, J. Glenn. *The Warriors: Reflections on Men in Battle.* New York: Harper and Row, 1970.

Griffin, Jasper. *Homer on Life and Death.* Oxford: Oxford University Press, 1980.

Griswold, Charles L. "The Vietnam Veterans Memorial and the Washington Mall: Philosophical Thoughts on Political Iconography." *Critical Inquiry* 12 (1986): 688–719.

Grossman, Dave. *On Killing: The Psychological Cost of Learning to Kill in War and Society.* Boston: Little, Brown, 1995.

Hachiya, Michihiko. *Hiroshima Diary.* Chapel Hill: University of North Carolina Press, 1955.

Hainsworth, Bryan. *The Iliad: A Commentary.* Ed. Geoffrey S. Kirk. Vol. 3. Cambridge: Cambridge University Press, 1993.

Halberstam, David. *The Best and the Brightest.* New York: Penguin, 1983.

Halperin, David M. *One Hundred Years of Homosexuality and Other Essays on Greek Love.* New York: Routledge, 1990.

Hammond, Martin, trans. *The Iliad: Homer.* Harmondsworth: Penguin, 1987.

Havelock, Eric A. *War as a Way of Life in Classical Culture.* Ottawa: Editions de l'Université d'Ottawa, 1972.

Heffernan, James A. W. *Museum of Words: The Poetics of Ekphrasis from Homer to Ashbery.* Chicago: University of Chicago Press, 1993.

Heller, Joseph. *Catch-22.* New York: Simon and Schuster, 1961.

Henderson, John. "Lucan/The World at War." In *The Imperial Muse: Ramus Essays on Roman Literature of the Empire,* vol. 1, *To Juvenal through Ovid,* ed. A. J. Boyle. Victoria, B.C.: Verwick, 1988.

Herodotus. *The Histories.* Trans. Aubrey De Séincourt, rev. by John Marincola. London: Penguin, 1996.

Herr, Michael. *Dispatches.* New York: Avon Books, 1980.

Hesiod. *Works and Days and Theogony.* Trans. Stanley Lombardo. Indianapolis: Hackett, 1993.

Hoare, Philip. *Oscar Wilde's Last Stand: Decadence, Conspiracy, and the Most Outrageous Trial of the Century.* New York: Arcade, 1997.

Hobsbaum, Philip. *A Reader's Guide to Robert Lowell.* London: Thames and Hudson, 1988.

Hofer, Philip. Introduction to *The Disasters of War,* by Francisco Goya. New York: Dover, 1967.

Howard, Michael. *Clausewitz.* Oxford: Oxford University Press, 1983.

Hughes, Robert. *American Visions: The Epic History of Art in America.* New York: Knopf, 1997.

Huizinga, J. *Homo Ludens: A Study of the Play-Element in Culture.* Boston: Beacon Press, 1955.

Hynes, Samuel. *Flights of Passage: Reflections of a World War II Aviator.* New York: F. C. Beil, Annapolis: Naval Institute Press, 1988.

————. "Personal Narratives and Commemoration." In *War and Remembrance in the Twentieth Century,* ed. Jay Winter and Emmanuel Sivan. Cambridge: Cambridge University Press, 1999.

————. *The Soldiers' Tale: Bearing Witness to Modern War.* New York: Allen Lane, 1994.

Janko, Richard. *The Iliad: A Commentary.* Ed. Geoffrey S. Kirk. Vol. 4. Cambridge: Cambridge University Press, 1984.

Jarrell, Randall. "The Range in the Desert." In *Poetry of the World Wars,* ed. Michael Foss. New York: Peter Bedrick Books, 1990.

————. *Selected Poems.* New York: Knopf, 1955.

Johnston, Ian C. *The Ironies of War: An Introduction to Homer's "Iliad."* Lanham, Md.: University Press of America, 1988.

Jones, James. *The Thin Red Line.* New York: Charles Scribner's Sons, 1962.

Katz, Jonathan Ned. *Love Stories: Sex between Men before Homosexuality.* Chicago: University of Chicago Press, 2001.

Keegan, John. *The Face of Battle.* Harmondsworth: Penguin, 1978.

————. *The Mask of Command.* New York: Viking, 1987.

Kermode, Frank. *The Sense of an Ending.* Oxford: Oxford University Press, 1967.

Kernan, Alvin. *Crossing the Line: A Bluejacket's World War II Odyssey.* Annapolis, Md.: Naval Institute Press, 1994.

al-Khalil, Samir. *The Monument: Art, Vulgarity, and Responsibility in Iraq.* Berkeley and Los Angeles: University of California Press, 1991.

Killens, John Oliver. *And Then We Heard the Thunder.* Washington, D.C.: Howard University Press, 1983.

King, Katherine C. *Achilles: Paradigms of the War Hero from Homer to the Middle Ages.* Berkeley and Los Angeles: University of California Press, 1987.

Kirk, Geoffrey S. *The Songs of Homer.* Cambridge: Cambridge University Press, 1962.

————, ed. *The Iliad: A Commentary.* 6 vols. Cambridge: Cambridge University Press, 1984–93.

Kirk, Geoffrey S., and J. E. Raven. *The Presocratic Philosophers: A Critical History with a Selection of Texts.* Cambridge: Cambridge University Press, 1963.

Lakoff, George, and Mark Johnson. *Metaphors We Live By.* Chicago: University of Chicago Press, 1980.

Larkin, Philip. Review of *The Collected Poems of Wilfred Owen.* London, 1963. Quoted in Andrew Motion, *The Poetry of Edward Thomas* (London: Routledge and Kegan Paul, 1980), 134–35.

Latacz, Joachim. *Homer, His Art, and His World.* Trans. James P. Holoka. Ann Arbor: University of Michigan Press, 1996.

Lattimore, Richmond, trans. *The Iliad.* Chicago: University of Chicago Press, 1951.

Lawrence, T. E. *Seven Pillars of Wisdom: A Triumph.* New York: Doubleday, 1935.

Lepore, Jill. *The Name of War: King Philip's War and the Origins of American Identity.* New York: Vintage, 1998.

Lessing, Doris. *Prisons We Choose to Live Inside.* New York: Harper and Row, 1987.

Lessing, Gotthold Ephraim. *Laocoön: An Essay on the Limits of Painting and Poetry.* Trans. Edward Allen McCormick. Baltimore: Johns Hopkins University Press, 1984.

Levi, Primo. *The Reawakening.* Trans. Stuart Woolf. New York: Collier, Macmillan, 1965.

———. *Survival in Auschwitz* [*If This Is a Man*]. New York: Collier, Macmillan, 1993.

Liddell-Hart, Basil H. *History of the World War, 1914–1918.* London: Faber and Faber, 1934.

———. *The Real War, 1914–1918.* Boston: Little, Brown, 1930.

Lin, Maya Ying. *Boundaries.* New York: Simon and Schuster, 2000.

Lincoln, Bruce. *Death, War, and Sacrifice: Studies in Ideology and Practice.* Chicago: University of Chicago Press, 1991.

Linderman, Gerald F. *The World within War: America's Combat Experience in World War II.* New York: Free Press, 1997.

Linenthal, Edward Tabor. *Sacred Ground: Americans and Their Battlefields.* Urbana: University of Illinois Press, 1991.

Logue, Christopher. *Kings: An Account of Books 1 and 2 of Homer's "Iliad."* New York: Farrar, Straus and Giroux, 1991.

———. *War Music: An Account of Books 16 to 19 of Homer's "Iliad."* New York: Farrar, Straus, and Giroux, 1981.

Lombardo, Stanley, trans. *Iliad.* Indianapolis: Hackett, 1997.

Lynn-George, Michael. *Epos: Word, Narrative, and the "Iliad."* Atlantic Highlands, N.J.: Humanities Press International, 1988.

MacCary, W. Thomas. *Childlike Achilles: Ontogeny and Phylogeny in the "Iliad."* New York: Columbia University Press, 1982.

Macleod, C. W. *Homer: Iliad, Book 24.* Cambridge: Cambridge University Press, 1982.

Manning, Frederic. *The Middle Parts of Fortune: Somme and Acre, 1916.* New York: St. Martin's, 1977.

Marg, Walter. *Homer über die Dichtung: Der Schild des Akhilleus.* 2d ed. Münster: Aschendorf, 1971.

Mariani, Paul. *Lost Puritan: A Life of Robert Lowell.* New York: Norton, 1994.

Marshall, S. L. A. *Men against Fire: The Problem of Battle Command in Future War.* New York: William Morrow, 1947.

Martin, Richard P. *The Language of Heroes: Speech and Performance in the "Iliad."* Ithaca, N.Y.: Cornell University Press, 1989.

Mauldin, Bill. *Up Front.* Cleveland: World, 1945.

McNamara, Robert S., and Brian Van De Mark. *In Retrospect: The Tragedy and Lessons of Vietnam.* New York: Times Books, 1997.

Mendelson, Edward. *Later Auden.* New York: Farrar, Straus and Giroux, 1999.

Merkle, Stefan. "Telling the True Story of the Trojan War: The Eyewitness Account of Dictys of Crete." In *The Search for the Ancient Novel,* ed James Tatum. Baltimore: Johns Hopkins University Press, 1994.

Mishkin, Tracy. *The Harlem and Irish Renaissances: Language, Identity, and Representation*. Gainesville: University Press of Florida, 1998.

Mitford, Jessica. *The American Way of Death Revisited*. New York: Knopf, 1998.

Monsacré, Hélène. *Les larmes d'Achilles: Le héros, la femme et la souffrance dans la poésie d' Homère*. Paris: Albin Michele, 1984.

Moore, James W. *The Low Country Engineers*. Charleston, S.C.: U.S. Army Corps of Engineers, 1981.

Morris, Ian. "Homer and the Iron Age." In *A New Companion to Homer*, ed. Ian Morris and Barry Powell. Leiden: Brill, 1997.

Morris, Ian, and Barry Powell, eds. *A New Companion to Homer*. Leiden: Brill, 1997.

Mosse, George. "The Process of Trivialization." In *Fallen Soldiers: Reshaping the Memory of the World Wars*. Oxford: Oxford University Press, 1990.

Moulton, Carroll G. "Homeric Metaphor." *Classical Philology* 74 (1979): 290–92.

———. *Similes in the Homeric Poems*. Göttingen: Hypomnemata 49, 1977.

Muellner, Leonard C. *The Anger of Achilles: Mēnis in Greek Epic*. Ithaca, N.Y.: Cornell University Press, 1996.

Murrin, Michael. *History and Warfare in Renaissance Epic*. Chicago: University of Chicago Press, 1994.

Nagy, Gregory. *Best of the Achaeans: Concepts of the Hero in Archaic Greek Poetry*. Rev. ed. Baltimore: Johns Hopkins University Press, 1999.

Nehamas, Alexander. *The Art of Living: Socratic Reflections form Plato to Foucault*. Berkeley and Los Angeles: University of California Press, 1998.

Nelson, Charles. *The Boy Who Picked the Bullets Up*. New York: Meadowland, 1990.

Newby, Eric. *Love and War in the Apennines*. London: Picador, 1983.

Ninh, Bao. *The Sorrow of War*. Trans. Frank Palmos. London: Secker and Warburg, 1993.

Norris, Frank. "The Green Stone of Unrest." In Stephen Crane, *The Red Badge of Courage*, ed. Sculley Bradley et al. New York: W. W. Norton, 1976.

Nuland, Sheldon. *How We Die: Reflections on Life's Final Chapter*. New York: Knopf, 1994.

Nussbaum, Martha C. *Upheavals of Thought: The Intelligence of Emotions*. Cambridge: Cambridge University Press, 2001.

Oates, Stephen B. *A Woman of Valor: Clara Barton and the Civil War*. New York: Free Press, 1994.

O'Brien, John Maxwell. *Alexander the Great: The Invisible Enemy*. New York: Routledge, 1992.

O'Brien, Tim. *The Things They Carried*. Boston: Houghton Mifflin, 1990.

Oguma Hideo. *Long, Long Autumn Nights: Selected Poems of Oguma Hideo, 1901–1940*. Trans. David G. Goodman. Ann Arbor: University of Michigan Press, 1999.

Osada, Arata. *Children of the A-Bomb: The Testament of the Boys and Girls of Hiroshima*. Trans. Jean Dan and Ruth Sieben-Morgen. New York: G. P. Putnam's Sons, 1959.

Ovid. *Ovid's Metamorphoses*. Trans. Rolfe Humphries. Bloomington: Indiana University Press, 1955.

Owen, E. T. *The Story of the Iliad: As Told in the Iliad*. Toronto: University of Toronto Press, 1946.

Paul, Allen. *Katyn: The Untold Story of Stalin's Polish Massacre*. New York: C. Scribner's, 1991.

Paz, Octavio. *The Bow and the Lyre*. Trans. Ruth L. C. Simms. Austin: University of Texas Press, 1973.

———. *The Labyrinth of Solitude: Life and Thought in Mexico*. Trans. Lysander Kemp. New York: Grove Press, 1961. Quoted in Susan N. Masuoka, *En Calavera: The Papier-Mâché Art of the Linares Family* (Los Angeles: UCLA Fowler Museum of Cultural History, 1994), 57–58.

Pease, Donald. "Fear, Rage, and the Mistrials of Representation." In *The Red Badge of Courage:*

American Realism: New Essays, ed. Eric J. Sundquist. Baltimore: Johns Hopkins University Press, 1982.

Pope, Alexander, trans. *The Iliad of Homer*. Ed. Maynard Mack. In *Poems*, general editor, John Butt, vols. 7–8. New Haven, Conn.: Yale University Press, 1967.

Porter, Horace. *Campaigning with Grant*. New York: Century Company, 1897.

Power, John W. *War without Mercy: Race and Power in the Pacific War*. New York: Pantheon Books, 1986.

Prier, Raymond Adolph. *Thauma Idesthai: The Phenomenology of Sight and Appearance in Archaic Greek*. Tallahassee: University of Florida Press, 1989.

Proust, Marcel. *Remembrance of Things Past*. Trans. C. K. Scott Moncrieff, Terence Kilmartin, and Andreas Mayor. 3 vols. New York: Vintage Books, Random House, 1982.

Pucci, Pietro. "Antiphonal Lament between Achilles and Briseis," *Colby Quarterly* 29, no. 3 (1993): 258–72.

———. *Odysseus Polutropos: Intertextual Readings in the "Odyssey" and the "Iliad."* Ithaca, N.Y.: Cornell University Press, 1987.

Pyle, Ernie. *Brave Men*. New York: Grosset and Dunlap, 1944.

Redfield, James. *Nature and Culture in the "Iliad": The Tragedy of Hector*. Expanded ed. Durham, N.C.: Duke University Press, 1994.

Rhodes, Richard. *The Making of the Atomic Bomb*. New York: Simon and Schuster, 1986.

Roeder, George H. *The Censored War: American Visual Experience during World War Two*. New Haven, Conn.: Yale University Press, 1993.

Rose, Jacqueline. *Why War? Psychoanalysis, Politics, and the Return to Melanie Klein*. Oxford: Blackwell, 1993.

Royster, Charles. *The Destructive War: William Tecumseh Sherman, Stonewall Jackson, and the Americans*. New York: Knopf, 1991.

Scarry, Elaine. *The Body in Pain: The Unmaking and Making of the World*. Oxford: Oxford University Press, 1985.

Schadewaldt, Wolfgang. *Von Homers Werk und Welt*. 4th ed. Stuttgart: Koehler Verlag, 1965.

Schein, Seth L. *The Mortal Hero: An Introduction to Homer's Iliad*. Berkeley and Los Angeles: University of California Press, 1984.

Scheliha, Renata von. *Patroklos: Gedanken über Homers Dichtung und Gestalten*. Basel: Benno Schwabe, 1943.

Schulte, Rainer, and John Biguenet, eds. *Theories of Translation: An Anthology of Essays from Dryden to Derrida*. Chicago: University of Chicago Press, 1992.

Scully, Vincent. "The Terrible Art of Designing a War Memorial." *New York Times*, 14 July 1991, 2:28.

Segal, Charles P. *The Theme of the Mutilation of the Corpse in the "Iliad."* Leiden: Brill, 1971.

Shay, Jonathan. *Achilles in Vietnam: Combat Trauma and the Undoing of Character*. New York: Atheneum, 1994.

Sheehan, Neil. *After the War Was Over: Hanoi and Saigon*. New York: Random House, 1991.

Sherman, William T. *Memoirs of General W. T. Sherman*. New York: Library of America, 1990.

Sihanouk, Norodom. *My War against the CIA*. New York: Pantheon, 1972.

Simon, Erika. "Der Schild des Achilleus." In *Ausgewählte Schriften*, vol. 1. Mainz am Rhein: Philipp von Zabern, 1998.

Slatkin, Laura. *The Power of Thetis: Allusion and Interpretation in the Iliad*. Berkeley and Los Angeles: University of California Press, 1991.

Sledge, E. B. *With the Old Breed at Peleliu and Okinawa*. Novato, Calif.: Presidio Press, 1981.

Stanley, Keith. *The Shield of Homer: Narrative Structure in the "Iliad."* Princeton, N.J.: Princeton University Press, 1994.

Stein, Gertrude. *Everybody's Autobiography.* Cambridge, Mass.: Exact Change, 1993.

———. *Wars I Have Seen.* New York: Random House, 1945.

Steiner, George. *Homer in English.* Harmondsworth: Penguin, 1996.

Stevens, Richard L. *The Trail: A History of the Ho Chi Minh Trail and the Role of Nature in the War in Viet Nam.* New York: Garland, 1993.

Storr, Robert, ed. *Dislocations.* Exhibition catalogue, Museum of Modern Art, New York, 20 October 1991–7 January 1992.

Strachey, Alix. *The Unconscious Motives of War: A Psycho-analytical Contribution.* New York: International University Press, 1957.

Sturken, Marita. "The Wall, the Screen, and the Image: The Vietnam Veterans Memorial." *Representations* 35 (summer 1991): 118–43.

———. "The Wall and the Screen Memory: The Vietnam Veterans Memorial." In *Tangled Memories: The Vietnam War, the AIDS Epidemic, and the Politics of Remembering.* Berkeley and Los Angeles: University of California Press, 1997.

Sun Tzu. *The Illustrated Art of War.* Trans. Thomas Cleary. Boston: Shambhala, 1998.

Tate, Allen. *Collected Poems, 1919–1976.* New York: Farrar, Straus and Giroux, 1977.

Tatum, James. "The *Iliad* and Memories of War." *Yale Review* 76 (autumn 1986): 15–31.

———. "Memorials of the America War in Vietnam." *Critical Inquiry* 22 (summer 1996): 634–78.

Terry, Wallace. *Bloods: An Oral History of the Vietnam War by Black Veterans.* New York: Ballantine Books, 1984.

Theweleit, Klaus. *Male Fantasies.* Trans. Erica Carter and Chris Turner in collaboration with Stephen Conway. Vol. 1. Minneapolis: University of Minnesota Press, 1987.

Thiep, Nguyen Huy. "The General Retires." In *The General Retires and Other Stories,* trans. Greg Lockhart. Oxford: Oxford University Press, 1992.

Thomas, Helen, with Myfanwy Thomas. *Under Storm's Wing.* Manchester: Carcanet, 1988.

Thong, Huynh Sanh, ed. and trans. *Heritage of Vietnamese Poetry.* New Haven, Conn.: Yale University Press, 1979.

Thucydides. *The Peloponnesian War.* Trans. Stephen Lattimore. Indianapolis: Hackett, 1998.

Trumbull, Robert. *Nine Who Survived Hiroshima and Nagasaki.* New York: E. P. Dutton, 1957.

van Wees, Hans. "Homeric Warfare." In *A New Companion to Homer,* ed. Ian Morris and Barry Powell. Leiden: Brill, 1997.

———. *Status Warriors: War, Violence, and Society in Homer and History.* Amsterdam: J. C. Gieben, 1992.

Vendler, Helen. "Art, Heroism, and Poetry: The Shaw Memorial, Lowell's 'For the Union Dead,' and Berryman's 'Boston Common: A Meditation upon the Hero." In *Hope and Glory: Essays on the Legacy of the Fifty-fourth Massachusetts Regiment,* ed. Martin H. Blatt, Thomas J. Brown, and Donald Yacovone. Amherst: University of Massachusetts Press, 2001.

Vidal-Naquet, Pierre. "Temps des dieux et temps des hommes." *Rèvue de l'histoire des religions* 157 (1960): 55–80.

Wace, A. J. B., and F. H. Stubbings, eds. *A Companion to Homer.* London: Macmillan, New York: St. Martin's, 1962.

Weil, Simone. *The "Iliad"; or, The Poem of Force.* Trans. Mary McCarthy. Wallingford, Pa.: Pendle Hill, 1956.

Westmoreland, William C. *A Soldier Reports.* Garden City, N.Y.: Doubleday, 1975.

Whitman, Cedric. *Homer and the Heroic Tradition.* Cambridge, Mass.: Harvard University Press, 1958.

Wills, Garry. *Lincoln at Gettysburg: The Words That Remade America.* New York: Simon and Schuster, 1992.

Wilson, Edmund. *Patriotic Gore: Studies in the Literature of the American Civil War.* New York: Farrar, Straus and Giroux, 1962.

Winter, Jay. "Setting the Framework." In *War and Remembrance in the Twentieth Century,* ed. Jay Winter and Emmanuel Sivan. Cambridge: Cambridge University Press, 1999.

———. *Sites of Memory, Sites of Mourning: The Great War in European Cultural History.* Cambridge: Cambridge University Press, 1995.

Wolf, Christa. *Cassandra: A Novel and Four Essays.* Trans. Jan Van Heurck. New York: Farrar, Straus and Giroux, 1984.

Wolf, Reva. "Onlooker, Witness, and Judge in Goya's *Disasters of War.*" In *Fatal Consequences: Callot, Goya, and the Horrors of War.* Hanover, N.H.: Hood Museum of Art, Dartmouth College, 1990.

Woolf, Virginia. *Mrs. Dalloway.* London: Grafton, Collins, 1976.

———. *To the Lighthouse.* London: Hogarth Press, 1927.

Xenophon. *Anabasis.* With an English translation by Carleton L. Brownson, revised by John Dillery. Cambridge, Mass.: Harvard University Press, 1998.

Yeats, William Butler. *The Collected Poems of W. B. Yeats.* Toronto: Macmillan, 1956.

Young, James E. *The Texture of Memory: Holocaust Monuments and Memory.* New Haven, Conn.: Yale University Press, 1993.

Zbarsky, Ilya, and Samuel Hutchinson. *Lenin's Embalmers.* Trans. Barbara Bray. London: Harvill Press, 1998.

CATALOGUE OF THE MUSES

Of all the post-worlds we presently live in, the post-Olympian is perhaps the most challenging. We must work hard to find our muses. They flee authors, and with good reason. What muse in her right mind wants to appear in a *catalogue?* Can we imagine Homer invoking such a goddess for an *acknowledgment?* The following ones tarried to help at various stages of this project.

William Cook brought me to Killens's *And Then We Heard the Thunder* and many other connections between African American literature and classics. Don Cameron urged me to publish the lecture that eventually turned into the project of this book. My thanks to the *Yale Review* for permission to use material from that beginning essay here. Other friends and colleagues have been generous with their help and advice: Robert and Florence Fogelin, Walter and Miriam Arndt, Betye Saar, Rita and Donal Cruise-O'Brien, Christian Wolff, Charles Wood, Harold Bond, Blanche Gelfant, James Cox, Donald Pease, Hans and Anna Penner, Brenda Silver, Mary Kelley, Marysa Navarro-Aranguren, Beatriz Pastor, Jeremy Rutter, Robert and Carolyn Connor, Edward Bradley, William Scott, Margaret Graver, Dennis Washburn, Peter Bing, Bryan and Janette Reardon, Gordon and Jay Williams, B. F. Hicks, Froma Zeitlin, Helene Foley, Jay Parini, David and Carol Rosen, Sandra Black, Randy Tatum and Suzy Hillard, Nick Barberio and Leonard Barkan, Martha Connell, Herb and Laurie Ferris, the Jacobsons (Nicholas, Geraldine, Antoinette, and Nora), Alan Farrell, and James Heffernan, who also read a draft of chapter 7. Nancy Vickers taught a course with me in the summer of 1990 on the *Iliad* and war, which Marilyn Young also attended. I am grateful to both of them for a memorable class in those beginning days of a war.

Dartmouth has supported the research and travel required for this project at every stage. I have taught the *Iliad* and war to every kind of audience there, from students in first-year seminars and courses in War/Peace Studies, to a

Humanities Institute for faculty and visiting scholars, to, last but not least, some trustees, one provost, and two presidents. Audiences elsewhere provided helpful advice. I am grateful to Willard Spiegelmann (Southern Methodist University, both at the beginning and the end of the project), David Konstan, John Bodel, and Michael Putnam (Brown University), David Cox and other graduate students at the University of Virginia, Alysa J. Ward (University of Georgia), Thomas Palaima, Douglass Parker, Paul Woodruff, Joseph Carter, and Daniela Bini (University of Texas), Harvey Yunis and Michael Maas (Rice University), Susan Stephens, Mark Edwards, and Stephen Orgel (Stanford University), Daniel Selden, Mary Kay Gamel, and John Lynch (University of California at Santa Cruz), Malcolm Bell (American Academy in Rome), Sharon Herbert (University of Michigan), and Barry Strauss and Hayden Pelliccia (Cornell University).

Visits to the monuments and memorials of war have been part of this book since its beginning. I have seen a great many more than could be included here, ranging from deconstructions of Maya Lin's design (in the Texas Vietnam Veterans Memorial at the State Fair of Texas, in Dallas), to Augusto Morer's remarkable, overlooked memorial to the *partigiana* (partisan woman) on the shore of the Biennale in Venice. I am grateful to Gordon and Jay Williams for a photograph from one site I have yet to visit, Atatürk's tribute to the British and Commonwealth dead at Gallipoli.

The most challenging part of this project was the search for the other side of the memorialization of the American Vietnam War, in Vietnam itself. Once again Marilyn Young was there. She put me in touch with the Indochina Reconciliation Project in New York, where Cathy Taromina proved to be immensely helpful in both Hanoi and Phnom Penh. The Vietnam-USA Society in Hanoi enabled me to see a staggering range of battle sites and monuments in a comparatively short time; I am particularly grateful to Dao Ngoc Ninh for his guidance and his on-site translations of Vietnamese memorial inscriptions. Marilyn Young also alerted me early on to Geoff Dyer's *Missing of the Somme* and thereby laid the groundwork for a visit to Lutyens's memorial at Thiepval, in itself an overwhelming experience that will deepen anyone's appreciation of Maya Lin's memorial. My special thanks to Bryan Reardon, who brought the sorrow of that particular battle and war vividly to life in his memory for it. Marilyn also accompanied me on expeditions to other Vietnam War memorials, the most important by far being closest to home, in the Vietnam Wall Experience in Northfield, Vermont.

For helping me take a poetic field trip to the vanished site of Battery Wagner outside Charleston I am grateful to a family friend of long standing, Julia Templeton. She drove me to the dead end of the last road in the sand dunes of Folly Island beach. As Julia allowed at the time, this was one of the more unusual excursions she has conducted for visitors to Charleston. She followed up that visit with an article some months later by Arlie Porter of the *Post and Courier* of Charleston, about the successful effort of environmentalists and historical preservationists to block a luxury condominium's development on the remnants of Morris Island. Mr. Porter in turn steered me to David Rich, of the U.S. Army Corps of Engineers for the Charleston District, who was most gracious and helpful, both in dispelling some of the sillier myths about the disappearance of Battery Wagner and in supplying me with information on the geology and engineering involved in Quincey Gillmore's jetties project.

For their help in securing photos and permissions for works from their collections, my thanks to Rey Antonio (Alderman Library, University of Virginia), Kristin Murray and Rebecca Pine at Art Resource (New York), Malli Kamimura at Magnum (New York), Donald M. Cole at the Fowler Museum of Cultural History (UCLA), Kathleen O'Malley at the Hood Museum (Dartmouth), and Jeffrey Nintzel for his photograph of the Shaw Memorial in Boston. Mark Austin-Washburn of the Dartmouth Medical School's Department of Photography and Illustration did expert work in preparing a wide range of prints for publication.

I thought I was near completing this book when I began a residency at the Rockefeller Research and Study Center at Bellagio. I am happy to report to Susan Garfield and others at the foundation that that honor probably extended the work on it by a number of years; this was a horizon-expanding time I would trade for nothing else. My thanks to the foundation and fellow residents for much inspiration and friendship: Betye Saar, Donal and Rita Cruise-O'Brien, Valerie Miner and Helen Longino, Lincoln and Marty Chen, Gautam Desgupta and Bonnie Maranca, Alfonso and Siri Montecino, John and Jan Vercoe, and Börje Ljunggren. I completed the first draft of this book while a visiting scholar at New York University. I am grateful to many friends and colleagues there for their wonderful hospitality, above all Catharine Stimpson and Leonard Barkan.

I am particularly indebted to all those who read drafts of the book in whole or in part and offered comments and suggestions, from the earliest stages of a proposal to the final draft. As anyone who has done it knows, this is hard work to do well. Special thanks, then, to those who read what I wrote and told me what they thought about it: Chris King, more than anyone; and then James Williams, Jocelyn Penny Small, Charles Rowan Beye, Carroll Moulton, Myra Jehlen, Marilyn Young, William Noble, Gregory Nagy, Pietro Pucci, Keith Stanley, Andrew Victor, and the anonymous readers for the University of Chicago Press. Jane Taylor and Gail Vernazza performed their usual magic in helping me prepare the final copy. Richard Isomaki was an expert copyeditor who also saved me from a number of errors far worse than lapses in style. My former editor at Chicago, Geoffrey Huck, worked energetically with me from the first proposal to the final draft. I owe him a great deal for his constant encouragement and sympathetic advice and regret his leaving the Press before we finished. But Alan Thomas stepped in, and did so most capably. I am grateful to Alan for picking up where Geoff left off, to Alan's assistant, Randolph Petilos, and to Christine Schwab for seeing the book through production.

As the appearance of her name many times in this catalogue will suggest, there has been no one more important to this book than Marilyn Young. Her deep learning in history and literature of the Cold War and Vietnam will be a familiar story to anyone who knows her, as will her generosity. My debt to Marilyn is exceeded only by the one I owe William Noble, whose own work lies in the realm of the country gods and in the making of gardens that delight the muses—so at least every visiting muse says. I have vegetated in this project as long we have known one another. It was Bill with his gardener's eye who started insisting that I find a way to prune it and then finish it, and he kept on insisting that it be finished, until it was. And so this book on the sorrows of war is dedicated to Bill Noble, maker of gardens.

INDEX

Note: Numbers in italic indicate references to figures.

abortion, 170–71

Achilles, 49–76; Agamemnon's quarrel with, 52–53, 55–56, 116, 186n. 22, 191n. 6; Andromache compared to, 163; battles of, 119–29, 153–55; characterizations of, after Homer, 96–97, 105–6, 182n. 26, 185n. 2, 186n. 26; competence of, 161–62; death of, 159; divine horses of, 159–60; grief of, 170, 191n. 7; Hecuba's hatred of, 165; incompetence of, 57–61; laments of, 191nn. 9–10; Nestor's strategies for, 75–80; Patroclus's love for, 79–80, 108–12, 144–46, 186n. 22; Penthesilea killed by, 96–97; Priam meeting with, 160–66; rage of, 33, 50–53, 83, 143–44, 180n. 11, 181n. 12, 182n. 26; shade of, in *Odyssey*, 164; shield of, xiii, 136–57, 174, 183n. 53, 188n. 7, 189nn. 10, 20; tears of, 79–80, 191n. 11; Thersites and, 73–74, 75; Troilus murdered by, 105; trophies of, 47–48, 135; warriors, later, compared to, xi, 58–59. *See also* Briseis; Dixon, Norman; fathers; Hector; killing; love; MacCary, W. Thomas; mothers; Patroclus; sex; Shay, Jonathan; Thetis; warriors; Wolf, Christa

aerial warfare, 24–26, 126–27, 131, 151–53, 155–57

Aeschylus, 106, 186n. 26

African Americans: Civil War, service in, 87–88; and Shaw memorial (Saint-Gaudens), 91–95; and Vietnam War, 41, 46; and World War II, 54–55

Agamemnon, 49–75; Achilles' quarrel with, 52–53, 55–56, 116, 186n. 22, 191n. 6; Calchas and, 182n. 17; celebrations of, 71–

74; flattery of, 162; military incompetence of, 56–62, 74, 149, 184n. 55; tears of, 79–80, 184n. 62. *See also* catalogue of ships; commanders; Dixon, Norman; Grant, Ulysses; Keegan, John; Nestor; Odysseus

Ajax, 138–39

Alexander the Great, 85, 182n. 38

Alexiou, Margaret, 191n. 10

American Way of Death Revisited, The (Mitford), 19, 179n. 30

America War (War against Americans in Vietnam), 22–28, 98–99, 179n. 37. *See also* Vietnam War; Vietnam Veterans Memorial

Andromache, 4, 47–48, 98–107, 115, 171–73; Achilles and, 163; Patroclus and, 97. *See also* Hector

And Then We Heard the Thunder (Killens), 54–55

ANZAC Cove (Ari Burnu), memorial of, 179n. 36

Ap Bac, battle of, 24

Aphrodite, 96, 115; affair with Ares, 97–98, 190n. 29

Apollo, 48, 82, 90–91, 150

Appomattox, 66, 67

Arab warriors (in T. E. Lawrence), 113

Arc de Triomphe, 16, 166

archaeology, 85–86

Ares' affair with Aphrodite, 97–98, 190n. 29

Aristophanes, *Lysistrata*, 99–100, 185n. 7

Aristotle, *Poetics*, 37, 39, 180n. 15

Arnold, Matthew, "On Translating Homer," xviii–xix, 177n. 4 (note)

Ars Poetica (Horace), 4

Astyanax, 102, 105, 158, 171–72, *173*